Roman Siege Warfare

ROMAN SIEGE WARFARE

Josh Levithan

The University of Michigan Press
Ann Arbor

Copyright © by Josh Levithan 2013
All rights reserved

This book may not be reproduced, in whole or in part, including illustrations, in any form (beyond that copying permitted by Sections 107 and 108 of the U.S. Copyright Law and except by reviewers for the public press), without written permission from the publisher.

Published in the United States of America by
The University of Michigan Press
Manufactured in the United States of America
♾ Printed on acid-free paper

2016 2015 2014 2013   4 3 2 1

A CIP catalog record for this book is available from the British Library.

Library of Congress Cataloging-in-Publication Data

Levithan, Joshua, 1976–
    Roman siege warfare / Joshua Levithan.
       pages   cm
    Includes bibliographical references and index.
    ISBN 978-0-472-11898-4 (hbk. : alk. paper) — ISBN 978-0-472-02949-5 (e-book)
    1. Siege warfare—Rome—History. 2. Siege warfare—Psychological aspects. 3. Siege warfare—History—To 1500. 4. Military art and science—History—To 500. 5. Rome—History, Military.   I. Title.
UG443.L47   2013
355.4′40937—dc23

2013025442

What an advantage that knowledge can be stored in books! The knowledge lies there like hermetically sealed provisions waiting for the day when you may need a meal. Surely what the Collector was doing as he pored over his military manuals, was proving the superiority of the European way of doing things, of European culture itself. This was a culture so flexible that whatever he needed was there in a book at his elbow. An ordinary sort of man, he could, with the help of an oil-lamp, turn himself into a great military engineer, a bishop, an explorer or a General overnight, if the fancy took him . . . he knew that he was using science and progress to help him out of his difficulties and he was pleased.

—FARRELL, *THE SIEGE OF KRISHNAPUR*

The story as represented (which will not require much apology because it expects but little praise) is Heroical, and notwithstanding the continual hurry and busy agitations of a hot Siege, is (I hope) intelligibly convey'd . . . And though the main argument hath but a single walk, yet perhaps the movings of it will not seem unpleasant.

—D'AVENANT, *THE SIEGE OF RHODES*

PREFACE

This book derives from my dissertation, "Siege Warfare and Combat Motivation in the Roman Army." It is primarily an attempt to describe Roman siege warfare as it was practiced and experienced; it also advances the idea that some general understanding of the usual course of a siege is necessary to a full comprehension of any single ancient account. Siege warfare was highly structured, and we should read siege accounts with close attention to the evolving expectations of the participants. Two further ideas shape the book: that combat motivation, rather than the contest of engineering and fortification, is the central dynamic of any siege; and that sieges were understood to inhabit a distinct moral sphere, one in which the responsibility for the escalating violence of the siege belonged to the besieged rather than the besiegers.

While there are several useful studies of aspects of Roman siege warfare, these tend to focus on physical events rather than processes, giving archaeology center stage and emphasizing technological detail rather than human experience. This book is a history of histories, a reading of the unfolding of historical events in time and narrative. While the most important and most compelling sieges will be discussed—from Livy's more or less imaginary story of the siege of Veii in the early fourth century BCE to Ammianus' eyewitness accounts of late fourth century CE sieges—I make no claims to comprehensiveness or even to evenhandedness. For some of the largest-looming sieges we have no surviving, trustworthy account, and I have omitted these in order to focus on those in which a good historian has a good story to tell.

Chapter 1 elaborates on much of this, while chapter 2 examines combat motivation among Roman soldiers in the context of the siege. Chapter 3 sketches the general progression that governed the practice of siege warfare and structured the historical narratives. Chapters 4–7 are case studies of the most significant sieges in the essential sources: Livy and Polybius, then Caesar, Josephus, and Ammianus Marcellinus. This book concludes with an epilogue that briefly discusses the sacking of besieged cities—at once a separate topic (and one badly in need of further study) and an essential element of any coherent understanding of the special moral atmosphere of siege warfare.

Abbreviations for classical texts generally follow the *Oxford Classical Dictionary*. Where not otherwise noted, translations derive from the Loeb.

For astute guidance and relentless encouragement during the writing of my dissertation I owe sincere thanks to John Matthews and Celia Schultz, and to Ann Hanson, Carlos Norena, and Edward Watts. I am very grateful to Christina Kraus, Nathan Rosenstein, and to my editor and the reviewers for the press for giving so much of their time and wisdom in shepherding this project toward book-hood. I would like to mention as well the members of my Kenyon College seminar on "The Siege in History and Literature," who were assigned far too many readings, subjected to an unpredictable barrage of hobbyhorses, interpretations, and approaches, and yet managed many challenging sallies. Finally—because they know that it's demanding—warmest thanks are due to the members of *Oh the Humanities!!!*

I should dedicate this book to those dearest to me, were it not for the fact that my inefficiency in producing it has long kept me from them; but I think of them the most, on toast.

Yet given that the actual reading and writing were solitary pursuits, some acknowledgment is due to the accompaniments that were most often piped in through tinny computer speakers. For some reason this project seemed to call for "rock opera," probably not so much because of the rocks or the *opera*, but because these are generally loud, violent, and loosely yet predictably structured works (never mind their disparate artistic merits). So here's to *David Comes to Life, Quadrophenia, The Black Parade, Der Ring des Nibelungen, The Wall, Southern Rock Opera,* and *American Idiot.*

CONTENTS

ONE　　　Introduction　1
TWO　　　The Moral Contexts of Siege Warfare　22
THREE　　The Siege Progression　47
FOUR　　 The Republic　80
FIVE　　　Siege Warfare in Caesar's Commentaries　119
SIX　　　 Josephus and the Siege of Jerusalem　142
SEVEN　　Siege Warfare in Ammianus Marcellinus　170
　　　　　Epilogue: The Sack　205
　　　　　Bibliography　229
　　　　　Index　239

ONE

INTRODUCTION

Roman warfare has drawn scholarly and popular attention for a very long time. This attention has usually been focused on major battles, despite the insurmountable difficulty of providing a comprehensible narrative of open-field battle. The siege, defined as much by the presence of a wall as a battle is by open country, has attracted far less attention. When a siege does become the object of study it is usually as a discrete historical occasion—rarely is the siege considered as a category of military event. This makes some sense in that a major siege is a site-specific performance and, often enough, the climactic operation of a famous war. Yet Roman siege warfare had its own structure, its own customs, and its own governing expectations, and the sources allow a diachronic and synoptic understanding of "the siege" much stronger and more secure than the oft-pondered "Roman battle." Even when Roman sieges are the subject of sustained study they tend to be sorted by their use of the special techniques and technologies of siege warfare rather than examined for the way in which the entire siege conforms to or diverts from the typical narrative and operational plotlines.

The idea here, then, is to rebalance the ledger by emphasizing the human elements—morale and motivation—rather than the engineering, and to recapture the sense of a siege as an event in progress which presents, at each stage, a range of possible attitudes, methods, and outcomes.[1] "The

---

1. Thus this book does not discuss technology in detail, nor does it summarize what is known of each Roman siege, nor again assess the place of the siege in the larger practice of

Roman siege" is an event—or, rather, a sturdily constructed event category—that was witnessed, described, and recounted in particular ways that both reflect how the history really was experienced and produce a narrative centered on the commander, whose decisions guided the unrolling of the siege along a few well-traveled paths.

THE SIEGE APART

Ancient siege warfare should not be approached as a fortifications-related variation on a general practice of battle, but rather as a fundamentally different sort of combat. Ancient combat was generally fluid, while the siege was sharply defined: in time, in space, and in operational terms. Neither the operational identity of the combatants—who was attacking and who defending—nor the identity of the objective could change, and there could be no disputing the result: the town was taken or the siege was a failure.

The pressure of these strictures formed a distinct mode of warfare, inaugurated when an army arrived before a walled town or city that had closed its gates against it, that was waged both in a different moral environment and with its own separate set of potential outcomes. While these were dictated by the circumstances of siege warfare and recognized, generally, throughout the classical world, in Roman hands the siege mode developed its own specifically Roman themes and rhythms, and much of the rest of this book is concerned with identifying them.

Like the formal open-field battle, Roman siege warfare was conducted within a set of expectations based not on purely rational expectations of efficiency but instead on a blend of military practicality and cultural preference. Yet several situations unique to siege warfare caused a cultural shaping of military practice both more intense and more broadly accepted than those affecting other operations.[2] The concentration of violent effort in space and the practical challenge posed by a high wall revealed the dom-

---

Roman warfare. Moreover, with the partial exception of chapters 7 and 8, it is a study of offensive siege warfare only. This is both because Rome was far more often besieger than besieged and because the progression of the siege was controlled, almost completely, by the besieging commander.

2. See Keegan (1993), especially chapter 1, for a general discussion of war and culture. See also Reddé (2003), 58–59, and Watson (1993b), 141, an occasionally perceptive comparative study, for the siege as "a near-formalistic kind of battle."

inant influence not of *Realien* (things, facts, physical realities) but rather of cultural and psychological factors.

This might seem counterintuitive: with the wall looming before us, we are likely to begin thinking like (or imagine that we are thinking like) military engineers. But whatever means were used to neutralize this paradigmatic obstacle, it still fell to one man to be the first to go over or through it, usually at a time and place that could be accurately anticipated. The will to combat was always much more important to edged-weapon fighting than tactical drill or high-level weapons skills, and this is all the more emphatically true of siege warfare. Yet long ago, at some point between the *Iliad* and *de Rebus Bellicis*, the narrators of siege warfare became besotted with machinery, a fascination that abides in military history generally and the study of Roman siege warfare in particular. The sources do make it abundantly clear that siege warfare tended toward a highly dangerous assault by a few individuals or small groups—but first they would like to tell you about the spectacular machines.

This we might call the gadgetary turn, during which writers began to lavish attention on artillery and wall-damaging techniques, fetishizing technology and obscuring the centrality of the assault to the siege and of human behavior to the assault. It surely begins in the Hellenistic period, which provided both new machines that could be lionized and a historical practice fond of digression and tableau.[3] The innovativeness of any gadget is made much of, but anything impressively enormous or on fire is worthy of celebration.[4] Siege narratives are interrupted with brief technology-smitten asides and long digressions, with descriptions of torsion artillery (invented during the fourth century and quickly becoming common) and of various variations on the siege tower theme (which tended to fail spectacularly).[5] As might be expected, the surviving technical treatises—

---

3. See Cuomo (2007), 41–76, for the "Hellenistic Military Revolution," during which there was a "redefinition" rather than a weakening of the central importance "of the traditional moral qualities of combatants" (43). Cuomo also corrects the habit of Marsden and many subsequent specialists in ancient artillery of neglecting the ancients' interest in the moral and aesthetic effects of their weapons.

4. Thucydides, ever influential, is thus a precursor of this historical habit. Although there was little in the way of effective siege machinery in his time, he makes the most of what he has, notably the earthworks and "engines" at Plataea (2.75–6) and the "flame-thrower" at Delium (4.100). See Davies (2006), 12, on size exaggeration in Roman accounts.

5. For brief gadget-notices, see, e.g., App. *Mith.* 4.26–7 or 11.73, where a complicated

which are not bound by narrative conventions—provide more practical details on the workings of siege machines, but we tend to overlook the element of fantasy in even the most knowledgeable authors.[6] A writer's inability to explain (or disinterest in explaining) how a machine really works is the tip-off of its gadgetary function: it is an impressive distraction. Here, as in many places throughout this book, there is a thematic echo between historical event and narrative. The gadgets were generally much more imposing than effective during the actual siege, and all the more so in the historical narrative. Even in the case of stone- and arrow-firing artillery, which certainly had real tactical utility, there is much more evidence that it was impressive than that it was deadly.[7]

---

ship-mounted siege tower is engaged to deliver a mere four soldiers to the wall top—a good example of technology distracting from the central problem of motivating a few soldiers against many defenders. Plutarch is particularly fond of calling attention to clever or spectacular innovations in siege warfare, e.g., *Brut.* 30; *Demetr.* 20 and *passim;* and *Marc.* 14, a gimmicky retelling of the siege of Syracuse, which can be compared to the more balanced version in Livy (on which, see chapter 4). Vegetius, who exerted enormous(ly undue) influence throughout the Middle Ages and on into the early modern period, is a major conduit of the gadgetary fixation. His section on siege warfare has a single paragraph, acute but perfunctory, on the moral impact of general assaults followed by several pages of machines and stratagems. A parallel (and much more entertaining) chain of transmission runs through epic history from Lucan's wall-shaking siege towers (2.505) and multiple-body-piercing ballista bolts (3.465–8) to Renaissance epic's preoccupation with the infernal machines of war and the threat they pose to true chivalry.

6. The most striking technological digression among Roman historians is Ammianus 23.4. Den Hengst (1999), 30, calls the passage a "literary *tour de force,*" and emphasizes that the problems with the technical descriptions are basically irrelevant. Ammianus was a knowledgeable military man, but here he was writing like a writer, drawing on his "book learning" rather than practical experience. Kelso (2003) speculates that the particular influence on Ammianus may in fact be Lucian. More important still is Whitehead's contention (2010, 30, paraphrasing Lendle; see also Whitehead 2008) that "different levels of practicability were an accepted feature of the *genus polioriceticum,*" with highly practical advice about ladders and artillery side by side with uselessly huge or complex machines. Without indulging in gadgetary fantasy (but also without explaining his machines sufficiently for the uninitiated to fully understand them), Caesar shows "an almost flamboyant engagement" with the narrative possibilities of technological digression, using descriptions of siege towers (as well as other feats of engineering) both to emphasize the psychological component of warfare and to attribute credit (usually to himself) for victories. See Kraus (2007), 375; Dodington (1980), 37–42 and *passim.*

7. See, for example, Zos. 1.70 and Procop. *Wars* (*Goth.*) 5.23.9. Josephus includes both testimony to artillery's effectiveness—for example, *BJ* 3.166–8—and impossible horror stories—*BJ* 3.245–6. The interest, and, one could argue, the author's sense of the readership's interest, in siege technology is even greater in modern archaeologically inflected studies than in the Roman historians. These latter-day works have for centuries been furnished

So let us set aside the machines. Siege assaults, much more than other military operations, depended upon the aggressive heroics of a few, and so we should focus our inquiry on combat motivation. A commander might choose the precise place and time of an attack and provide himself with a good vantage point. But after that, all he could do was watch. Those who led the assault would be highly visible, up against the wall. The number of witnesses—comrades, commander, officers in charge of writing reports,

---

with lavish illustrations of towers, machines, artillery, etc. Campbell (2005) and (2006) and Davies (2006) are, of recent English-language works on Roman siege warfare, the best illustrated, with photographs, diagrams and, for what they are worth, imaginative visual reconstructions. An excellent archaeological study—in French—of Caesar's famous investment of Alesia is Reddé (2003). Topographical information and images of equipment are useful aids and should be sought out in those books, but the long and loving study of military hardware usually comes to overshadow the cultural and psychological aspects of historical experience, and the tangibility of objects encourages overconfidence in imagining their historical use or in throwing the tenuous lines of potential trends across the vast chasms in our knowledge. Kern (1999, 273), for instance, notes the "minor role" of siege machines in the Second Punic War, but goes immediately on to claim that siege engines had become so useful "that Roman siege warfare had reached a new level," despite flat contradiction in the sources (App. *Pun.* 5.30). The use of modern military vocabulary can also lead to subtle but damaging anachronisms, such as the hopeful reconciliation of spotty sources to possibly indicate that "the Roman battering assault was accompanied by an artillery barrage" (Campbell 2006, 121), despite the fact that this was an assault in 142 BCE, a period in which Roman artillery was far too scarce to mount anything like a "barrage," even if the term is ever appropriate to low-velocity direct-fire weapons. Campbell (e.g., 2006, 72–73, 92) also devotes a great deal of time and energy in sketching out ancient designs that do not quite make sense and may, in some cases, be imaginary. An archaeologist who must be exempted from these criticisms is James (2004, see especially pages 3–4, although I disagree on the relative proximity of texts and skeletons to the "real experience" of Roman soldiers; and 2011a), who consistently strives to keep the physical from outweighing the cultural and psychological elements of historical experience, and has only been tempted, in a semi-gadgetary vein, so far as to (plausibly) suggest Sassanian chemical warfare (2011b).

A gadgetary turn naturally engenders a Rube Goldberg or a Heath Robinson, and we must be wary of continuing to let the machines loom so large in our stories of ancient siege warfare. Even in the case of the machines we can reconstruct, we still know next to nothing about how they were devised or about how the expertise in constructing and using them was passed on, and so we must deal synchronically with such technologies, as they appear in narratives by authors who understood the context of their use. Here I will give only brief explanations of the practical matters of siegecraft (towers, mines, catapults, etc.) and only when necessary to a basic grasp of the physical details of the environment inhabited by the people whose actions we are trying to understand. Similarly overindulged-in in accounts of siege warfare, especially in the ancient sources, is the use of ruses and stratagems—these are the "gadgets" of narrative, flashy possibilities that distract from the larger, more subtle problems at hand, and therefore will not be dealt with in any depth here.

sometimes even the historians themselves—provided motivation. An analogy with the theatrical stage is inescapable, and historians reflexively record the names of the featured players of the assault, as well as their deeds.[8] Fame and fortune awaited the survivors.

Finally, the siege differs from other military actions in that it is not merely a concentration of warfare-as-usual but also in some sense a transgression of or against it. Greco-Roman military culture preferred the consensual engagement in the open field, and city walls should be seen as part of this system, enclosing an area from war and providing a secure base of operations. But when the gates were closed and no army marched out to defend the walls, the defenders were signaling their rejection of the preferred mode of combat and their willingness to move to a different one.

This was the point of departure for our specifically Roman idea of siege warfare: instead of a "fair fight" in the open, the attackers were now forced to make an undesirable choice between the time and expense of blockade (aimed at starving the defenders into surrender) and the blood and expense of a siege (taking the town or city by assault, with or without extensive engineering). "Rome" was now in a difficult position. To retreat in the face of defiance would be unmanly, but to invest a city and fail to take it would be a great embarrassment, and careful calculation was needed to avoid undertaking too difficult a siege. And indeed, Rome only very rarely failed to take a place deliberately besieged. This was a common practical problem—cutting losses is politically and cognitively difficult in any context—but Roman cultural preference doubled down, in effect, on the strategic gamble by insisting on success and devoting enormous resources to its sieges.[9] "Failure is not an option" is and was a silly piece of rhetoric, but the Roman practice of siege warfare effectively transmuted the idea into a moral buttress against the physical and tactical difficulties of a siege.

---

8. Stage analogy: *BJ* 6.146. See also Livy 31.24.12–3; Polyb. 7.17; and App. *Pun.* 71, where Scipio Aemilianus, in the unusual position of watching a battle as a spectator, likens his perspective (which would be analogous to the commander's view of a siege) to that of the gods in the *Iliad*. See also *Orlando Furioso*, 40.22.

9. Although, as we see in chapter 7, Rome became acclimated to lower-stakes siege warfare in the East and in late antiquity, even this was still different from the constant transactional simmer of feudal warfare, where threats and bravado during a siege were part of a long-running performance rather than moral tactics that usually immediately preceded a decisive outcome. Duby (1984), 80, describes the flamboyant declaration by the father of the young William Marshall that his son, held hostage by the besieged, may as well be killed because he has the "hammer and anvil" to make another, as "une telle réplique appartient au livret classique de ce grand opéra qui se jouait, à beaux cris, à beaux gestes, sur le théâtre de la guerre féodale."

Motivation for this necessary success derived, too, from the conviction that it was the defenders—who had closed their gates in shameful fear—who were responsible for the rigors of the siege and must be not simply conquered, but also punished. Long sieges almost always ended with a ferociously violent sack that involved rape, pillage, and, less frequently, mass murder. Such acts are often attributed to the ugly release of the pent-up stress of the besieging troops, but they also, often enough, carried strategic intent. Destruction was retribution for not submitting to the quick defeat of open battle against Rome and a warning to future targets of Roman campaigns that marching out or capitulating were both to be preferred to submitting to a siege. The message that fighting on from behind walls is to be punished by cruelty and death, though, came from the soldiers as much as from their general, who could hardly have restrained them in any case.[10] Battle is essentially consensual: it could only take place when many on each side desired it. But no one really wanted to be at a siege.

THE FACE OF THE SIEGE

The tradition of treating military history as a subset of political history—with the attendant focus on politician generals and the winning moves they devised in their decisive battles—was already well established when the first Roman historians were writing. This sort of battle writing overlooks the experience of the individual participants, making soldiers into passive nodes between their commander's will and the violence of their weapons.[11] Intervening, of course, is the mind of the soldier as well as the complex and changeable collective psychology of a group of soldiers, as mediated by their common culture. In other words, morale. A soldier's desires—foremost among them the desire to survive—did not often harmonize with his commander's operational goals, which budgeted some number of casualties in a favorable exchange for victory. This conflict of interest has been largely ignored by previous studies of siege warfare, which focus primarily or exclusively on tactics and technologies. I hope to examine the siege synoptically without eliding the gap between the individual point of view and any notional unity of military purpose. The "typical Roman soldier at a siege" is notional, too, of course, but any attempt at a historical understanding of Roman siege warfare must rest first on the perceptions and experience of the human being in harm's way.

---

10. On which see chapter 8.
11. See Keegan (1976), 53–72; Goldsworthy (1996), 172–73; Morillo (2006), 11–70.

This approach follows John Keegan's *The Face of Battle,* urtext of the "new military history." According to Keegan, "since we appear to know a great deal more about generalship than we do about how and why ordinary soldiers fight, a diversion of historical effort from the rear to the front of the battlefield would seem considerably overdue."[12] A host of academic military historians have charged into the fray behind this inspirational leader, seeking to come to grips with overlooked aspects of Roman warfare. The siege poses a different problem, and the metaphor must adapt: although there is a sharp fight at the end, the approach to the siege must be methodical—real Romans, after all, win with the *dolabra* (pickaxe) as much as the sword.[13]

Yet there are two reasons why it is actually easier to catch a glimpse of the face of the siege. First, the general's tactical control of the operation—initially static and generally predictable—is much more secure, and thus there is less reason to disassociate the decisions made at the rear from the action in front. Second, the siege is simply clearer. Describing the intense combat of the assault remains a challenge to narrative, but less so the secure identification of "what happened, and why." "Some individuals may recollect all the little events of which the great result is the battle lost or won; but no individual can recollect the order in which, or the exact moment at which, they occurred, which makes all the difference as to their value or importance."[14] But this is much less true of our "battle on a stage," and siege warfare is not as badly obscured by euphemistic description of chaotic action, or indeed by fundamental uncertainty about the many small-scale actions that make up an engagement. Because the outcome of a siege was indisputable and binary, ancient historians could describe what had taken place without seeding their narratives with justifications for the result: the decision could not be so easily "spun."[15]

Most fundamentally, the events of a siege were more easily seen. Any

---

12. Keegan (1976), 51; see also 35–45, 72–77. Kagan (2006), 15, provides a useful summary (and critique) of Keegan's approach.

13. Frontin. *Str.* 4.7.2.

14. The Duke of Wellington, from a letter to John Croker of August 8, 1815. Tolstoy held a somewhat similar view of the complexity of battle, and wrote much the same thing, although in greater depth, with very different historiographical intent, and with a different conclusion about the nature of human freedom. And rather less concisely: see the final twelve chapters of *War and Peace.*

15. Since "sieges are formulaic by nature," literary convention might actually work to bolster, rather than erode, the historicity of a narrative. Kraus (2009), 172; see also Roth (2006).

accurate interpretation of historical events must generally go all the way back to the eyes of a witness, and sieges serve history well in this regard.[16] Interestingly, we tend to overlook the general's ability to overlook his own sieges, often from a single, secure vantage point allowing a full view of the action at hand—a thing hardly ever possible during other types of combat. This is also the point of view preferred by our historians, most of whom stood beside a besieging commander at some point in their lives. This is problematic when we wish to understand what the desperate action at the wall was like, but it is very useful for the project that occupies much of this book. The battlefield general made his dispositions, signaled the initial engagement, and then lost tactical control over all but his reserves. During a siege, however, he was firmly in control of the sequence of events, able to choose each new tactic, plan each assault, and observe and respond to any individual action.

So there is much to be learned from a new approach to the siege, yet relatively little has been written along these lines. Recent monographs on the Roman army occasionally include a chapter on the methods of siege warfare, but the discussion is either limited to a short time period or to a particular strategic context.[17] Other books have provided an archeological overview of Roman siege works and synchronic summaries of each era.[18] These are products of the prolonged effort made, during the second half of the twentieth century, to understand the material remains of the Roman army in its barracks, forts, and camps—an effort that has greatly enhanced

---

16. This is not to say that historians wrote without the influence of literary tropes or other event-deforming expectations, only that "we mostly go about our business as if the contrary of what we profess to believe were the truth . . . we shall continue to write historical narrative as if it were an altogether different matter from making fictions or, *a fortiori,* from telling lies" (Kermode 1979, 109). This is philosophically and theoretically impure, but it is the only practical way to do ancient military history; tropes and other narrative impingements on pure chronicle will be discussed throughout; see especially the discussion of Livy in chapter 4.

17. See Southern and Dixon (1996); Gilliver (1999); Keppie (1984); Webster (1998); Goldsworthy (1996); Roth (2009).

18. Davies (2006) is a good complement to the discussion of the heavily engineered assault in chapter 3, clarifying and categorizing the technologies, and setting the stage for the action—the experience of the participants. See also Davies (2001), for a semiotics-inflected consideration of siege warfare that leaps almost directly from the functional to the symbolic, with perhaps not enough consideration of the (intervening?) quotidian psychologies of siege warfare. Kern (1999) is a comprehensive survey, but more given to paraphrase of the ancient accounts than to analysis.

our understanding of the careers of Roman soldiers and the conditions under which they lived. This work provides crucial foundational and background work—but archaeology, epigraphy, and papyrology can't depict the soldier in the midst of combat.[19]

Archaeology, both traditional and experimental, can, however, aid the imaginative reconstruction of the physical parameters of a siege. Ancient history in general depends upon both *Realien* and thoroughly subjective elements of human experience, and thus upon the two distinct disciplines that deliver objects to museums and texts to libraries. Siege warfare is, more than most things, a marriage of these extremes, the physicality of fortification and the psychology of highly focused combat. Yet while archaeological remains may hint at process, they cannot fill in the essential details of context and chronology. Without movement in time and space there is no experience of history. As intriguing as it can be to ponder the exact course of Caesar's siege lines or to try to reconstruct Vitruvius' ram-tortoise, these are only elements of the scenery—the human experience is the play. Since the action is only preserved in historical narrative we are entirely dependent upon the writings that survive.[20]

Without getting bogged down in theoretical debates about the nature of historical truth, it should be possible to accept that, because culture (broadly construed, essentially, as non-*Realien*) mediates the contemporary understanding of events as well as their representation in our source texts, the facts in the ground and the dictates of military logic cannot really speak to the experience of human history; and yet however loosely the cerements of a historical text are draped around the corpse of bygone events, they still reveal their shape. Written history, then, is something of a

---

19. Although a few really exceptional exceptions to this rule do come close—for instance, the skeletons excavated where they fought and died in a mine below the walls of Dura or the *Perusinae glandes,* which preserve the quite explicit words literally hurled (from legionaries' slings) in siege combat. Nevertheless, sieges are only "slightly more likely than battles to produce archaeological evidence" (Whitby 2007, 76–77) and should not be approached as potential positivist panaceas. If the archaeology of Roman military sites has become "en effet . . . une science autonome" (Reddé 2008, 280), the conclusion that excavations must be interpreted along with relevant texts is welcome, if seemingly both belated and so roundabout as to be inverted.

20. Historical texts are more effectively comparable, too, knowing their predecessors and engaging in conversation, while archaeology may be either voluble or mute. Of sieges discussed at length in this book, Amida (Diyarbakir) has not been thoroughly excavated, Alesia (Alise-Sainte-Reine, see Reddé 2001, among others) has been the subject of antiquarian excavations since the days of Napoléon III, and Jerusalem has received partial but intensive archeological attention (see Price 1992).

zombie. However, since the life of the real historical event is irrevocably lost, and since animated corpses are more interesting than buried ones, this is not such a bad thing. The philosophy of history sometimes overlooks the simple fact that it is possible to aim well at an imperfect target, and so the goal of a book like this should be (and is) to tell a story, conscious of the story-like nature of history, that nevertheless aims at truth. This is, to strip our metaphorical gears, not a matter of having our cake and eating it too, but rather of baking half a cake with the unspoiled ingredients available to us. In any case, writing history with a careful eye on the source narratives and an optimistic view of their rootedness in fact is the only sensible way to write the history of combat. Our possibilities of understanding ancient fighting are rigidly limited by physical constraints (which are very easy to understand), yet it is so difficult to know the cultural and emotional realities of this experience that we need the intrusions and explanations of the authors at least as much as we resent them.[21]

So we're stuck with narrative, since the events of ancient military history can be found nowhere else, but the goal is not to cut the fossilized facts free of the surrounding matrix. On the contrary, a proper understanding of events depends almost entirely on our comprehension of cultural context.[22] In this, the twenty-first-century reader of military history is often badly served by our own culture's valorization of scientific reason and confidently objective analysis. The pervasiveness of game theory—and of strategy expressed in colorful, simplistic visuals—has introduced a historical blind spot, leading us to imagine clarity and logic where chaos reigned. The tendency to treat warfare as if governed by a "universal Higher Logic of War" with immutable principles, a competitive game in which all players relentlessly seek the best possible outcome, had become too deeply rooted in modern military history.[23]

---

21. As Whitby (2007), 69, points out, even historians writing about combat that took place within their own lifetimes err by relying on faulty or contentious memories, and even Thucydides, "our best ancient military narrative . . . presents a literary text informed by subjective analysis which must be treated with caution at all times." These problems and more afflict even the best of our Roman sources.

22. Keegan (1993) has also been influential in his later emphasis on the fact that warfare is a cultural construction—an enlightening restatement of the obvious.

23. "Universal Higher Logic:" Keegan (1976), 21. We are taught from an early age, now, to defer to rationality as represented by hard science—and well we should, in most cases. But we should not go so far as to surrender the psychological subtleties of humanism. The nineteenth- and early-twentieth-century Western fixation on man as a rationally motivated

But war is no more a science than an art, and certainly no game. This is a principle so broad as to be unwieldy, but it is a necessary correction, since any new insights in ancient military history depend upon eliminating the pretension to universality of the rationalist school of "military science." Happily, the last two decades have produced much good work on the Roman army that moves along these lines, and this book aims to follow by giving siege warfare the necessary treatment as a separate category of warfare with its own structure and moral expectations.[24]

THE SOURCES

The major sources of this study are the historical works of Polybius, Caesar (including his continuators), Livy, Josephus, and Ammianus Marcellinus. Although a wider range of texts is consulted in chapters 2, 3, and 8, the four chapters that treat specific sieges in significant depth are structured around these authors, for three basic reasons. First, enough of the writing of each survives to allow for some nuance in our understanding of their language and literary tendencies. Just as cultural context is necessary to understand events, literary context is necessary to understand the way events are handled as they are worked into elements of narrative. By the time of Polybius there were already enough expectations specific to siege narratives that historians "are forced to display all the contrivances, bold strokes, and other features of a siege; and when they come to [describe a sack] . . . they must draw on their own resources to prolong the agony and heighten the picture."[25] Polybius here is inveighing against his predecessors and asserting his own commitment to unvarnished truth, but both parts of

---

actor produced a vision of battle as the rational performance of idealized tactics. The unhappy blending of descriptive and prescriptive interests in military history (that is, academic historians and professional officers—with one man sometimes filling both roles) contributed to the clearing of emotional and psychological factors from the battlefield. This is one of the reasons that I avoid discussion of troop numbers: our sources are rarely reliable and it is almost always impossible to get a sense of how many men were actually engaged in combat. Yet numbers beg to be computed, and we are overly impressed by their stolid testimony. Surely it is right to expect the side with a quantitative advantage to win? But we do not know; just as we do not usually have solid information on food supplies or objective assessments of the strength of fortifications. For these reasons, and to keep this book to a manageable size, I pay scant attention to the archaeology of fortifications or to logistics.

24. Most notable is Goldsworthy (1996), and many subsequent publications. See also Van Wees (1992), (2004) on Greece, and Lendon (1997) and (2005) on both Greece and Rome.

25. 29.12.7–9, trans. Shuckburgh. See also Tac. *Ann.* 4.32.

the equation are worth emphasizing: we need writers who try to tell it like it was, but we need to be able to read carefully through those scenes which were likely, nevertheless, to elicit authorial embellishment, and that requires volume(s). Second, each of these authors, except for Livy, had personal experience of warfare, possessed specialist military knowledge, and had been present at sieges.[26] Finally, they all wrote of events in the recent past, relying at times on written sources but more often on autopsy or the testimony of living eyewitnesses. The fact that their works appeared within living memory of the sieges encourages confidence in the basic factual accuracy of the accounts. These authors are the best qualified to accurately represent Roman siege warfare.[27]

Despite the dangers of commenting broadly on a phenomenon that changed greatly over the centuries, synoptic analysis of Roman siege warfare over a period of about six hundred years is possible. Of the major sources for this book, Polybius (2nd second century BCE), is the earliest writer, and Ammianus (late fourth century CE) the latest. There are good reasons for choosing precisely this period. Although it embraces enormous political and social change—Rome transformed itself from an oligarchic republic relying on semiprofessional soldiers into a monarchy employing hundreds of thousands of professionals—the practice of Roman siege warfare is marked by both cultural continuity and technological near-stasis. Equipment and weapons did change over time, but the basic technologies, with the one exception of torsion artillery (and this was well-established by Polybius' time) date to the Middle Bronze Age (in Mesopotamia) or earlier. Such changes as there were did little to alter the facts of siege warfare: the striking but relatively superficial differences in narrative technique may, like the minimally relevant gadgets, draw the attention away from fundamental similarities. The basic idea, of choosing to go either over a wall by means of ladders or through it after causing it some damage, equally well characterizes the siege warfare of the Mediterranean for a thousand years before or after our chronological boundaries. What makes

---

26. Livy is merely inescapable when considering the republic. Yet, just as the politics of Caesar and the apologies of Josephus can be peeled away from their combat narratives, so too Livy's stories of early Roman heroes and legendary battles can be sifted to reveal more about the contemporary understanding of siege warfare than would a brief historical description of an actual first-century siege. See, for example, 4.22 or 5.5–7.

27. Not that this is enough to ensure the security of the actual event from narrative interference, just as no number of burly men in yellow-on-blue "EVENT SECURITY" shirts can keep you from telling a great-but-not-quite-accurate story about what happened on the field.

the period at least basically cohesive and at the same time distinct from earlier and later warfare is the essential cultural conservatism of Roman warfare. If we push back before Polybius, we not only run out of good sources, but we get beyond torsion artillery and toward something like a more legitimately "heroic" culture. If we strike out beyond Ammianus, we find that the increasing prestige of both Christianity and cavalry overstrains the basic cultural unity.

These good reasons for choosing our roster of central authors trump certain drawbacks, notably Polybius' emphasis of the (Scipionic) general's control over events, Josephus' lies and exaggerations, and Caesar's propagandistic dissimulation. Ammianus, although he is prone to digression and favoritism and writes in a baroque style that is not to every taste, delivers vivid depictions of siege combat much more accurate in human terms than the reserved tactical narratives which have usually been preferred. Caesar, Josephus, and Ammianus in particular share a willingness to write about fighting on its own terms that the other extant historians of Rome do not. Events in battle appear as isolated incidents spotlighted amidst the chaos and are not used simply to illustrate larger narrative threads. For example, Josephus' chapters on the siege of Jerusalem are frequently interrupted by melodramatic polemics about the zealots or paeans to Titus, yet when he dramatizes moments of real combat, the fighting stands clear of the political context.

A wider range of texts, including other histories, biographies, and military handbooks, can provide context or lend choral support to insights drawn from the major sources, but, as they lack either sufficient military interest and experience or extended siege narratives, these must remain secondary. Among the historians, Tacitus and Cassius Dio remain useful,[28] while Sallust, despite his poor grasp of military affairs, sheds light on several important aspects of siege warfare. Appian is untrustworthy, but he preserves otherwise-lost details that derive from reliable sources. Of the biographers, Suetonius provides a few details, the famously inaccurate *Historia Augusta* is best ignored, and only Plutarch is much use. The sheer extent of his surviving works, as well as his abiding interest in human nature, provide a number of interesting details and insights into ancient combat. Of the military handbooks, it is Vegetius, Frontinus, and Onasander who are

---

28. As preservers of historical evidence rather than providers of cogent narratives: Dio's brief descriptions of battles read like rote distillations of his predecessors, while Tacitus, Mommsen's "most unmilitary of writers," cannot write clearly about warfare.

most relevant. Despite their nonnarrative format, these very practical texts (explicitly intended, in some cases, for the use of nonprofessional senatorial commanders), often address themselves to particular situations that are easily identifiable in terms of the siege progression outlined in chapter 3.[29] The handbooks are also a useful compendium of psychological insights, which together reveal much of the basic Roman cultural assumptions about motivation and morale. Valerius Maximus, who compiled historical anecdotes for rhetorical purposes, is similarly helpful as a reflection of first century CE attitudes toward such subjects as courage and fortitude.

THE SETTING OF THE ROMAN SIEGE

During its centuries of conquest, Rome conducted many sieges. Practical concerns came first, and Roman siegecraft was rooted in the logic of logistics and the possibilities of each unique site. But long practice leads to habit, and Roman siege warfare, while always sensitive to individual operational realities, congealed into a rough and replicable repertory. Roles and stages were rigid and clearly defined, and there was a general sense that the defenders, in refusing open warfare, were shamefully "forcing" the besiegers to fight at a tactical disadvantage. The moral complications of this stance is examined in greater detail in chapters 2 and 3, but it is worth emphasizing the Roman conception of this "asymmetrical" aspect of siege warfare. We tend to understand fortifications as mandated by logic—force multipliers that the defender acquires when ceding initiative and mobility. In Roman eyes, a wall was a barrier, but also a fighting platform that gave an advantage that was unfair, unworthy, and unmanly. This view was not unique to Rome—Plato discusses the idea that merely having a good city wall causes softness and complacency among the citizenry—but it loomed unusually large, and the commitment to open aggression was taken further than in other ancient Mediterranean societies.[30]

---

29. Renewed interest in the handbooks is largely due to Campbell (1987); see also Gilliver (1999). It is quite likely that with the help of Marsden (1969; 1971) the modern student may learn more about the functioning of artillery than most legionary legates did. The typical Roman senatorial commander was surely dependent on the advice of his experts when it came to mining or other issues of engineering. What he knew (or should know) was how to motivate and lead men—this is the missing "expertise" that the ancient social system was counted upon to provide. See, for example, Caes. *B.Gall* (hereafter *BG*) 7.24. Yet even some of the more technical handbooks contain a mixture of fact and hopeful fantasy, on which see Whitehead (2008), 146 and *passim*.

30. *Leg.* 6.778e–779a. Sparta famously flaunted the dominance of its phalanx by refus-

Walls were originally built, it could be said, to keep war out there in the fields, where it belonged.[31] The use of technology, even something as simple as a pickaxe or a ladder, to extend violence through space or through an obstacle—beyond, that is, the approved "fair fight" between adult males in an unbounded space—is often greeted with hostility in premodern cultures. There is the intermittent Homeric discomfort with archery, the chivalrous hatred of the crossbow, Japan's giving up the gun: in each case, the ability to show martial virtue by closing the open space between oneself and a deadly adversary is abrogated. Sallust echoes these ideas when he describes Roman soldiers under attack within a hostile city: they are penned in, attacked by women and children throwing roof tiles, and the brave and the cowardly die alike. Fear of unheroic random death at the hands of women or children is also a Spartan justification for avoiding siege assaults.[32]

---

ing to construct walls, but Aristotle (*Pol.* 1330b33–1331a17), writing—not coincidentally—after the development of siege artillery, took a much more practical approach to the value, and values, of fortifications. Or recall Duby's take on medieval siege warfare (note 9), in which moral posturing was itself the main event. In Roman warfare it was always intended as a prelude to the killing.

31. Without becoming mired in a complex debate based on scanty evidence, it seems possible to generalize that walls in preclassical southern Europe were seen primarily as deterrents to raids and encouragers of open battle rather than as fortifications that would in due course be attacked. Serious fortifications and real siege warfare came only with the influence of Persia and the very ancient tradition—with very different cultural baggage—of Near Eastern siege warfare. Massive walls, and the massive undertaking of taking them, were prestigious because they were proper to the majesty of kings, and, circularly, because only kings could or would undertake them, in pursuit of prestige. Yet these traditions had limited impact in the central and western Mediterranean, and it is important to note that both the extreme aggression of Roman siege warfare and the difficulties Rome later encountered when dealing with large-scale stone fortifications in parts East have to do with the low-tech, more-symbolic-than-tactical fortifications of ancient Italy and its Gallic and German neighbors. On the other hand, the Roman ability to muster the skill, the resources, and the aggressive will—the Roman oligarchic competition for glory replacing the Near Eastern drive for royal or imperial prestige—to conduct ongoing and extensive siege warfare was unprecedented in Europe. It is also worth mentioning that the most famous decision to force siege instead of accepting battle—Pericles' insistence on staying within the long walls—was an act that would not have been politically survivable for a Roman republican politician.

32. Sall. *Iug.* 67. Sparta: Plut. Comp. Lys. and Sull. 4.3. A concern also for the biblical siege commander Abimelech (Judges 9:52–54) who, mortally wounded by a millstone dropped by a female defender of the tower he was assaulting, ordered a servant to finish him off in order to avoid the ignominy of being killed by a woman. Sometime later (1218 CE), the villainous Simon de Montfort was killed by a shot from an artillery piece operated by

So the Roman adversary who chose siege over open war or capitulation was acting shamefully, and some of this shame contaminated the besiegers, who were forced to take up tools and penetrate the fortifications, to fight their way into the interior space of civilization, and to carry violence across the boundary that normally separated naked force from order (it is difficult here not to think of Achilles' shield) and fighters from noncombatants.[33] A common and very important special circumstance of siege warfare, too was the presence of noncombatants as witnesses and potential victims. We frequently meet with scenes of women, children, and old men watching the fighting from atop the walls, which is held to be a motivator of the most intense sort. To fight because you fear to die in the sight of your loved ones—and because your failure is likely to lead to their rape, enslavement, or murder—is to fight with true desperation: something different from the prospect of death or defeat in open warfare. Siege assaults, then, are exceptionally visible affairs, with the besieging general and the besieged families each able to bear witness. This "public" dimension changes the moral terms of otherwise intimate close combat, and the fact that failures might be witnessed—and jeered—by noncombatants added to the sense of forced embarrassment.[34]

Yet despite the distastefulness of having to engage in a siege assault, there was never any question that the true shame belonged to the defend-

---

the women and maidens of Toulouse (*Song of the Cathar Wars,* laisse 205). Both sieges were lifted immediately thereafter. A similar, albeit later still (and fictional) intermingling of the themes of male anxiety over virility, female agency, and the material demands of siege warfare is reflected in the incident of young Tristram and the sash window, on which see Sterne (1759–67), in particular volume 5, chapter 17.

33. Rarely, in the ancient world, were assault troops killed by women (although see Lynn 2008, 202–8) or children, but they did often provide immediate assistance to the fighters. Plut. *Pyrrh.* 34.2 does have a mother who kills with a roof tile. App. *Hann.* 5.29 reports a sally by woman fighters, but this likely to be an invention; see also Diod. Sic. 13.56. Yet to fight males who were supplied and exhorted by women was bad enough; see, for example, App. *Hann.* 6.39; Plut. *Pyrrh.* 27.4–28.4. The fact that we so often hear of women giving their hair to repair mural artillery (catapults could indeed be powered by twisted hair) points to the irresistibility of a detail that combines female involvement with war, siege desperation, and high technology. See Caesar, *BC* 3.9; App. *Pun.* 13.93; "Heron of Byzantium" *Bel.* 112; Vegetius, IV.9; Flor. 1.31.10. See also Marsden (1969), 87–88.

34. Mothers and wives watching combat from the walls is a trope as old as the *Iliad,* and the hypothetical situation of fighting under the eyes of wives and children can also be evoked as imaginative motivation; for example, at Livy 21.41.15–16. See chapters 5 and 6 for women at Gergovia and Jotapata. Vergil repeatedly imagines the fate of dying in sight of family on the walls: *Aen.* 1.94–6, 11.877–8, also 11.475–6, 12.593–613; see also Hor. *Odes.* 3.2; Luc. 7.369–70.

ers, who had refused to fight openly, like men. Livy, for instance, makes much of this. In a speech given to a sturdy Roman legionary, he represents the army—mutinous because its commander is pursuing a (strategically sound) Fabian strategy—as shamed by its inactivity, insulted by the enemy "as though we were women cowering behind our rampart."[35] Even recently defeated Romans should display an unconquered spirit by camping before the walls rather than behind them or by sallying out against now-overconfident enemies.[36] When Roman armies (or Roman heroes) strike fear into their enemies, they demonstrate their shattered morale by hurriedly building field fortifications or by staying within them "as if besieged by their own fear."[37] Cincinnatus was said to have degraded a consul for waiting safely in his fortifications for relief, "for he held a man unworthy of the highest command whom moat and rampart had protected, not his own valour, and who had felt no shame that Roman arms be kept in terror behind closed gates." In the late fourth century, at the very end of the period covered in this book, the emperor Julian, playing on already ancient tropes, claims that the very existence of a wall saps courage and strength.[38]

Although they were not as systematic in viewing the siege as a distinct mode of warfare, many of Rome's enemies—Celts, Germans, Greeks, and Persians—shared these values and likewise preferred to fight in the open, with the loser accepting the "decision" of the battle, at least for the moment, and surrendering some measure of wealth and political indepen-

---

35. 7.13.6. Note also the priority given to morale in Livy's soldierly rhetoric: *exercitum tuum sine animis, sine armis, sine manibus iudicas esse*. See also Luc. 10.441 and 489–91, where Caesar is aware of the shamefulness of having to shut himself within an Alexandrian palace and seems to recover his military honor by acting with aggression despite having been forced into the defensive role—the besieged as besieger.

36. 6.2.7, 7.7.2. See also 8.19.6–9, 23.16.3. Thus the "backs to the wall" cliché holds up under some scrutiny. To fight with your back to the wall is to fight with desperate courage. To fight from behind the wall might be much better from a tactical point of view, but it indicates moral defeat and will be punished in a way that honest "sporting" combat will not.

37. 6.2.9, 10.11.5. Conversely: 3.26.3–4. Livy uses *munimenta* to tell the story of morale—he is not unaware that later Roman armies saw no shame in habitually fortifying their camps. Machiavelli, a close reader of Livy, noticed and ratified this equation of the acceptance of battle with political confidence, and was therefore suspicious of the usefulness of fortresses. See *The Prince* 10; *Discourses* 2.24.

38. Cincinnatus: Val. Max. 2.7.7; see also, App. *B Civ.* 4.123; Plut. *Caes.* 19.2–3; Luc. 2.494, 10.439ff; or Plut. *Cat. Min.* 58.4–5, where Cato's philosophically practical willingness to stand siege and let time work against Caesar—a point of view presented as both intelligent and tragically out of step—is mocked and rejected. Julian: *Or.* 2.75D–76A.

dence.[39] This is practical: power had been tested (the physical power of human groups as well as the implied verdict of divine support) and refusing to accept the result of the test would push ordinary aggression toward total war. So it was wrong to lack the strength to fight and win and yet fail to capitulate.

This commitment to open battle may seem both hypocritical and foolish to us, yet, if we adopt the ancient mindset so far as to accept the moral value of military courage and to disregard the political right to exist peaceably without suffering aggression, we can perceive the logic. This way of doing things also had the undeniable benefit of keeping fighting away from urban centers, and it worked in symbiosis with Rome's sociopolitical traditions, rewarding Roman elites for seeking battle. It also limited its own damage by linking war (even defensive war) to a critical moral mass—that is, to the ability to assemble enough fighters with the confidence to risk battle. Sieges only took place when this system broke down, when a specific psychological level had been reached: a population must have morale low enough to refuse to fight but high enough to refuse to capitulate. Therefore, while a city under siege by a Roman army may be the victim of aggression, its decision to close its gates indicated an "immoral" refusal, as well as a rejection of a possible limitation of the war. By the logic of this loose "system," a city that refused either to fight in the open or to surrender—even if it was ultimately the victim of aggression—bore the responsibility for its own destruction. In any functional system the penalty for resistance needs to be worse than the situation that was refused—hence the punitive quality of the violence of the sack.[40]

---

39. In practice, of course, stratagem, duplicity, and indirect action played major roles—but to point out that cultural limitations tended to unravel toward "true war" is not to deny their fundamental importance. An argument, lately much contested, for violent open-field battle as a system for the limitation of warfare is found in Hanson (1989). On fighting before the walls, see Van Wees (2004), 124, 126ff. See also Keegan (1976), 296, 309. On Persians (Parthians), see Tac. *Ann.* 6.34.

40. See pages 50–60, for more on gate closing. See chapter 8 for the ancient interest in mass suicide by the besieged—a striking way to opt out of this system, and one that should bring attention back to the fundamental inhumanity here, which was at the service of Roman might, brutality, and nearly boundless appetite for conquest.

The same very general expectations of siege warfare were shared to at least some degree by classical Greeks (See, for example, Xen. *Cyr.* 7.5.73 or Polyb. 2.58.6–7; Polybius here, as elsewhere, distinguishes between "laws" [νόμοι] and "custom" [ἔθος], but not with much consistency) and ancient Hebrews. In fact, Deuteronomy 20:10–20 proclaims the identical laws: there is no right to avoid the siege, but surrender at contact wins the people of the city their lives, as slaves. If they close the gates and resist then the men may be killed and the

Despite this fact, Roman siege warfare was not "total war" in the modern sense—several possible points of limitation were in fact prescribed. Rather, Roman sieges were in some essential sense not quite war at all, at least in as much as "war" has open battle as its paradigmatic event. That a siege, with men and machines outlined by forbidding fortifications, looks different from a battle—that it requires a different setting—is quite obvious and very true, but the visual should not be overemphasized. "Siege" should evoke not just walls and machines, but also a different moral atmosphere, which is no less real even if we must describe it in cultural and psychological terms. And then there is the fact that the special dangers and labors of the siege led to another unique scene: the transgressive, utterly undisciplined sack, a sort of fugue state of military behavior.

These are the crucial contexts, the cultural setting of the Roman siege "scene." With this separate mode of warfare came very specific expectations about the progress of the siege. Much of this book, beginning with chapter 3, aims to demonstrate that each siege operation followed the same series of stages, sharing a formalized and widely accepted plot, a progression or forward-moving pattern that held despite many variations in its specific components and events. This progression was predicated on the initial refusal of open warfare, which allowed the besiegers to feel justified in predicating the level of violence meted out to the resisting city (when it surrendered or was taken) on the extent of their own suffering—predicating, but also amplifying, out of retributive retaliation and pent-up rage.

This book seeks to explain what happened during Roman sieges rather than to explain why it is that the Romans were so often victorious. Yet it would be strange to ignore the importance of effectiveness—an issue of significance to participants, after all. There is an answer (or one best answer among many) but it is not the familiar one. Rome exceeded contemporary societies in its ability to organize labor and deploy high technology, factors which mattered much during sieges.[41] Yet the Roman army's preeminence

---

women and children enslaved. There is also here an injunction against cutting fruit trees for siege works, a passage often invoked—without reference to its context—to demonstrate a traditional Jewish respect for trees. Fascinatingly, the *JPS* translation of 20.19—"Are trees of the field human to withdraw before you into the besieged city?"—seems to imply the same justification for the violence of the sack, exempting the trees from destruction (although they, like people who surrender at contact, must render tribute) because they did not flee.

41. Only the engineers of the Parthian and Persian empires might match their Roman

in these areas was not the most significant or most decisive element of Roman success. Because the assault of a palisade or wall was necessarily led by a few of the most aggressive or glory-hungry soldiers, and because their success or failure was often witnessed by much of the rest of the force, and, more importantly, by its commander, such an assault was the Roman soldier's greatest chance to be recognized and rewarded. Logistics and technology enable victory, but in virtually every siege the final achievement of victory depended on psychological advantage—on morale.

---

counterparts in skill. Roman soldiers, too, were usually inured to hard labor, while high-status warriors of other cultures did not generally expect to dig.

TWO

THE MORAL CONTEXTS OF SIEGE WARFARE

"À la guerre, les trois quarts sont des affaires morales."[1]

Maps adorned with colorful blocks and sweeping arrows, the firm persuasion of force strengths and distances, the eye-popping dimensions of military hardware—these traditional metrics of warfare are tangible, concrete. Beside them, mere morale seems ephemeral. Certainly, highly motivated soldiers must have fought better than unwilling conscripts—the aggressively brave better than spooked or demoralized men. But how much could that matter, when armored legions collided? And if motivation resists quantification, how can a historian accurately describe its effects? But combat motivation did matter, immensely. And it can be assessed: carefully and without certainty, but free, at least, from the dangerously misleading false certainties that arise from apparently objective data considered in isolation from human experience.

Morale, understood broadly as the confidence and willingness to fight, is more fundamental to the conduct of war than tactics or strategy, which, after all, presuppose the active participation of soldiers. Since the willingness of the group to enter combat is the basic prerequisite for battle, mo-

---

1. Correspondance Militaire de Napoléon Ier (1876), 5.1061.

rale precedes tactics.² Morale also supersedes tactics: a group of unconfident or demoralized soldiers given an excellent tactical plan will generally be defeated by highly motivated troops who force direct engagement, even at a tactical or material disadvantage.³ The nature of battle with edged weapons demands a willingness to close the physical distance between oneself and the enemy. This closing of distance is the fundamental moral⁴ obstacle of premodern warfare, and the soldiers who do it, assuming great personal risk in order to kill, are the ones who bring victory.⁵

---

2. Often hidden in plain sight is the simple fact that cultural expectation and social pressure enable military obedience: a large group of armed men cannot really be forced to go to their deaths by a handful of officers.

3. Goldsworthy (1996), 201–5.

4. I use this adjectival form in the hopes of evoking both "morale" and "morality," words that have strayed apart in recent centuries and must be brought back into overlap if Roman sieges are to be understood. "Morale" entered English from French, which makes the reconversion to the earlier and more familiar adjectival form somewhat dissonant, but in a useful way. No less a master of English prose than Edmund Blunden (1928), 38, apologized for using the adjectival form in this manner, in part to avoid coining a new, unambiguous adjectival equivalent of "morale." I find that the ambiguity* forces the reader to remember that military action cannot be removed from human culture. Roman-era understanding of the morality of siege warfare is closely tied at several points to the construction of military morale, and "moral" preserves this connection.

*This corresponds to Empson's (1930) fourth type of ambiguity, with perhaps some echoes of the first type. That the appreciation of this connection between morality and morale is to some extent the moral of this book is a mere painful pun, of the third type.

5. The importance of reckless disregard for personal safety as an element of aggression is demonstrated by the fear reflected in many ancient writers of fighting a truly desperate enemy. In a modern battle, nothing is more sought after than an encirclement at range, after which the enemy can be made to surrender or destroyed with artillery. In ancient battle, however, generals feared trapping their foe, lest desperation create "battle lust" in a previously demoralized opponent, thus delaying victory and increasing casualties while achieving little, since a routed army was hardly more of a threat than a slaughtered one. Total envelopment—the dream of most generals since Hannibal—might impress as a tactical tour de force, but it was also likely to bring a more costly victory than would a simple frontal attack. Livy loves the trope of the desperate foe (e.g., 6.3.9, 9.14.15, 37.32.6, or 9.23.8, where the dictator Q. Fabius conceals the arrival of a relief army, thus stimulating the aggressiveness of his besieged men by leading them to believe that combat is their only possible escape). The Greek historians are fond, too, of pointing out the inadvisability of fighting against desperate courage. See, e.g., App. Hisp. 90; Polyb. 16.32–3; or Josephus, who returns again and again to this theme as a way of explaining stiff Jewish resistance (BJ 3.113, 149, 153, 208–9, and 260–1 cite desperation during the siege of Jotapata; for the siege of Jerusalem see chapter 6). The special moral situation of siege warfare stems, to a great degree, from the fact that it begins in this situation of complete envelopment and that it in-

COMBAT MOTIVATION

We are focusing, then, on one dominant, yet elusive, element of morale, variously called "aggressiveness," "the will to combat," "bloody-mindedness," or, simply, "fighting."[6] Classical writers also had a wide variety of words to draw on in describing this phenomenon, but they often reached for the basic positive adjectives of manliness: *andreia* and *virtus*. To show aggressive courage in battle was to be emphatically manly.[7]

Military historians now generally recognize the distinction between this sort of "combat motivation" and other aspects of morale.[8] Combat motivation tends to focus on high-performing soldiers and their choices, while morale is often assessed as an average or general state throughout a large unit or army. Because this book is about siege combat, we will pass over the aspects of morale that pertain to keeping an army happy and willing to accept battle. The deadly fight at the end of a siege assault involved only a small percentage of the troops present, so Roman siege commanders were primarily concerned to stimulate the extreme aggression of a few rather than the confidence of the many.[9] The central question, then, is one

---

sists thereafter on the desperation of the defenders. See pages 64 and 113–15, below. See also Vegetius 4.25, Milton, Paradise Lost 2.45.

6. Will to combat: Keegan (1976), 114–17. Bloodymindedness: Baynes (1967), 97–100. Fighting: Egbert et al. (1957); Marshall (1947).

7. See pages 37–40.

8. Kellett (1982), 6: "(Combat) motivation is . . . the conscious or unconscious calculation by the combat soldier of the material and spiritual benefits and costs likely to be attached to various courses of action arising from his assigned combat tasks. Hence motivation comprises the influences that bear on a soldier's choice of, degree of commitment to, and persistence in effecting, a certain course of action." Grinker and Spiegel (1943), 37, 48, treated this "nucleus of morale" under the heading of "Motivation for Combat," recognizing what would come to be called "combat motivation" as "the psychological forces within a combat group which impel its men to get into the fight" and "the willingness to endure any sacrifice necessary to achieve success in battle."

9. See Kellett (1982), 9, on the "disproportionate" effect of "a very few highly committed men." Egbert et al. (1957), proposed that among American infantrymen 15–20 percent were responsible for all conspicuous cowardice and another 15–20 percent for all conspicuous bravery and voluntary crisis-leadership. Pennington (1943), has 10 percent fearless and 10 percent unredeemable cowards. The (dubious) accuracy of these numbers is of little moment—more important is the recognition that stories of exceptional whole-unit combat motivation do not make much sense. As for Rome, see Goldsworthy (1996), 264–71; Sabin (2000); Lendon (2005).

of combat motivation: why did some soldiers choose a much greater risk of death merely in order to do violence to strangers?[10]

The central question, but not the only moral challenge. In many sieges the decisive assault took place only after the besiegers drew heavily upon a different sort of morale, the required physical and psychological endurance necessary for prolonged labor, often under missile fire and the constant threat of a sally by the defenders.[11] This endurance morale is, like morale generally but unlike aggressive combat motivation, fundamentally supported by unit cohesion.

UNIT COHESION

The Latin *disciplina* bore a wider range of connotations than does its English descendant. It indicated a complex of ideas similar to the range of military virtues described by endurance morale, including "not merely obedience and punishment, but nearly every military excellence that was not encompassed under *virtus*."[12] A central meaning was learned self-discipline in combat—self-discipline, that is, within the group. This is an important correction of the old stereotype of Roman discipline as extremely brutal, typified by the horrifying, but very rare, punishment of decimation.[13] Ro-

---

10. Short of morale sinking to the level of mutiny, it was only this handful of exceptionally motivated fighters that really mattered. Cohesion might help an army stand under the slings and arrows of their enemies, but such missile fire is far less dangerous than the sword or spear blows of men defending themselves in close combat, especially when these men can fight unwinded and protected by fortifications.

11. Endurance morale is broadly similar to the primary twentieth-century connotation of "morale"—the tough-minded endurance of the long horrors of modern combat—that required the invention of the term "combat motivation" to describe voluntary aggression. Since ancient combat, almost always very short in duration, lacked this sense of endurance, we have good reason to insist on the replacement of the evocative Gallicism with a clunky bit of jargon.

12. Lendon (2005), 176–77, 190, 220–21, defines *virtus* as nearly identical to aggression, or the motivation to kill. For another view of military masculinity, see Phang (2001), 352–54. It is also interesting to note William McNeill's idea that drill—or any rhythmic, muscular, group activity—creates a "sense of pervasive well-being . . . a sort of swelling out, becoming bigger than life, thanks to participation in collective ritual," McNeill (1995), 2.

13. Decimation was the selection by lot of one man from ten, to be beaten to death by the other nine. The grotesque combination of intensely personal violence, collective punishment, and randomization has always fascinated, but the killing should not: most mod-

man soldiers endured under fire because of their training and their fear of acting unmanfully. Roman soldiers in a good unit also endured because of the carefully nurtured bond with their fellow soldiers. Discipline is not produced by a stick-wielding, schoolmasterish centurion, but rather is intimately connected to "unit cohesion." The orders of officers, and their enforcement by violence, strengthened the bonds among the men of the unit in several ways. Collective discipline could work to forge collective identity both by fusing the men together and by emphasizing the separation of the unit from the rest of the world. Unit cohesion distributes the pressure of the command to join battle onto a strong lattice of horizontal bonds, supplementing the motivation of fighting "against" the enemy with the sense of fighting "for" comrades. This increased moral strength is positive, then, but it is also motivated by fear of the ostracism that will follow "letting your buddies down." Roman soldiers continued to swear the old *sacramentum,* a formal oath of obedience, which surely retained at least a touch of religious awe long into the imperial period and which bound a man to his comrades.[14] Group morale bolsters individual motivation, providing a safeguard against fluctuations in the individual's will to combat.

And what were these groups, these units? The Roman army appeals to readers of military history in part because of its standardized hierarchy of units—the century of up to eighty men, commanded by (and called after) its centurion; the cohort of several hundred; and the legion itself, up to 5,000 or so strong, commanded by a senatorial noble. Writers can't resist using the adjective "regimental" here, invoking the special pride placed in maintaining centuries-old traditions specific to the unit. Yet we know little about the continuity of identity or tradition in the legions of the Republic prior to the first-century BCE civil wars, when long-serving legions began to acquire nicknames (and reputations) to go along with their numbers.[15] Even with the legions of the empire, we must tread carefully. It is

---

ern armies retain the death penalty, and most used severe corporal punishment as recently as the last century. What is most different about the Roman punishment is the role of shame, turning soldiers into the murderers of their comrades and treating them thereafter like mere beasts: the survivors of the decimated unit were afterwards fed on barley—animal fodder rather than food for men. See, e.g., Livy 2.59; Polyb. 6.38; see also Vegetius 1.13. Lendon (1997), 265 convincingly argues that a modern soldier might find many things familiar in Roman military culture—but not the role of "paralysing shame."

14. See Watson (1969), 44–50; Campbell (1984), 19, 23–32; and Phang (2008), 117–20. The changes in the oath(s) over time and the extent to which bonding to commanders or to comrades was emphasized are vexed questions.

15. See Webster (1998), 102–7, or Keppie (1984), 142–43.

too easy to make anachronistic assumptions about the consistency of Roman bureaucracy or the nature of its leadership, and terms like "regimental tradition" do not help. The permanent legions of the empire did add unit-specific celebrations and emblems, including the legionary eagle.[16] Yet the evocation of English county regiments, with their peculiar traditions, uniform quirks, and carefully cherished histories suggests more than the evidence will bear. Certainly, Caesar made much of his tenth legion, motivating it by announcing his favoritism, and its sense of corporate identity seems to have been important in the civil wars.[17] Yet this is an exceptional (and exceptionally well-attested) case, and there is no evidence that soldiers of later generations took personal pride in the legion's past accomplishments. This is somewhat beside the point: there are rousing anecdotes of heroic battlefield acts done in the name of the legion, but it is still difficult to draw a straight line from "regimental pride" to siege-assault heroism.[18]

The legion's primary relevance for our purposes is in the way signs and ceremonies might shape the worldview of its soldiers during their long years of service. The early emperors sought to insure loyalty by reminding their soldiers of the imperial presence: the image of the emperor was carried in battle and appeared on the coins of the soldiers' pay, imperial birthdays were added to the military calendar. Such propagandistic efforts might forestall rebellion or mutiny by reminding a soldier of his duty to his imperial patron, but this is hardly the equivalent of Henry's "once more unto the breach."

A century numbered at most eighty: men who knew each other's names and faces, who labored, ate, and slept in close proximity and who took their communal identity from their centurion. The centurion was surely an important figure in peacetime. He was involved in discipline and training, but neither a drill sergeant nor (necessarily) a hyper-effective fighter, as the popular image has it.[19] Rather, he was a petty bureaucrat who had

---

16. Lee (1996); Bishop (1990).

17. BG 1.40, 4.25; BC 3.91; B Afr. 16; BHisp. 31.

18. *Contra* Holmes (1985), 311, who suggests that modern soldiers could escape death anxiety via a belief in the "life" of the regiment, arguing that "group narcissism" might help a soldier "accept" both his own death and the destruction of his primary group in the knowledge "that his regiment will live on as a mystical entity." There is no Roman evidence that the relatively weak bonds of esprit de corps could make significant inroads against such an existential issue.

19. Associations of enduring toughness or "killing machine" destructiveness predominate—the British Centurion tank, or the fearsome automata devised by Cylon and

likely won his place through connections (or through the possession of skills such as literacy). His social status was much higher than that of his men, as was his pay. Nevertheless (and the Romans would have seen nothing odd in such a transformation), the centurion became a battlefield leader in the literal sense: wherever he went, there the century was supposed to follow.[20] Anecdotes of extraordinary valor by centurions are common, and such casualty statistics as we have would seem to bear out the idea that they were first into danger.[21]

While centurions embodied combat motivation, representing, in a sense, the collective *virtus* of their men, the unit itself was represented by its standard. "Standards," small decorated images carried on poles, translates the more suggestive *signa,* a category of objects that included both the legionary eagle and each century's own standard. The eagle—which displayed the legion's battle honors, played a role in army cult observances, and stood guard over the soldiers' savings deposits when the legion was in barracks—was clearly a generator and focal point of "regimental" pride for its legion. But it was not a static object of mild veneration: it was carried into battle, which meant that esprit de corps could be parlayed into an immediate cause of combat motivation. To lose the eagle was the ultimate disgrace, so the sight of the *aquila* advancing into battle both signified confidence and demanded aggression from the legionaries.[22] Roman commanders often played on unit pride by purposefully endangering the standards, turning battle into a game of "capture the flag." Frontinus preserves the old story of the young Servius Tullius throwing a *signum* into the enemy ranks to encourage his lackluster troops, and many more such stratagems are remembered in the sources. "It is recorded that the consul actually threw a standard inside the stockade to make the soldiers more eager

---

Dwemer alike—yet the image of the centurion as a backward projection of the drill-sergeant archetype also endures, thanks in no small measure to Brian Cohen's ill-executed Latin graffiti.

20. See, e.g., BG 7.12, B Afr. 82.

21. See, e.g., BG 5.44, BHisp.23. For statistics, see BG 7.51 (nearly 700 men and 46 centurions lost, a casualty rate about six times higher), BC 3.71 (960 men and 32 centurions and tribunes), or BC 3.99 (200 men and 30 "brave centurions" in the victory at Pharsalus).

22. The eagle "was" the legion in a metonymic sense that exceeds the otherwise broadly similar way in which battle colors could inspire and rally modern troops. See Suet. Claud. 13, where the inability to pull standards from the ground is taken as a prodigy and prevents a mutiny. The prestige of the *signifer* persists in many military cultures—the 26th North Carolina lost fourteen color-bearers at Gettysburg, and still found a fifteenth volunteer. Kellett (1982), 51.

to assault it, and in trying to recover it the first breach was made."[23] Such dramatic gestures were not standard practice, yet it was necessary for the eagle to be borne into each battle. This put it in some jeopardy, and heroism might fall to the *aquilifer* (eagle-bearer) who, like all standard bearers, would become the target of ambitious enemies and might be forced to avoid "military disgrace" by trading his life for the safety of the eagle.[24] These wild stories together should signal clearly that some men value these symbols and abstractions more than their own lives, and that their example could be a powerful source of immediate motivation.

FORTUNE AND FAME

The frequency of *signum*-related heroics signals the relevance of Roman esprit de corps, but it also points to the indirect workings of two more powerful forces: small unit cohesion and the competition for honor and glory. A standard-bearer charging ahead might well be seeking personal glory more than the honor of the "regiment," but it was the bonds of group cohesion that pulled more hesitant comrades in his wake.[25] Leaders could yoke together these two motivations, causing those men who would not fight for glory or a gilt eagle fight for the solidarity of their unit and the lives of their comrades. This was the middle voice of morale: not simply the minimal confidence of the army on the field or the aggression of the hyper-motivated individual, but the use of the whole matrix of threats, rewards, and bonds to ensure that groups of men were yanked along—behind the leaders, but ahead of the mass. The simplest way to effect this was to promote an ambitious man and hand him a *signum:* if he was aggressive and lucky he would soon find himself atop a wall as the rest of his unit swarmed up behind him.

But so far we have only redirected the central question into the Roman

---

23. Most *signa*-throwing stories do not involve the eagles themselves—Caesar's story of the *aquilifer* leaping into the surf and taking his eagle alone into Britain (BG 4.25–6) is exceptional. See also Livy 34.46.12; Val. Max. 3.2.20; Frontin. Strat. 2.8; Plut. Aem. 20; and Lee (1996), note 64. Harris (2006), 310 sees the standard-throwing stratagem as "making things still more difficult," but this is true only from a purely tactical point of view. Since tactical difficulties are often considered potential sources of great moral advantage, these are motivational gambles aimed at victory.

24. BG 5.37; BC 3.64.

25. Despite the much greater deadliness of modern combat to men moving in the open, at least one psychologist, Gal (1987), 154, has found that "unit cohesion . . . may serve . . . as a 'generator' of heroic behavior among the unit's members."

rank-structure. It bears repeating: what motivated a man—centurion, standard-bearer, or common soldier—to lead at the risk of his own life? Neither unit cohesion, nor any sort of generalized pride in the greatness of his unit or his emperor, was likely to drive one man to be the first up a ladder or into a breach.

There are two sorts of answers. First, he might take the lead because this type of aggression was lavishly rewarded. Most military cultures develop monetary and/or prestige awards that are geared to eliciting high-aggression behavior, and Rome was an early standout, using its hierarchy of ranks to make tangible promotion a desirable reward and also arriving at a system of stable, recognizable decorations.

Exceptional rewards are very often won, not surprisingly, in siege assaults. The first man to reach the top of an enemy wall received a prize that combined both high value and great prestige: the *corona muralis* or "wall crown."[26] The crown had been awarded as early as the Middle Republic and was sometimes supplemented by monetary rewards for the runners-up. Onasander is probably thinking of the long tradition of awarding wall crowns when he prescribes a special prize for the best men, as encouragement to volunteer to assault a strong point.[27] Caesar, usually content to claim that risky deeds of valor were done out of love for him, admits to offering monetary rewards (*praemia*) to the first men to overtop the wall at Avaricum. This offer was so enticing that the centurion L. Fabius, who later distinguished himself in the storming of Gergovia (until his excessive zeal carried him too far), "was known to have said that day among his men that he was spurred on by the rewards [offered earlier] at Avaricum, and would allow no one to mount the wall before him."[28] Josephus gives Titus a major speech, in the attempt to exhort volunteers for an assault on a formidable section of Jerusalem's walls, which touches on pride and the glory of heroic death before ending in a frank promise of wealth and promotion for any successful survivors.[29] In a less happy version of this scenario, the beleaguered Emperor Julian faced near mutiny when he prom-

---

26. If he survived. As with the *corona vallaris*—bestowed after the storming of a camp rampart—the scarcity of eligible survivors meant that the crown was infrequently awarded, and eventually the object lost its connection to actual assault heroics; see Maxfield (1981), 76–78. See also Polyb. 6.39.4, and pages 102–4, below.

27. Livy 2.20; Onasander 42.16; Maxfield (1981), 55–66, 76–80. For variations on the theme, see Herodotus 1.84.1; Livy 10.44.3–5; Plut. Brut. 31 (32); Herodian 8.4.9.

28. Or so Caesar tells us—see BG 7.27–8, 47.

29. BJ 6.33–54.

ised his army insultingly small cash prizes.[30] Cash considerations must have loomed large, too in the frequent promise of promotion, which might bring the former *miles* as much as five or ten times his current salary, with a huge grant upon retirement.[31] Officers, who were more likely than soldiers to act with an eye toward promotion, would be disproportionally motivated to keep themselves at the forefront of assaults. Thus the reward structure reinforced what was in any case desirable, namely a good representation of the formal leaders at the sharp end of the combat.[32]

Horace does the historian a great service by rolling together greed, anger, *virtus,* and cynical heroism in a comic story of the storming of a city for pecuniary gain:

> A soldier of Lucullus's, they say,
> Worn out at night by marching all the day,
> Lay down to sleep, and, while at ease he snored,
> Lost to a farthing all his little hoard.
> This woke the wolf in him—'tis strange how keen
> The teeth will grow with but the tongue between—
> Mad with the foe and with himself, off-hand
> He stormed a treasure-city, walled and manned,
> Destroys the garrison, becomes renowned,

---

30. Ammianus 24.3.3.

31. Roman army pay is a thorny problem, and there is very little evidence for the pay of centurions—but it was clearly a path to what any ordinary soldier would consider considerable wealth.

32. One of the officers decorated and promoted at the end of the siege of Jerusalem was a centurion named C. Velius Rufus, the subject of a much-discussed career inscription; on which see especially Kennedy (1983). His career before the promotion is unknown to us, but he advanced very rapidly afterward, and the conclusion that a demonstration of prowess at Jerusalem brought him the continued favor of the Flavian emperors is nearly inescapable. The eighteenth-century British navy provides an interesting point of comparison in that it, too, expected both competence and bravery from its officers, yet recognized really spectacular courage, preferably in elective combat against superior force, as a way to leap ahead in an otherwise ossified career structure. Since strict adherence to seniority made late-career promotion difficult, a great advance at the beginning of a career had long-lasting effects, and a young officer could, perhaps like C. Velius Rufus, make his career with one death-defying feat. When one John Bray captured a larger French vessel, personally lashing its bowsprit to his own ship, he was promoted to post captain by the admiralty and the midshipman who helped him was promoted to lieutenant by royal dispensation, despite not having the statutory time served. Rodger (1987), 295–97.

> Gets decorations and two hundred pound.
> Soon after this the general had in view
> To take some fortress, where I never knew;
> He singles out our friend, and makes a speech
> That e'en might drive a coward to the breach:
> "Go, my fine fellow! go where valour calls!
> There's fame and money too inside those walls."
> "I'm not your man," returned the rustic wit:
> "He makes a hero who has lost his kit."[33]

A good joke, but not at the expense of the soldier, who (though evidently thickheaded, brave, and foolhardy) ends up well compensated for the risks he ran. It is also an amusing foreshadowing of a favorite modern soldier figure, the cynical campaigner who rises to the occasion. But Horace's nameless rogue is an intentional break with the dominant and dead serious ancient tradition of celebrating heroic deeds motivated by a desire for fame and honor. Ovid, reaching for a simile, takes it for granted that a soldier who is first to scale the wall and finds himself all alone within an enemy city is "all aflame with love of fame." Vergil's episode of Nisus and Euryalus provides the most famous representation of the sober, highbrow approach to heroic volunteerism by ordinary (at least by the standards of epic) soldiers: the poet promises the "fortunate pair," killed while trying to break out through siege lines, that "if there be any power/ within my poetry, no day shall ever/ erase you from the memory of time."[34]

This promise to the fictional characters has been kept, as long as the *Aeneid* (or, now, of course, this book) continues immortal. Yet the number of still-remembered names of otherwise obscure real-life siege stormers is striking. Every one of the sources that Tacitus drew upon informed him that one G. Volusius of the third legion was the first man into the Vitellian camp at Cremona.[35] Caesar preserves for us the names of the valorous

---

33. Epist. 2.2.26–40, trans. Conington.

34. Ov. Met. 11.525–8, trans. Mandelbaum. Verg. Aen. 9.446–9, trans. Mandelbaum. It is a remarkable coincidence that the only line of the *Aeneid* found by archaeologists within a Roman military installation is 9.473, in which Rumor brings the news to Euryalus' mother. This may have been a writing exercise assigned to the son of Flavius Cerialis, commander of the fort at Vindolanda in the first years of the second century; see Birley (2002), 141–42.

35. Tac. Hist. 3.31. When reporting a similar act of volunteer heroism—two soldiers who died while disabling a huge artillery piece that threatened their units—Tacitus takes

centurions: Pullo, Vorenus, Scaeva, and Crastinus, as well as Fabius and Petronius, the stormers of Gergovia. Those who survived were promoted, and the fame they must have enjoyed at Rome, as men not only "mentioned in dispatches" but in the published version of Caesar's memoirs, would have been considerable. The authors of the empire followed suit,[36] and Josephus was a particularly avid preserver of names,[37] perpetuating the fame of Sabinus, a scrawny, dark-skinned Syrian; Julianus, a Bithynian centurion; Pudens, the auxiliary trooper who was defeated in single combat by the despicable Jonathan, and even a considerable number of their valorous foes.[38] The practice long predated Rome,[39] and it continued in late antiquity and beyond. Ammianus gives us the names of the first three men to emerge from the tunnel into the town of Maoizamalcha: the common soldier Exsuperius, the tribune Magnus, and the *notarius* Jovian. Moreover, he identifies an officer, Aelianus, by referring to a feat he had once accomplished: it seems that this was a famous man, known throughout the army as "that Aelianus who once led the rookie horsemen out from Singara."[40]

However flattering literary immortality may have been, most men certainly put more stock in a transient and local sort of fame, namely the recognition of their valor by the commander in chief in the presence of the

care to explain that their names are lost because they were using the shields of fallen comrades and thus could not be identified.

36. See, e.g., Plut. Sull. 14.2; Arist. 14.3–6; Pyrrh. 30.4–6; Val. Max. 3.2.22, 3.2.23a (among many others). The centurion Scaeva—he of the shield with 120 holes—is remembered in Valerius Maximus, Suetonius, Caesar, and Plutarch: he was a celebrity (see note 72, below). The best later compendium of literary testimony to the Roman willingness to risk life and limb for fame and eternal glory is surely Burton (1652), pt.1, sec. 2 mem. 3, subs. 14.

37. A fact which, given his likely lack of Latin and questionable status during the siege of Jerusalem, indicates reliance on the *commentarii* and thus lends support to the idea of an institutional habit of recording such names.

38. BJ 6.54; 6.81, 6.92; 6.169–76; 6.227; 5.474. See also 5.312.

39. One Dagan-Mushteshir, for instance, distinguished himself in a successful sally at Hiritum in 1764 BCE. Hamblin (2006), 231. Thucydides (3.22) names Ammias, son of Coroebus, as the first Plataean to overtop the contravallation during the breakout, while Arrian (Anab. 2.23.5, 2.27.6) preserves the names—Admetos and Neoptolemos—of the first men over the walls in Alexander's assaults on Tyre and Gaza.

40. 24.4.23; 18.9.3, the feat itself occurring in one of the lost books. Some of the Gallic troops who sallied from Amida (19.6.9) were later honored with statues. See also Procop. Pers. 2.3.22–26, 2.26.26. Medieval and early modern witnesses are just as interested in preserving names—see for instance the Crusade chronicles of Fulcher or Ambroise, or Balbi di Correggio's account of the siege of Malta.

assembled army. After the sack of Jerusalem, Titus, "eager to commend the army for its achievements and to confer the appropriate rewards on those who had especially distinguished themselves" praised the army, promising in particular that

> he would at once confer on them honors and rewards, and not a man who had chosen to exert himself more than his comrades should fail to get his due. He would give his special attention to this, since he was more concerned to reward valor than to punish malingerers.
>
> He accordingly ordered the appointed officers to read out the names of all who had performed any brilliant feat during the war. Calling them each by name he applauded them as they came forward, exulting as if their exploits were his own. He placed crowns of gold on their heads, gave them golden torques, small gold spears and silver standards, and promoted each man. He also assigned them silver and gold and clothing and other objects out of the booty.[41]

Poor Julian, standing on a platform knocked together deep in Persian territory, was only able to offer 100 pieces of silver for the lives of his soldiers, and so his expostulations on the higher value of glory were rather forced. But the basic principle was sound: reputation was tremendously important to soldiers. And it seems to have worked, since after that next town (Maiozamalcha) was taken, we read of an award ceremony that seems self-consciously in tune with even older precedent. Ammianus, in an odd little digression, mentions the old story of a siege assault that was successful largely due to the efforts of one huge soldier who single-handedly carried a ladder up to the wall. When on the next day this soldier could not be found, it was put about that Mars himself had borne the ladder, and Ammianus writes that: "If he had been a soldier, from consciousness of a memorable exploit he would have presented himself of his own accord." Human heroics performed without the desire for public praise are unimaginable. "But although the hero of this splendid feat remained wholly unknown, on the present occasion those who had fought valiantly received

---

41. BJ 7.11–15, trans. adapted from Thackeray. Caesar also paraded his troops after victories, and peacetime emperors settled for the next best thing—public praise of the efforts of soldiers in their warlike drill performances. See B Afr. 86; BG 5.52. For the empire, see the *adlocutio* of Hadrian at Lambaesis, ILS 2487.

siege crowns, and according to the ancient custom, were praised in the presence of the assembled army."[42]

Thus, despite the possibilities of cash gifts, gold crowns, and lucrative promotions, the primary value of these awards was measured in social status.[43] Fame and glory—in the eyes of the larger society but most particularly in the world of the army—were the essential reward for exceptional combat motivation. While we know little about the mental life of ordinary Roman soldiers, we know, as they did, much about the aristocratic culture of honor and shame. Throughout the republic, Roman leaders advertised their martial achievements in their speeches and on their monuments, and combat bravery was a prerequisite to social esteem and political success.[44] Polybius saw this as a Roman cultural-military advantage, since repeated public mention of noble deeds "inspires young men to endure the extremes of suffering . . . in the hope of winning glory." The best proof of this cultural conditioning was that young Roman leaders believed so strongly in the immortality of their fame that they, like Horatius at the bridge, were quite willing to die in battle.[45]

Still, it is difficult to determine to how much the values of later professional soldiers were influenced by republican aristocratic lore. Certainly, the gap between the city and the army grew rapidly throughout the principate: the soldiers who besieged Jerusalem with Titus in 70 CE did not grow up admiring the statue of Horatius in the forum or the ancient spoils that bedecked the houses of illustrious families. But, as we will see, they were still the products of a culture that emphasized the competition for glory: they knew the old stories of heroism and they watched the dramatizations of violent skill and *virtus* in the face of death that took place in the arena. Perhaps they too, like Alexander the Great, dreamt of Hercules reaching to them from the wall of a besieged city.[46]

Leadership and Siege Warfare

But Roman generals in our period did not lead siege assaults, as Alexander or Pyrrhus had.[47] Instead, they made a series of decisions that determined

---

42. Ammianus, 24.4.24. Ammianus has, rather touchingly, mistaken the ancient usage: they should have been awarded mural crowns, not the siege crown. See chapter 7, note 83.
43. See Maxfield (1981), 55ff.
44. Harris (1979); Lendon (2005).
45. Polyb. 6.54–55.
46. See Lendon (1997), 237–66. Alexander: Plut. Alex 24.3.
47. If we can believe Plutarch (Pyrrh. 22.6), Pyrrhus was the first to mount the wall of

the course of the siege and delegated actual combat leadership. Yet even as his tactical role atrophied, the commander's moral leadership grew in importance. He needed to assess the combat motivation of troops who might be called upon to assault, learning "whether or not they had fighting morale."[48] Once an assault was launched, there were essentially two ways in which a Roman commander functioned as a manager of morale: he sought to inspire his troops, to raise their energy level in expectation of battle—and he served as a witness of their behavior.[49]

This second, rather more passive role was more significant, as the many references to it attest. During a siege, the commander, even the emperor himself, might securely observe all that went on. As Severus would do many years later, Tiberius "took his seat on a platform in full view of all, in order to watch the struggle, since this would cause his men to fight more zealously."[50] The motivational effect of the commander's gaze should not be dismissed as mere propaganda or literary wishful thinking: it might inspire, but it was certainly the source of those very tangible crowns, promotions, and bags of coin. During the desperate moments of a siege assault, the commander's field of vision became a sort of mobile lottery for the daring and ambitious.

The siege could become a stage for the performance of leadership, too. Scipio Aemilianus exhorted his men from within missile range of New Carthage, protected by three attendants holding large shields, and Polybius explains that "the fact that he was in full view of his men inspired them to fight with redoubled spirit." Trajan's column also shows the emperor viewing the walls of a city while soldiers surrounded him with shields, and Josephus emphasizes the presence of his imperial prince in the danger zone near the walls (although he certainly falsifies the extent to which Titus endangered himself). Julian consciously sought to emulate Scipio.[51]

Eryx, killed "heaps" of defenders, and "proved that Homer was right and fully justified in saying that valour, alone of the virtues, often displays transports due to divine possession and frenzy." Trans. Perrin.

48. BAfr. 51.

49. MacMullen (1984), 449–51; Goldsworthy (1996), 162–63; see also Campbell (1984), 59–69.

50. Severus: Cass. Dio. 76.11.4; Tiberius: Cass. Dio. 56.13.4.

51. New Carthage: Polyb. 10.13.1–4, trans. Walbank. Column: scene 114 (Cichorius plate 85). There is an even clearer representation—but much abraded—of Marcus Aurelius sheltering behind upraised shields in scene 10 of his column; see Coarelli (2008), 130. Titus: see chapter 6. Julian: see pages 198–99.

VIRTUS AND COMPETITION

The commander stood ready to reward the glorious heroes of the assault. Yet the social and cultural forces at work are far less pleasant and seemly behind the scenes of the Roman competition for glory. For one thing, the goad behind the man who chases after immortal fame was the simple fear of shame. For another, this competition for fame and fortune was not abstract or metaphoric, but a real contest waged between comrades.

Whether he sought glory and promotion or merely to avoid embarrassment, every Roman soldier was "stirred to courage (*virtus*) by desire of praise and fear of disgrace."[52] Irrational as it might be to value honor over life, it was militarily useful: with men who feared shame so completely, Livy's description of a general rallying fleeing troops by "shaming them out of their fear" rings true.[53] In this way, as in so many others, combat was an intensification of the public world.

At the center of this nexus of honor and shame was *virtus,* another concept with wide currency in the Roman world. Often translated as "valor" or "courage," *virtus* could describe a range of different behaviors, from worthy, dignified rectitude to rash, athletic, death-defying military aggression.[54] Each soldier was under external pressures of duty and discipline but probably felt even greater internal pressure to prove himself: bravery in combat was not just one aspect of masculinity but its core constituent, and so the appropriate punishment for the failure to demonstrate courage was a denial of that masculinity.[55] Conversely, *virtus* was found in

---

52. BG 7.80; see also Lendon (1997), 239. Only a few words earlier Caesar had described the Gauls, too, as being strengthened in morale (*animos confirmabant*) by the shouts of supporting troops, as the Romans would have been if they were fighting before their own walls.

53. Livy 2.65.4.

54. On *virtus,* see Eisenhut (1973); Rosenstein (1990); Goldsworthy (1998); Lendon (1999). McDonnell (2006), 24, argues for a specific military sense. Of the examples of this usage, "most denote an aggressive type of physical courage, fewer the courage needed to withstand attack."

55. Julian forced a unit of fleers to dress in women's clothes, "thinking this a punishment worse than death for manly soldiers." Zos. 3.3.5, trans. Ridley. A fascinating glimpse of an "outsider" view of Roman discipline is Phaedrus App. 10 Perotti, the story of an effeminate soldier scorned as a *cinaedus* (passive homosexual) and believed incapable of a recent theft, since such an act required aggressive courage. Yet when a barbarian challenges the Roman army, he volunteers for single combat, while his comrades hesitate. The effeminate soldier is permitted to go, but only because, should a "worthy man" (*fortem virum*) be killed in the duel, the commander (Pompey, no less) might be open to the charge of rash-

acts that were violent, dangerous, athletic, and effective, and so its central meaning became "an aggressive quality credited to men who stormed cities, or killed opponents in single combat."[56]

Exemplified in the few leaders of a siege assault, then, this sort of *virtus* had to generate an aggression that must have looked much more like insane rage than the responsible courageousness of a respectable Roman man. The mental state necessary to charge into extreme danger had nothing to do with probity or military discipline—it was the state whose recognition in other cultures has given English the words "berserk" and "amok." In Latin, non-Roman instances of this behavior tend to be described as beast-like, while Romans are often fierce or metaphorically burning. These are men who, unlike encircled troops or the defenders in a last stage of a siege, *choose* to fight at the pitch of desperation. Roman culture reabsorbed such pre-civilized behavior by drawing this potentially destabilizing rage into the context of essential manliness.

It is strange, then, to realize that the comrades who charge the wall of a city are not cooperatively seeking success or making independent statements of their own *virtus* so much as they are competing: "The Romans, under the eye of Caesar (Titus), vied man with man and company with company, each believing that the day would lead to his promotion, if he but fought with gallantry."[57] Here, and more effectively in other siege situations, competition between groups could be used as a motivation—Titus made the construction of siege works around Jerusalem into an intramural competition, with each of his four legions tasked with building their own siege ramp as quickly as possible.[58]

Yet whatever competition between units is going on, the real competition is interpersonal: we seem to be seeing something like the opposite of unit cohesion.[59] Iliadic heroes rushed out in front of their admiring armies in search of men to kill in order to add to their personal glory: so did Roman soldiers, driven by cultural demands not all that dissimilar.[60]

---

ness (*temeritas*). When he kills and beheads his enemy, this manly act earns him a reward—and retroactive guilt for the theft. See Phang (2001), 285–87.

56. McDonnell (2006), 62, which also discusses the somewhat different sense of *virtus* as steadfastness or moral courage.

57. Josephus, BJ 6.142. See also Tac. Hist. 3.27.

58. BJ 5.466–8. There are numerous examples of the exploitation of military rivalries. See, e.g., BG 1.39, 2.27, 7.17, 8.19, 8.28; B Alex. 12; B Afr. 51; ILS 5795; Ammianus 29.6.13.

59. See Lendon (1997), 244–47, and especially (2004), 444–45.

60. Van Wees (1992), (1996), and Lendon (2005). For non-Roman examples, see also Arr. Anab. 2.27; Julian Or. 2.64B; Plut. Crass. 21.6–7.

> There were two most gallant centurions . . . Titus Pullo and Lucius Vorenus. They had continual quarrels together (over) which was to stand first, and every year they struggled in fierce rivalry for the chief posts. One of them, Pullo, when the fight was fiercest by the entrenchments, said: "Why hesitate, Vorenus? Or what chance of proving your pluck do you wait for? This day shall decide our quarrels." So saying, he stepped outside the entrenchments, and dashed upon the section of the enemy which seemed to be in closest array. Neither did Vorenus keep within the rampart, but in fear of what all men would think he followed hard.[61]

The two men kill several of the enemy and, in Caesar's telling, take turns rescuing each other, thus combining comradely support and competitive slaughter. They return to their own trenches *summa cum laude* ("with utmost praise") and no one can say whose *virtus* is the greater. This feat raised the morale of the troops, but accomplished nothing tactically. Sallust, too, sees competitive killing—and siege assaults—as the epitome of true Roman bravery:

> To such men no toil came amiss, no ground was too steep or rugged, no armed foe formidable; courage had taught them to overcome all obstacles. To win honor they competed eagerly among themselves, each man seeking the first opportunity to cut down an enemy or scale a rampart before his comrades' eyes. It was by such exploits that they thought a man could win true wealth—good repute and high nobility.[62]

Yet it is possible to see cohesion, too, at work in such acts, generating the bonds that drag other soldiers—in rivalry or fear of shame, certainly—after the most aggressive leaders. Or, just possibly, they could also be motivated by loyalty, following to fight "for" instead of "against." This is

---

61. BG, 5.44. In a nice example of ancient name preservation leading to enduring fame, the two centurions were borrowed by HBO's *Rome*, with Pullo suffering the indignity of demotion before being compensated with the plum job of *virtus* tutor to the young Octavius.

62. Sallust, BC 7, trans. Handford. The same emphasis is found in the twelfth-century Syrian warrior and writer Usama Ibn Munqidh (2008), 168, who notes that "when a man becomes known for his audacity . . . his ambition demands that he perform noteworthy deeds that his peers cannot accomplish."

why Onasander believes that friends should be stationed beside each other in battle, because they will then fight "more recklessly."[63] Psychologists have argued that "the dominating motivating factor for acts of courage can be found in the structure of social relationships within the primary group," (i.e., a group of some ten or twenty men).[64] Yet the Roman army did not have units this small, a fact that has led to the assumption (despite the lack of evidence) that groups of eight tentmates fought together as a formal squad.[65] But the search for a Roman "squad" is misguided: we do not need the unit to have the cohesion. The motivation we seek most of all is the motivation to approach danger: the leader closes distance with the enemy and some of his friends and fellow soldiers struggle to close or maintain their distance with him, driven by the possibility of fame and fortune, by the fear of shame, and by the affective bonds of comradeship.

Prospective Mortality, Altruism, and the Volunteer

But these men were likely to get themselves killed, which is all well and good if they have, like Sarpedon (or Servius Tullius, or a republican aristocrat for that matter), been living the life of a Homeric *promakos*, fighting among the foremost because they enjoy high social status.[66] But were ordinary Roman soldiers the victims of a system that won wars on the cheap by eliciting self-destructive behavior from the few unfortunates foolish

---

63. Onasander, 24.

64. Gal (1987), 32. The "small group" loomed very large in morale research following the Second World War, but is no longer receiving as much attention. See also Kellett (1982), 9, 44–45.

65. Keppie (1984), 173. MacMullen (1984), note 22, adduces some evidence; Harris (2006), 304, raises important questions. That Vegetius' organizational scheme uses *contubernia* in this fashion demonstrates either that tent-mates fought together or that an affective term later became a technical term meaning "squad," but not both. The Vindolanda tablets demonstrate that *contuberbalis* (as well as *frater*) was used in affectionate correspondence among soldiers. That these bonds were intimate is suggested by the migration of the word from its military context to mean first a close friend (in, e.g., Cicero and Pliny) and then a favored concubine or beloved partner. Such bonds among soldiers on the battlefield are generally passed over in our major sources, but see the exceptional B Alex, 16.

66. Il. 12.310ff. Van Wees (1996), 24, notes that superheroic glory is typified in Homer by only a handful of different acts: "Slaying a rival in single combat before the assembled army, or being the first to breach the wall in an assault on fortifications; . . . an ἀριστεία; or killing a warrior of great stature." Given that only the second was regularly possible in historical Roman practice, Roman siege *virtus* seems quite Homeric. See also Aen. 9.525 ff.

enough to throw their lives into such a lottery? They must have been (as soldiers often are), unless we can argue that fame and fortune were worth the mortal risk (this would be difficult to do), or that a common, elective, self-destructive behavior came about "naturally." These are, for a modest humanist, waters at least as treacherous as the Cartagena Lagoon, but could psychology or evolutionary biology suggest an explanation?[67]

In the last few generations, self-sacrificing acts have come to dominate major military awards for valor, and it has been argued that altruistic sacrifice is an unexceptional thing: "Dying for one's comrades . . . is a phenomenon occurring in every war, which can hardly be thought of as an act of superhuman courage. The impulse to self-sacrifice is an intrinsic element in the association of organized men in the pursuit of a dangerous and difficult goal."[68] This is something more than rivalry, surely, but before we ask whether Roman soldiers might have agreed with such a statement we should recognize the technological differences that make a comparison nearly impossible. It is very difficult to assess the actual deadliness of ancient combat, but major open-field battles rarely resulted in more than 5 percent fatalities on either side.[69] Most of these occurred among the aggressive men who fought with hand weapons at the very front of the battle, while the masses behind were relatively safe. But modern acts of heroism tend to involve leaving cover and venturing onto the much more deadly "empty battlefield" for purposes other than battle-winning aggression. The Medal of Honor, in fact, is most often won either for rescue attempts or sacrificial acts, with enlisted men and junior leaders being most likely to act to save other members of the primary group rather than to harm the enemy.[70] There is an odd sentimentalism here: the recent military hero,

---

67. Like many in the humanities, I am an avid spectator of the more public contests over aspects of social evolution, group selection, reciprocal altruism, and other tempting concepts—and happy to remain safely in the grandstand rather than join the scrum. Cartagena Lagoon: see chapter 4, pages 99–107, with note 66.

68. Gray (1959), 91.

69. See Sabin (2000). Even 5 percent losses may have been unusual; the significant exception being fatalities among the defeated when their army is trapped, enveloped, or pursued during a prolonged rout.

70. See Egbert et al. (1957), Blake (1976). Blake's statistics on Vietnam-era Medals of Honor support these generalizations, but no rigorous statistical survey has been attempted. Interestingly, as the rank of the recipient rises so does the chance of the act being aggressive rather than sacrificial ("war winning" rather than "soldier saving," although these classifications are built on odd groupings of the subcategories). And the percentage of posthumous awards falls dramatically. Rome recognized soldier saving actions with the coveted *corona civica*—but only if both rescuer and rescued survived.

especially if he or she is of relatively low rank, is often recognized for an act of enormous courage and devotion to the primary group, but one that does not take place in a context of military success. The quintessential act is falling on a grenade. This demonstrates our cultural commitment to believing that war can reveal great goodness or nobility. But it has nothing to do with combat motivation.[71]

Rome, too, recognized self-sacrificing valor: Caesar gives Petronius action-movie-worthy last words as he charges into a group of Gauls, dying to save his men, and there is the famous pseudo-*devotio* of Cassius Scaeva.[72] Self-sacrifice was celebrated then as now, but the emphasis in Roman culture was very different: valor was encouraged and recognized because it brought glory, and glory meant success. Holding out, covering a retreat, falling on a grenade: these things enable a future victory, at best. Ideally, a modern battle would be won without any such actions, but no Roman battle was won without demonstrations of high combat motivation—leading, fighting first, killing. More to the point, no Roman siege could end in victory unless a soldier qualified for the *corona muralis*. But how many of these men lived? How deadly were Roman siege assaults?

This, question, unfortunately, is both very important and very difficult to answer. There are no formal siege assault casualty reports in the sources. Moreover, the degree of risk would have varied depending upon the nature of the site and the skill and morale of its defenders. As we will see, Jerusalem proved extremely deadly, yet at the other extreme Tacitus claims that none were killed and only a few wounded when Corbulo stormed Volandum.[73] A siege assault involved an approach under plunging missile fire to fortifications that had to be penetrated on a narrow frontage, the width of a ladder, tunnel, tower, gate, or breach. An attacker would not necessarily

---

71. Blake (1976) has around two-thirds of all awards to enlisted men for "soldier saving" actions. Sixty-one men enlisted men, NCOs, and lieutenants won the medal for throwing themselves on a grenade (or other explosive) in order to save others.

72. Petronius: BG 7.50, but see note 28, above: Caesar is praising the sacrifice in part to deflect our attention from the ill-considered assault. Scaeva: App. BCiv 2.60 (and Plut. Caes. 16.2; Suet. Div. Jul. 68; Caesar BC 3.53) with a fascinating epic fictionalization into an avatar of evil *virtus* by Lucan 6.140ff. This was not technically a *devotio*, the ancient rite in which a nobleman/priest consecrated his life to the gods before battle and then sought death. Besides, Scaeva survived. Appian wants us to read the episode as a grenade that failed to explode: shame propelled his men to rescue him, so Scaeva's sacrifice failed, but he succeeded in motivating his men.

73. Tac. Ann. 13.39.4. Jerusalem: see chapter 6; other than in Josephus there are very few enumerations of assault parties.

be able to shield himself or use his own weapon effectively, especially if he was climbing. Even a general assault with multiple towers, many ladders, or fighting at several gates would involve, at most, a few score men in actual combat at any given moment. Even if a man killed the first defender he met, he still occupied the inescapable focal point of the fight and would, if the defenders were not disheartened, face another foe immediately. Even if he were wounded or exhausted, there was no tide of battle to pass: the assault had to go through him.[74]

Bereft of statistics, it is necessary to fall back on a two-part argument. There is much anecdotal evidence from the Roman period for the fact that, in any sort of intense combat, the bravest or most aggressive fighters are more likely to be killed. Tacitus frequently points out that victorious armies become uncertain and easily defeated once their *fortissimi* have been killed;[75] so too in Polybius, where those foremost in danger suffer first.[76] If the bravest and best are more likely to die in fluid battle, this must be even more true of an assault, which isolates them against more numerous, rested, sheltered defenders. It remains to show that these men in fact led the attack. An assault could be carefully planned and initiated in good order; nothing prevented a commander from picking the unit(s) he wanted. Yet there is not a single account in the sources of a particular century, maniple, or cohort being ordered to attempt a narrow siege assault.[77]

It seems plain that the standard Roman practice was to assemble a group of volunteers. Even if no such group was recognized before a unit made a general assault, the same process of self-selection—by closing the distance to the target more quickly—would bring the most highly motivated soldiers to the wall first. Sallust's description of the assault of Zama in 109 BCE makes it entirely dependent upon the motivation of unspecified individuals: "The Romans fought according to their temperament, some standing off and slinging stones or bullets, others charging up to the

---

74. This combination of concentration on an individual and dramatically high mortality is why the assault on fortifications is one of the characteristic heroic acts in epic, on which see note 66. Hamblin (2006), 448–49, finds fear of the deadliness of the siege assaults as far back as the Egyptian Old Kingdom. Also worth noting is the biblical association of personal faith and the act of scaling a wall (e.g., 2 Samuel 22.30/Psalms 18.30: "With You, I can rush a barrier,/With my God, I can scale a wall").

75. Tac. Hist. 4.33, 5.21, Ann. 12.38, Agr. 34. See also Ammianus 31.15.7.

76. Polyb. 5.98–100.

77. There is a partial exception at Livy 32.17.10, but this is an unusual assault, through a large breach that had been cleared after the initial assault temporarily succeeded before being driven back. See also 10.44.5.

wall and trying to dislodge it or climb it with ladders because they were eager for hand-to-hand combat . . . Even those who were fearful and unwilling to go near the walls did not escape without injury, for they were hit by spears thrown by hand or launched from machines; thus the danger, although not the glory, was shared by the good men and fearful men alike."[78] Sallust here glosses over an important distinction: whatever the threat from distance weapons, hanging back under missile fire was nowhere near as dangerous as attacking a defended wall. In another attack on a formidable fortress he gets it right: "the best men were getting killed and wounded, while the rest grew more afraid." For the most part, the cowardly were at the risk of injury, while the fighters courted death.[79] Even more so than in battle, it was the fastest and the most reckless who volunteered to lead the assault, taking on "the largest share of toil and danger."[80] Onasander counsels against committing an entire force to an assault against a difficult objective, assuming that volunteers will be drawn to such a task. He sees this as a positive cost-benefit exchange: "I do believe that certain soldiers of the army must be allowed to run desperate risks—for if they succeed they are of great assistance, but if they fail they do not cause corresponding loss."[81] And while a general can encourage destructive behavior, he cannot persist in ordering individuals or very small units to suffer long odds. Volunteers were essential.[82]

And these volunteers often died: how deadly were Roman siege assaults? Deadly enough to remark upon, but rarely deadly enough to deter a well-motivated force from victory. This is most explicit in Polybius, who, although he never gives numbers, does describe siege assaults as involving "combats of so desperate a character, that at times more men fell in these encounters than usually fall in a pitched battle." It is often clear that such casualties are considered high but that, nevertheless, there will always be volunteers rushing to take their fallen comrades' place on the

---

78. Sall. Iug. 57.4–6. Trans. adapted from Handford.

79. Sall. Iug. 92.9. See Handford (1963), 9–10: Sallust is a better informant on Roman cultural assumptions than on more technical military matters.

80. Val. Max. 3.2.6b. The prospect of such high casualties could be exaggerated into an equation between *virtus* and disdain for life. Val. Max. 2.7.9, makes the desire for life dishonorable. Moreover, at 3.2.7, *virtus* is personified and opinionated, considering any "submission to fortune worse than any fate." "Manliness," then, can be twisted into something that seeks out spectacular ways to die.

81. Onasander, 32.3. See also BHisp. 13, where a problematic portion of the text describes an assault, initiated by confident troops apparently without orders, that seems to result in the capture of the would-be heroic volunteers.

82. See Gilliver (1996), 154; and (1999), 144.

ladder.[83] The most aggressive went first, but their comrades—other pre-assault volunteers, the only slightly less *fortissimi* of their unit—followed. Whatever their motivations, every man who pushed his way onto the ladder or through the breach also spared his "buddies" that particular danger. There is a hint here of reciprocal altruism, but the outcome, rather than the heroic tragedy of the grenade, is the seizing of the fortified objective. In the end there is no pressing need to choose between cohesion and competitive ambition: in either case, the presence of close comrades was a powerful motivational force channeled in a useful direction.

STORMING THE WALLS

But who were these volunteers? Why did they really choose to do what they did? A young, habitually aggressive officer discusses the motivation behind the choice to lead a desperate attack on enemy fortifications:

> When I look back now to that blind dash across the open against a choice and well-furnished position, I see that we must have been inspired by a quite improbable degree of recklessness. And yet, where would be the success of war if it were not for individuals whom the thrill of action intoxicates and hurls forward with an impetus not to be resisted? It seemed often as though death itself feared to cross our path.[84]

Alas, there is no surviving account written by an experienced Roman soldier that describes combat from a personal perspective—if, indeed, anything like that was ever written down. The writer here is Ernst Jünger, and the action he describes took place in Flanders in 1918.[85]

Jünger believed that success in close combat could only be achieved by

---

83. Polyb. 1.42.13, trans. Paton/Walbank. See also 10.13 and 8.37—both sieges discussed in chapter 4—and especially 4.71, although these are Macedonian troops.

84. Jünger (1929), 260. Trans. Creighton.

85. Often decorated and more often wounded, Jünger enjoyed leading out small groups of men to seek combat and finished the war in command of a unit of storm troopers. After his unrepentantly nationalistic memoir, *In Stahlgewittern*, made him famous, he was for some years a public anti-Semite, ultra-nationalist, and Nazi fellow traveler before breaking with the Nazis and regaining international regard as an expressionist writer. He died in 1998 at the age of 102—unusual longevity for a dedicated "front fighter" who had actively sought combat in a military situation that had all of the asymmetries of siege warfare (including the dominance of the defense and the high rate of casualties among junior officers) with none of its decisiveness.

the irrational and undisciplined aggression of those few who found themselves, as he says in fine Homeric fashion, "among the foremost." Such actions, so vivid in poetry, would be invisible to the historian's eye, and were often passed over in descriptions of open battle. But when the scene was set and the general was watching, we can still occasionally catch a glimpse. During the Third Punic War, the walls of Megara (an outer section of Carthage), were too well defended for a general assault, but a group of the "most daring young men" rushed the wall from a tower and climbed down to open a gate and admit the army.[86] Many stories survive of famous generals having led such actions in their pre-command youth: Plutarch tells us that the young Antony led a volunteer assault, reaching the ramparts first and killing many.[87] Scipio Aemilianus, fighting in Spain under Lucullus, was said to be the first to climb the walls of Intercatia, and when he came to command he noticed the valor of Marius at the siege of Numantia.[88]

The Roman army was disciplined, professional, and capable. Its thoroughgoing organization, seemingly so modern, has always attracted the admiration of military writers who love a well-ruled checkerboard. But even in battle, once the fighting began, tactical subordination only existed at the back of the formation, where discipline and duty kept the less brave in step. While discipline played a role in siege warfare, enabling the approach, the assault depended upon the high combat motivation of a few, who fought with primal ferocity. We know of the auxiliary Sabinus not just because his rush to death and glory was dramatic but also because it was effective. Sabinus was killed, but his army, despite repeated failures against Jerusalem's high, fiercely defended walls, continued to find volunteers, and so it was eventually victorious. Rome's long record of success in such endeavors was the product of a culture and a military system that encouraged such valor in many ways. The siege-winning decisions were made not (or not only) in the minds of the commander, but in the minds of those few who chose to risk themselves most in the race to the wall. The survivors stood in rank and file again when they received their golden prizes of valor.

---

86. App. Pun. 117.
87. Plut. Ant. 3.1; see also Lys. 28.5.
88. Val. Max. 3.2.6b. Appian, Hisp 53, does not have the same story—instead Scipio fights a single combat. Numantia: Plut. Mar. 3.2, but not during an assault (see pages 113–15). In addition, a young artillery officer named Bonaparte was wounded during the assault on Toulon in 1794.

THREE

THE SIEGE PROGRESSION

Ancient warfare was usually fluid, but a siege was contained, confined, and circumscribed. The beginning and end were easily recognized as such, and so the siege was experienced as something like a finite narrative: it began, and tension built steadily toward a clear conclusion. The longer and more difficult a siege the greater the motivational challenge, and the greater the moral cost. The besieging commander, instead of simply setting a battle plan in motion and hoping to commit his reserves at the right point, was able to control each stage of the siege, deliberately choosing each new tactic or method of approach. These distinct properties of siege warfare are fairly obvious to a careful reader of the ancient sources. Attracting less notice, though essentially a sum of these parts, is the fact that Rome (and by this I mean both Roman culture and the men of its armies) preferred battle to the rigors of siege warfare, and linked the extreme violence of the sack to the defenders' refusal to fight openly.[1]

There is one more important difference: far more than any other sort of ancient conflict, the siege followed a regular, predictable pattern—a progression that was in the mind of the commander as he began the siege and which informed the observations of eyewitnesses. This chapter seeks to add to our understanding of Roman siege warfare by sketching the general

---

1. Not only was the siege contained in time and space and confined within the expectations of its linear progression, but it was also circumscribed by the conventions of writing about siege warfare, which irremediably mediate our understanding of the historical events themselves. See chapter 1, and chapter 4, particularly notes 29–34.

course of the siege progression and recovering, as it were, a long-lost ancient thought artifact. While ancient narratives and modern studies almost always treat the siege as a major operation in the course of the campaign under discussion, here we examine the Roman siege synoptically. Although we lose (for the moment) the details provided by strategic context, we gain important insight into the event category itself, the way it was shaped by the expectation and understanding of the commander, the participants, and the writers who describe it to us. The progression must be flexible if it is to approach comprehensiveness, but it will be subjected to closer scrutiny in the following four chapters.

THE ONE-WAY SIEGE

The intensity of a siege could be counted upon to increase: steadily, with the passage of time, but also in large, predictable increments as new tactics and technologies were tried. The representation of such a process takes great narrative skill and thus can be hard to perceive, yet each day that a siege dragged on damaged both other strategic goals and the reputation of the men prosecuting it. But we can see—quite plainly, in most historians' work—the increase in violence that occurred as each new method of approach, usually more labor intensive or potentially more dangerous than the last, was first attempted.

The progression of a siege from one stage to the next is something like a ratcheting gear: the wheel turns steadily and more energy enters the system, but only as it clicks through a tooth on the receiving gear is a new level of tension stored in the machinery.[2] When the siege ends, the tension in the tightly wound gear—the psychological and physical price paid by the besiegers—is released, and the clicking of the unwinding wheel measures out the violence of the sack. Looked at in this way, the tactical and technological panoply of Roman siege warfare is subordinate to its moral state, and the assembling of a stage-by-stage progression in this chapter can be seen as the erection of a structure for making sense of morale.

The commanding general did, of course, make a careful assessment of the fortifications and the practical strengths and weaknesses of each possible mode of approach. He then chose whatever tactic seemed to provide a decent chance of success at minimal cost in blood and treasure. If this

---

2. See Murakami (2011), 497: "Gears that have turned forward never turn back. That is one of the world's rules."

failed, he moved on through the progression, all the while calculating and recalculating the morale of the fighters on both sides. Each new application of risk and effort by the besieger promised more violence, and ratcheted up the level of tension not only between besieger and besieged, but in the contract of assent between besieging soldiers and their commander.

Broadly speaking, there were two ways to take a fortified place: a mass assault on the fortifications or a laborious attempt at victory through engineering. Each of these methods was more stressful for soldiers than the mutual violence of open-field battle: most, if not all men, are much better able to psychologically prepare themselves for short periods of intense danger than for prolonged exposure to attrition.[3]

Roman legionaries were accustomed to regular heavy labor, but not while under fire. Even when not digging or building, Roman soldiers hated to face harassing arrow or sling-stone fire, despite the fact that long-range missile fire, especially against men equipped with large shields and helmets, was not nearly as dangerous as a mêlée.[4] The wear and tear of attrition, often in the form of slight wounds from nearly spent sling stones or partially deflected arrows, was combined with the constant threat of a surprise sally. Stress accumulated because legionaries under harassing fire could not respond in kind. Exhaustion, brought on by the demands of siege labor—digging and tunneling; cutting and hauling timber, earth, and stone; building all sorts of screens, sheds, and towers and then dragging them into position—also undermined morale. Finally, and perhaps most importantly, there was no compensatory chance to earn fame and fortune. A legionary was salaried and inured to hard labor and discipline, but open combat gave some leeway to choose greater risk and reward or to remain relatively safe. Siege work provided no such chance.

But a siege assault did, particularly if it was an assault on the narrow frontage of a breach or bit of wall top, made approachable only by weeks of labor and engineering. Such an assault provided a greater opportunity

---

3. See Grinker and Spiegel (1945), and chapter 2, note 11. Holmes (1985), 216, writing of modern and early modern military history, notes that "sieges, too . . . seemed to bruise men's tolerance more than battles in open field." See also Holmes (1985), 138–40; Van Wees (2004), 144; Lenski (2007), 229.

4. Hence the clichéd scene of Roman soldiers begging for the general engagement to begin, because delay subjected drawn-up heavy infantry to the missile fire of skirmishers. For hatred of arrow fire in a siege-like situation, see Caesar *BC* 3.44. For troops clamoring for a battle to begin, see, e.g., Caesar, *BG* 7.19, *BC* 3.90; Ammianus 16.12.13. See also Wheeler (2001).

for glory, and for converting stress into violent action, than any other.[5] A Roman general could expect that competent command decisions, appropriate leadership, and regular pay would ensure the willing performance of ordinary duties. But given the stresses of siege warfare his soldiers would expect additional payment, and he therefore had to weigh the degree to which normal expectations were being exceeded, giving thought not only to the motivation level of the minority of soldiers who might seek the opportunity of the assault but also to the basic morale of the majority, who would enable and support it. In a sense, he was mortgaging the loyalty of his men for their good service, and the debt would be paid at the end of the siege: in return for exceptional effort came the exceptional payment—in both a pecuniary and psychological sense—of the sack.

The violence of the sack thus stems first from the collective psychology of the besieging army, but it can also be seen as a mechanism of retribution.[6] Ancient writers casually refer to the "laws" of war, meaning a set of customs that loosely guided the expectations of combatants.[7] These customs could always be violated by the stronger party, but they served the interests of the aggressor in any event, ordaining the protection of civilians only if they surrendered. If a city closed its gates, however, it forfeited civilian status: males of military age immediately became combatants without the right to surrender, and women and children might be sold as slaves. Prolonged resistance earned greater punishment when the sack took place, sometimes extending even to the massacre of the population and the obliteration of the city. As horrifying as these rules were—brutal, unjust, admitting no right of peaceful independence—they did have the effect of placing some limitations on violence, using the leverage of terror to force early capitulation and thus protecting soldiers from sieges and civilians from the sack.[8] Superficially, this demonstrates a willingness on the part of the Romans and neighboring cultures to accept, for lack of a better word, the fact of war.[9]

---

5. See chapter 2.

6. See page 19, and chapter 8.

7. See Oakley (1997), I, 419–20. The laws of siege warfare are most often invoked in justification of the sack (see pages 214–15, below) but the existence of reliable formalities is often quite clear; see, e.g., Polyb. 2.58.6–7; App. *B Civ.* 5.41, *Hisp.* 79.

8. The Roman fetial customs and the early stages of "just war" theory fall outside the scope of this study. Suffice it to say that Roman laws against purely aggressive war were nearly as successful as the Kellogg-Briand pact of 1928.

9. This approach was in most ways more practical than modern rules: it accepted the destructive impulses of an invading army but extended protection from personal violence

Envisioning the Progression

Much of the rest of this chapter is devoted to sorting the descriptions we have of stratagems, assaults, and feats of engineering into the categories of the siege progression. It is impossible to know exactly how Roman commanders conceived of the range of choices they would have to make, stretching outward in time and upward in intensity, but a useful modern analogy is the flowchart. Each decision to escalate the intensity of the siege cut off a whole host of other options and opened the way to either victory or a narrowing set of untried or repeatable methods.[10] The idea, then, is to think through the siege along with the commander, bearing always in mind the moral, as well as material, demands of movement to a new level of the progression.

Although the flowchart embraces many different tactics and technologies, there are still only a handful of basic categories, a few ways to conquer a fortified place. The first and most fundamental choice was whether to conduct an active siege or a passive blockade.[11] As we will see below, it is

---

to noncombatants. To the victor was owed spoil and submission, but an invading army that murdered civilians in the open would be faced with a desperate resistance. So this was wrong: to treat people who had not closed their gates and persisted in a siege "as is usual in a city taken by storm" (Polyb. 3.86.11) was generally considered an outrage. Examples of this behavior or of similar breaches of promise are often remarked upon (e.g., Livy 2.17.6, 9.31.2, 24.19.9–10, 28.3.11–13). Plutarch disapproved (*Aem.* 29) of Aemilius Paullus' sack-by-stratagem of the cities of Epirus in 167, "an action perfectly contrary to his gentle and mild nature," and Sallust commented (*Iug.* 91.7) that the sack of Capsa was "against the law of war." See also Pomeroy (1989), Oakley (1997), I, 420–21.

10. The "decision tree" would be another possible analogy, but as these appear to be consistently binary, it is less apt than the flowchart, which might contain manifold options at a certain point, allow for some repetition, and return to the same sort of option at different levels of the progression. I do not suggest that a graphic representation of the siege progression ever existed, only that this might be a decent analogue of the mental model. Roman commanders were not familiar with good maps or complex schematics, but they were used to organizing large sets of independent items and probably had familiarity with hodological representations (such as the *Tabula Peutingeriana*), which bore strong visual and logical similarities to a flowchart. See also Campbell (1987), 20, on the military handbooks and the use of sets of *exempla* in education.

11. The ancient sources are almost always very clear about the distinction and the binary choice: see, e.g., Veg. *Mil.* 4.7; Livy 37.5.5; Tac. *Hist.* 5.13.4; Caesar's assessment of Alesia at *BG* 7.69; or, while we're at it, Luc. 9.273. English is slightly problematic because of the naval or economic resonances of "blockade" and the much stronger associations of "siege" with static or attritional warfare and thus the suffering and starvation of the besieged. The primary words in Greek and Latin were more balanced, evoking both grim offensive engi-

sometimes impossible to clearly separate the two, especially since the distinction hinges on the intent of the besieging commander: hunger leading to surrender is the goal of a blockade, while active sieges aim to take the place by force, even if blockading tactics and the weakening effects of hunger aid this effort.[12] Blockades were a rarity, and will be briefly considered at the end of the chapter.

Many writers see one further subdivision, leaving us with three basic approaches: aside from the blockade, we have sieges that succeed "by stealth" or "by storm."[13] But looking at the successful tactic without regard for the stage of intensity that the progression has attained yields little useful information: the character of stealth or surprise actions depends on previous engineering (if any) and assaults, as well as the defenders' expectations, which derive in part from their understanding of the rhythms of siege warfare. Stratagems pose another problem, since they are predicated on political and ethnic context (the solicitation of treachery is the most important subcategory of stratagem) as much as on the siege progression. Those that are essentially assault techniques will be considered as a separate category of assault, but others, too much intertwined with the broader context of the particular siege, will not be discussed here.

So, setting aside blockade and stratagem and focusing on force, we find a more useful trinity: assaults that go "over, through, or under the wall."[14] That is, the wall will be neutralized by an escalade without significant engineering aid, penetrated through a breach made by mining or battering, or circumvented by tunneling. This prepositional scheme for determining the assault/wall relationship is superficially appealing, but it omits both the fourth dimension of siege warfare and the single most important conse-

---

neering and suffering. In practice, Greek authors were careful to modify πολιορκία with words denoting the actual tactic—hunger or violence. Latin had the blanket term *obsidio* but also *obsessio* (more likely to signal a blockade, but also used of sieges generally), each of which could be modified—"by hunger," "by siege works"—as well as *oppugnatio*, which could mean any sort of attack or assault, including individual siege assaults, yet, significantly, could also be used to describe the entirety of an active siege: "the taking of a fortified place by storm" is an *expugnatio*.

12. See Lenski (2007), 225, on Veg. *Mil.* 4.7.1–2. In addition, the presence of lines of circumvallation is often taken to indicate a blockade, but this is not the case: see pages 65 and 77–79, below.

13. Goldsworthy (2003), 188. *RE*, "Festungskrieg" also opts for a tripartite division, as does Appian, at *Pun.* 6.33.

14. Goldsworthy (2003), 188, the three subcategories of "by storm." Identical are Eph'al (2009), 68; Davies (2006), 117; and McCotter (1995), 149, and Milton, Paradise Lost 11.656-7.

quence of the moral context, namely the degree of aggressive combat motivation required of the assault troops. Going under the wall through an intact tunnel to surprise the enemy and secure a gate or wall section is a very different action from mining under a wall to cause a breach and a consequent assault at/through the wall—one requires a small band of volunteers; the other, a general assault.[15]

Really, though, the exact number of tactics and methods is legion, and any sorting system will fail when the more complex and difficult sieges are considered.[16] What we need to keep in mind is both the amount of time spent on enabling the approach and the technological enhancement (or prior damage to the fortifications) that the method of assault requires. The most basic conceptual division used by ancient authors is the most useful: the assault of unsupported infantry as opposed to the engineered approach.[17]

The progression moves, then, from the hope of capitulation to light assaults and on to the assaults which use embankments, towers, and rams. These methods approach only a small area of the wall, which allows the defense to concentrate, making the eventual attack more deadly. Tactics cannot be fluidly interchanged as in open combat: the progression to a new level of effort precludes a return to a less intense tactical and moral stage—the gear wheel did not budge.[18]

Progression and Narrative

The literary accounts of Roman sieges often emphasize the transitions in the progression even while eliding the long intermittent periods of labor

---

15. And both were rare in Roman practice. See pages 87–88, 96–97, 117, and 202, below.

16. Watson (1993b), 138, counts four methods; Campbell (2006), 11, five. Yadin (1963), 16, and Bleibtreu (1990), 41–44, on ancient Mesopotamia, both also have five; Bradbury (1992) on the European Middle Ages, has six (and all are alliterative); but the ancient Chinese philosopher Mo Tzu takes the cake with twelve—see Needham (1994), 413. Machiavelli, *Discourses* 2.32, anticipates this chapter quite nicely: first he gets rid of blockades and surrenders, then he divides the pure assault from an assault mixed with fraud and explains that the general assault would be tried before heavy engineering was resorted to.

17. To Tacitus, *Hist.* 5.13.4, these are the "quick attack" and the more laborious type of assault that depends upon, at the very least, mantlets and other protective constructions.

18. This is not to say that advantage in a siege flows steadily from one side to the other. Besiegers can suffer setbacks from sallies or the undermining of their work, and narratives of sieges commonly feature an ebb and flow of fortune which, however much a literary convention, can also reflect fluctuation in the perceived "chances" of victory for each side—a perception which would move in close coordination with morale.

and waiting, giving us something like a series of stop-motion pictures of the siege. Narrative markers—pauses, digressions, bursts of dramatic prose—can also point to important transitions. Yet a certain suspicion is appropriate here: dicing narratives into episodes, then sorting and reconstituting them into a composite "progression" might render wholesome histories into unsavory sausages whose claim to composite factuality might seem less "historical" than the original chunk of text.

And so it does, which is why the bulk of this book consists of readings of individual siege accounts. Yet there are two good methodological defenses of this chapter. First, it provides an opportunity to bring in other sources of evidence—military handbooks in particular—to supplement the major narratives. Given that the narratives often presume a broader familiarity with the principles and customs of Roman warfare than we now possess, it behooves us to assemble all of the evidence we have in order to help us read between the lines, as knowledgeable Romans would have. Second, because a high-altitude view can reveal subtle contours that are hard to see at ground level—collecting as many sources as possible for the many centuries of Roman siege warfare will permit such a perspective. So, while the stages of the progression can be easy to appreciate in the sources, it should be made clear that the terminology used here—the categories and coinages—do not, unless otherwise noted, have any historical reality themselves, other than as rough approximations of terms and concepts in ancient minds. The goal of this classification scheme is twofold: to trace the siege commander's decision making and to understand the Roman siege as it was experienced by participants.[19]

THE SIEGE PROGRESSION: PRELIMINARIES

The Pre-Contact Stage

Every siege has a preface. The army approaches a fortified objective either because of its strategic value or because the army it seeks to bring to combat has retreated within it.[20] In the latter case, in the course of an active campaign, the pre-contact stage is usually skipped: the war is "on," so there

---

19. Ideally, this progression of siege techniques would be accompanied by a thorough typology of target sites: the size, fortification strength, and cultural importance of a site—from the humblest hill fort to the temple at Jerusalem—are important physical constants that clarify the moral movements of the siege progression.

20. Goldsworthy (1996), 102, provides a representative and diverse list of such instances.

is no possibility of completely avoiding the conflict. Not only would the Roman commander be unlikely to seek to discuss the situation when his opponents have fled the battlefield, but most foes, having taken the step of implicating a fortified place by defending it, would probably prefer to test the issue before yielding.

The pre-contact stage was normal during civil wars, wars of conquest, and wars of position against a familiar foe, in which detailed conventions of campaigning may develop.[21] Envoys are sent from one side to the other, or a herald formally warns the city of the costs of noncompliance. Such formality, though, is more typical of late Roman siege warfare than the centuries when Rome was more actively expansionist.[22] Still, the opportunity to allow surrender to an envoy before the arrival of the army was important—it was less shameful than capitulation in the face of force and usually obtained more favorable terms.[23]

The pre-contact stage, although it usually passed unremarked, was a distinct moment in the one-way march of siege time, the operational pause when a siege was in the offing but the besieging army was not.[24] An excellent example, from Nero's war with the Armenian king Tiridates, is the capitulation of Artaxata to Corbulo in 58 CE. At the conclusion of a campaign that included both assaults followed by massacres and preemptive capitulations, Corbulo sent light-armed men ahead to the city to cordon it off while the army and siege train were brought up. Yet as soon as the advance party was spotted, the citizens of the city opened their gates "willingly" (i.e., before any coercion was applied). Despite the brutality of the campaign, this quick action saved the inhabitants from massacre, although their town was destroyed.[25] Similar behavior saved the townspeople of Tigranocerta, who opened their gates to the envoys and were ready with gifts

---

21. For the last category see especially chapter 7.

22. Gilliver (1999), 155. See Bradbury (1992), chapter 10, on the conventions of medieval siege warfare, which bear some resemblance to the Roman-Persian sieges of late antiquity.

23. On the *deditio* as falling fundamentally outside of the context of war, see Watson (1993), 50.

24. Most of the imperial-era examples of a request for surrender actually occur later, during or after the intimidation phase of the siege. There are then two general differences: there must be extenuating circumstances for the defenders to still obtain favorable terms, and, even though massacre after surrender is rare, there can be no expectation of a guarantee of safety. The sort of endemic but limited warfare in which many pre-contact capitulations occur is reflected in the early books of Livy (e.g., 6.25.7, 9.40.18).

25. Tac. *Ann.* 13.41. See also Ammianus 16.4.1–2.

and compliments. "Nothing was done to humiliate the city, that remaining uninjured it might continue to yield a more cheerful obedience."[26] Although any real consideration of the many ways and means of surrender is not possible here, it should be noted that the terms of negotiation took their initial shape from the point at which the siege progression had been arrested. Mercy for a long-resisting city was possible if the besieging commander had good reasons, while on the other hand waiting even a short time and attempting to surrender at the point of an initial assault might result in disaster—but these were exceptions to a rough and widely understood rule.[27]

Contact and Intimidation

Contact occurs when the main body of an army marches into view of the fortifications. In the pre-contact stage the defenders might choose their course, but when they closed their gates they ceded initiative, irrevocably, to the approaching army. Closed gates indicated defiance and were all the grounds a commander needed to order an immediate assault.[28] Such assaults directly from the line of march were relatively rare, though, since to attack without any preparation would require fresh and highly motivated

---

26. Tac. *Ann.* 14.24, trans. Church. An incidence, then, of successful strategic intimidation. See also Campbell (2006), 112, with Livy 31.27.4, 31.40.1 and 31.45.3.

27. See App. *Pun.* 15 for brutality in the face of late surrender—reminiscent of "too late, chum" stories from the First World War. See also Livy 21.12–4; App. *Ill.* 24, and *Pun.* 73—the relevance of the breach in the Livy example brings to mind the early Modern customs concerning surrender. See Bradford (2005), 130, and Hamblin (2006), 225 for the similar workings of siege "laws" in the early modern Mediterranean and Near Eastern Bronze Age, respectively.

28. On gates, see Oakley (2005), IV, 525–26. The closed gate mentioned in passing: Livy 28.19.5; App. *Pun.* 92, or his matter-of-fact description of the sack of Gomphi, *B Civ.* 2.64 (which contrasts with Caesar's account, *BC* 3.80–1, where the exemplary sack functions as an effective means of strategic intimidation). The citizens of Brundisium send a message by closing their gates (App. *B. Civ.* 5.56) and the Apollonians drive out their Pompeian garrison commander by refusing to close theirs (*BC* 3.12), while the Sulmonenses open their gates as soon as they see Caesar's standards (*BC* 1.18). See also Livy's (6.3.5) use of the lack of troops drawn up before the wall and the observation of open gates as twin indications that a city will not be defended. *BHisp* 27 reports that Cn. Pompeius burned Carruca because it "closed its gates to his forces," and its military-man author describes gate-closing as a "crime" (*BHisp* 36). Herodian (8.2.2,5) notes not only the all-important closing of the gates of Aquileia to Maximinus's advance force, but also the reclosing of the gates after some hasty repairs. See also Ammianus 20.6.2.

troops, as well as a very low estimation of both the fortifications and the morale of the defenders.[29]

Instead, most armies deployed to begin building their camp and to begin the intimidation of their opponent. This stage of the siege has been dramatized since Aeschylus, who devotes much of the *Seven Against Thebes* to the intimidating displays and statements of the titular attackers.[30] As a Roman army approached its target, it might display its strength and competence by deploying before the walls in a brisk and aggressive manner. The purpose was to refocus and prepare the troops, to heighten their morale through drill and display, and also perhaps to win a bloodless victory. At once an appeal to reason (the facts of army size and equipment) and the beginning of psychological warfare, the intimidation phase allowed the defenders time to weigh their options and to choose immediate surrender over the much harsher terms that would apply later.[31] Of course, there was also the possibility that the morale of the defenders was so high that they might preempt the intimidation phase by sallying out to attack the deploying army or to offer battle before their walls.[32]

The fundamentally moral nature of siege warfare is now very much on display. Vegetius describes the hopes of the attacker that the high casualties of an assault might be avoided through moral victory: "For the side wishing to enter the walls doubles the sense of panic [within the city] in hopes of forcing a surrender by parading its forces equipped with terrible apparatus in a confused uproar of trumpets and men."[33] Noise was intimidating,

---

29. But Caesar often dared; see pages 123–24. Onasander, 39.4–7, also emphasizes the value of an unexpected appearance followed immediately by assault, but the few explicit examples in the sources are predicated on unusual moral advantages. Q. Petillius Cerialis (Tac. *Hist.* 4.71) both "despised" his opponents and thought highly of his troops' *virtus;* Livy (10.41.12–14) has a commander gamble on an assault in the aftermath of a battle.

30. For biblical precedent, see Eph'al (2009), 48–54.

31. Caesar's parade of sixty-four war elephants before the walls of Thapsus (*B Afr.* 86) both presented proof of military capability and launched a serious psychological assault. Josephus (*BJ* 3.127, 146) writes explicitly about Vespasian's hopes that intimidating parades and camps will bring immediate surrender.

32. See, e.g., Tac. *Hist.* 5.11, *Ann.* 14.25; Livy 23.16 (where the use of skirmishing to test morale is explicit), Josephus *BJ* 3.113–4, and numerous examples in chapters four and six. Even in long, heavily engineered sieges, the rather Homeric practice of low-intensity fighting between the fortifications might still be seen.

33. Veg. *Mil.* 4.12. Trans. Milner. Cicero, interestingly enough, gives a good itemized list, *Caec.* 43, of the components of an army's intimidating power, in an effort to prove, as

but a silent menace may have been more so. Something very like the shi-kiri, the period of ritual and silent intimidation before a sumo match, took place during the Persian siege of Amida, where the army encircled the city in full battle array only to stand silent and motionless for an entire day, before retiring in perfect order.[34] The emperor Julian reconnoitered the town of Pirisabora and, despite his intention to parley before assaulting, began to prepare the siege "hoping that this would be enough to deter the people of the town from any thought of resistance."[35] Titus paraded his legions before the walls of Jerusalem:

> So the troops, as was their custom, drew forth their arms from the cases in which till now they had been covered and advanced clad in mail, the cavalry leading their horses which were richly caparisoned. The area in front of the city gleamed far and wide with silver and gold, and nothing was more gratifying to the Romans, or more awe-inspiring to the enemy, than that spectacle . . . even the hardiest were struck with dire dismay at the sight of this assemblage of all the forces, the beauty of their armor, and the admirable order of the men.[36]

All of the essential elements are present: the display of sheer numbers, the invigorating effect of the parade on its participants, the menacing effect of disciplined movement (i.e., well-executed drill), and the flashing magnificence of military display.[37] The same elements can be seen in the deployment of the rebel Julius Civilis before the legionary fortress at Vetera, which "utterly confounded the besieged," and in Ammianus' reaction to the Persian army before Amida.[38]

Many Roman commanders chose to intimidate with a characteristically Roman demonstration of intent: they dug in. At the very least, imperial

---

part of a legal argument about private violence, that threats can have as real an effect as actual combat.

34. Ammianus, 19.2.2–5. See page 189. See also Josephus *BJ* 3.148.
35. Ammianus, 24.2.9, trans. Hamilton.
36. Josephus, *BJ* 5.350–53.
37. See also Bishop (1990), 26. Nor should the actual optical effect of flashing be discounted, since it testified to well cared-for weapons: Veg. *Mil.* 2.14, was of the opinion that "the glitter of arms strikes very great fear in the enemy." Trans. Milner, who cites Ammianus, 31.10.10 and Donatus, commenting in precisely the same words as Vegetius on *Aeneid* 7.626, which of course alludes to the flashing of Achilles' armor in the *Iliad*.
38. Tac. *Hist.*, 4.22, trans. Church; Ammianus, 19.2.3–4.

legions always encamped upon reaching the siege target, and often the construction of the first siege works would begin simultaneously with encampment. This intimidated by displaying both skill and seriousness of intent. Even if the commander's intention was to end the siege by an early assault, this physical labor paid moral dividends: it destroyed the defenders' hopes of an easy victory.[39] No Roman adversary could match the combination of logistical skill, political will, and social cohesion that Rome brought to the long labor of the siege. The great Julio-Claudian general Corbulo was speaking of intimidation as much as the tactical value of entrenchments when he remarked that the *dolabra* (pickaxe) rather than the sword, conquered.[40]

While any garrison that closed its gates must have at least hoped to survive a first assault, the sight of siege engines was sometimes enough to force surrender. Two Gallic towns capitulated to Caesar's feats of engineering: Noviodunum, because of the speed with which the works were built, and the *oppidum* of the Atuatuci when a siege tower begin to roll up an embankment before their disbelieving eyes.[41] At Pirisabora, during Julian's Persian campaign, the sight of a huge tower rising beside the city caused the surrender of a garrison that had been fighting well.[42] Appian is particularly fond of dramatic intimidation: he describes Sulla granting a town an hour to deliberate surrender, then spending that hour piling wood against their walls; he also notes a surrender at the sight of siege engines crawling up a ramp, and he even mentions ships (mysteriously) rigged so as to intimidate the besieged.[43]

Another common feature of the intimidation stage was the display before the walls of captives taken in previous operations.[44] During campaigns with sequential sieges, this living evidence of a recent sack was often brought forth in an effort to terrorize the defenders into submission; or

---

39. The best example of building for psychological effect is, probably, "the grossly over-engineered circumvallation thrown around Masada." Davies (2001), 70.

40. Frontin. *Str.* 4.7.2.

41. Caesar, *BG* 2.12 and 2.30–1. Polybius credits Philip V with similar, albeit slower, intimidating prowess: "By an energetic use of earthworks, and other siege operations, he quickly terrified the people into submission, and the place surrendered after a delay of forty days in all." 4.63, trans. Shuckburgh.

42. Ammianus, 24.2.18–20. See also Davies (2001), 69–70, on the psychological impact of siege ramps. Josephus, *BJ* 3.175, has Roman besiegers disheartened by the raising of the city wall in response to the siege ramp they are constructing.

43. App. *B Civ* 1.51, 4.72, *Hisp.* 48.

44. See Caesar *BC* 3.81, Tac. *Hist.* 4.34, or Ammianus, 20.7.3–4, 19.6.1.

alternatively, unharmed captives might be presented as evidence of prior leniency and an argument for swift submission.[45] More gruesome was the custom of displaying (or, at a slightly later stage, catapulting) the heads of captured citizens or hoped-for rescuers.[46]

The end of the intimidation phase, when the first assault was in preparation, was generally the last point at which defenders could negotiate terms, and thus was a good time to surrender. The basic requirement was that the defenders give up their arms and open their gates in exchange for their lives, but not necessarily their freedom, and only rarely their property. When Romans offered decent terms of surrender after fighting had begun there was usually a political or strategic explanation. Both Titus and Septimius Severus offered terms to defenders on the occasion of a new breach that threatened a famous temple, while Caesar, overextended and contending with the shifting alliances of the Gallic tribes, was occasionally lenient.[47] Under normal circumstances, however, the beginning of the siege proper foreclosed the possibility of negotiated surrender, and this rule had to be generally enforced in order to render future threats credible.

Engagement

Now the commander decided how to engage the enemy. In rare circumstances, preparation for a heavy assault began immediately, but usually the choice was between an initial assault and some form of skirmishing. This involved an exchange of missiles, possibly including artillery.[48] The town of Pirisabora, for instance, "surrounded on all sides by the river," could not easily be stormed, so Julian ordered his troops to spend a day (needed in any event to prepare the siege engines) contesting the moral situation

---

45. See, e.g., Polyb. 3.13, 5.9; Livy 7.19, 21.5.4. See also Plut. *Brut.* 30–2, *Marc.* 14; App. *B Civ.* 4.80–1.

46. See, e.g., Frontin. *Str.* 2.9.2–5. This is also how the Trojans, including the mother of Euryalus, learn of the death of Nisus and Euryalus. Vergil, *Aen.* 9.465–6.

47. Severus at Hatra, Cass. Dio 76.12.1–2; Titus at Jerusalem, among other occasions, Josephus *BJ* 6.96–128. See also pages 157–68. In Livy, "acts of humanity by the besieging commander sufficient to prompt the surrender of the defenders" should be treated with suspicion, as a rather common literary trope. Davies (2006), 19.

48. See Goldsworthy (1996), 145; Lendon (1999), 298–99, citing *BG* 7.36; *BC* 2.31, 3.84; *B Alex.* 31. This also explains the occasional, otherwise puzzling report of cavalry "attacking" a walled city or camp, e.g., *BG* 5.26; Cass. Dio 68.31; Ammianus 19.7.4–8.

through missile skirmishing and taunting.[49] Skirmishing could reveal gaps in moral commitment, as when Germans approaching a Roman camp broke off their attack "without any discharge of missiles, when they saw the cohorts in close array before the lines and no sign of carelessness."[50] The Roman ability to draw up in good order allowed them to gain the upper hand in the contest of morale without any physical conflict even taking place.[51]

A simple assault this early in the siege (lacking, that is, any technological support other than ladders and, perhaps, covering fire) is probably best thought of as a probing or testing assault, more an extension of the intimidation phase than a first serious stab at victory. The main intent of a testing assault is to test the capabilities of the defenders and the morale of both sides rather than to take the city (although the city might suddenly fall if the defenders panicked).

This category of assault is difficult to securely identify among the brief notices of nondecisive actions, but the best indications are an early position in a longer siege, a lack of exhortation by the general or of tactical detail in the assault narrative itself, and the presence of a following note about its effect on morale.[52] Casualties, then, were typically low, but the early feedback on morale could have great impact on the commander's subsequent decisions. The hope was that the testing assault might stimulate heroic volunteerism; that highly motivated men, willing to expose themselves at the front, would emerge from the group.[53] Tacitus described another German assault as follows:

> The tribes took up their position, each by itself, to distinguish and so the better to display the valour of each; first annoying us by a distant volley; then, as they found that very many of their missiles fixed themselves harmlessly in the turrets and battlements of the walls, and they themselves suffered from the stones showered down

---

49. Ammianus 24.2.9,11. More skirmishing: App. *Hisp.* 53, *Mith.* 24, *B Civ.* 5.33; Caesar, *BG* 5.57; Polyb. 5.100, 9.3.

50. Tac. *Ann.* 2.13, trans. Church. See also Ammianus 19.2.6–11.

51. One of the best descriptions of a testing assault, by one of Caesar's legates on a Gallic *oppidum,* can be found in Viollet-le-Duc (1874). It is, one should note, imaginary, the book being an interesting and rather odd "historical novel of fortification."

52. See, e.g., App. *Mith* 30, *Ill.* 19, *Pun.* 97; Josephus *BJ* 3.111, 132.

53. See pages 29–32.

on them, they fell on the entrenchment with a shout and furious rush, many placing their scaling-ladders against the ramparts, and others mounting on a testudo formed by their comrades.[54]

Precisely the same technique had been practiced the previous year by the Flavian general M. Antonius Primus in his assault on a Vitellian camp before Cremona. As Tacitus explains it, Antonius chose the assault because the men were clamoring for the offensive, exhibiting morale so high that they forced their general's hand. A skirmish was followed by a competitive testing assault.

> At first they fought from a distance with arrows and stones, the Flavians suffering most, as the enemy's missiles were aimed at them from a superior height. Antonius then assigned to each legion the attack on some portion of the entrenchments, and on one particular gate, seeking by this division of labor to distinguish the cowardly from the brave, and to stimulate his men by a competition for honor.[55]

That this is a testing assault and not a general assault is indicated by the fact that, after some of the legions are successful, there is a delay while tools and implements are fetched and a proper assault prepared. Vegetius, too, sees the testing assault as something like the last phase of the intimidation stage.

> Then, because fear is more devastating to the inexperienced, while the townspeople are stupefied by the first assault if unfamiliar with the experience of danger, ladders are put up and the city invaded. But if the first attack is repelled by men of courage or by soldiers, the boldness of the besieged grows at once and the war is fought no longer by terror but by courage and skill.[56]

And so, with this first moral test past, there comes a major, irrevocable step in the progression, from mere preliminaries to the full-blown siege.

---

54. Tac. *Hist.* 4.23, trans. Church.
55. Tac. *Hist.* 3.27. See also Josephus *BJ* 3.112–3, 132 for testing assaults with opposite results.
56. Veg. *Mil.* 4.12, trans. Milner.

Circumvallation

Although the sharp end of any siege operation will always involve a few individuals in desperate combat, the beginning of the siege proper is signified by communal labor. This is also perhaps the most Roman stage of the siege, where discipline paved the way, sometimes literally, for *virtus:* more than its forebears or competitors, more than its medieval successors, the Roman siege was characterized by the willingness to undertake extensive works.[57]

The commander now decided whether circumvallation,[58] the encirclement of the target with a continuous line of fortifications, was called for. The operational benefit of circumvallation is that it makes reinforcement and resupply of the defenders virtually impossible and allows a much smaller force to guard effectively against sallies or breakout. The drawback is the enormous expenditure of time and labor on works that do nothing to directly aid the assault.[59] Yet, by the late republic and certainly during the principate, the habit of digging lines of circumvallation had become entrenched.[60] It lost the commander nothing but time, and to skip it

---

57. The story begins, in a way, with Livy's account of Veii. See pages 86–88. On *virtus* and *disciplina* see pages 24–29. This is as good a place as any to note that, *contra* Le Bohec (2006), 135 and (2009), 60, the Romans did not prefer sieges to battles and certainly not because siege labor was a preferable trade-off for the greater bloodshed of open battle. Leaving aside the facts that general assaults were at least somewhat likely to be bloodier than successful battles and that engineered assaults caused high casualties among the best troops, the Roman view of siege labor was not that it replaced bleeding but rather that it enabled it even when cowardly enemies refused battle. See chapters 1 and 2.

58. I am indebted to Campbell (2005), 50–51, for clearing up a pervasive confusion in the literature. Amusingly, the confusion is rooted in nineteenth-century Franco-German antagonism: the French used *contrevallation* (contravallation) to refer to single lines, while *circonvallation* (circumvallation) referred to a second, outer ring that protected the besiegers against relief armies. The Germans didn't like this, and made "circumvallation" the dominant term for the (far more common) single line. Nevertheless, it makes better prepositional sense, when a second, outer line is built, to switch systems, redubbing the inner ring the contravallation. It should be noted, also, that "circumvallation" is a modern coinage; ancient Latin lacked an equivalent of the Greek περιτειχισμός and made do with verbal descriptions and frustratingly broad use of the terms *munitiones* (fortifications) and *opera* (works of any kind, often including machines). For the physical form of Roman lines of circumvallation, see Davies (2006), chapter 5; Caesar *BG* 7.69–74; or App. *B Civ.* 5.33.

59. Onasander, 40.2–3, shrewdly points out that these fortifications will remind the besieging army that they too are in danger. Typically, Caesar is explicit about the positive and blithe about the negative; see *BC* 1.19, and pages 136–41.

60. Roth (1999), 316. There seems to have been a decline in the frequency of circumval-

seemed sloppy, an offense against Roman doggedness that might invite sallies by the besieged—and if no sallies were forthcoming and the enemy seemed demoralized, the works could always be temporarily abandoned and a quick assault attempted.[61]

A conundrum of military morale is whether it is a good or a bad thing to corner the enemy, to make him believe that victory, or even survival, is impossible. Some authorities tend to warn against this—arguing that men with nothing to lose are more dangerous combatants—while others consider that creating a feeling of despair in one's enemy is a shortcut to moral victory.[62] It seems sensible to conclude that both cases may obtain, depending on other aspects of the moral and tactical situation. It seems unquestionable that men fight differently when fighting to avoid death than when fighting despite the hopelessness of survival.[63]

Yet there is a third condition: desperation motivated by the knowledge that only victory will bring survival. This is probably the most morally advantageous position for the defenders, a fact that explains the speed with which Rome sought to turn the issue from lenient surrender terms to the absolute despair of certain death. Hasdrubal's gruesome logic during the defense of Carthage offers additional evidence: he tortures Roman prisoners atop the walls for the explicit purpose of inciting the Roman besiegers

---

lation in the later empire, indicating both the deterioration of some military skills and the changed character of moral statements in endemic warfare against familiar foes.

61. See Livy, 9.4.8, 9.37.10, and 21.25.5. The discovery of lines of circumvallation (in Judaea) unmentioned in the histories supports the idea that historians might omit mention of circumvallation because it was, as a standard operating procedure, implied; see Gilliver (1999), 149. Abandon: see App. *Ill.* 25.

62. Desperation had a positive effect on motivation/performance: *BC* 2.6; Livy 4.28.5, 9.23.7–17, 37.32.6; Plut. *Alex*, 16.7; Tac. *Ann.* 4.51, 12.31; Ammianus 20.11.18,22; Veg. *Mil.* 3.21, 4.25. Arguing that assaults against trapped siege defenders should be avoided: Onasander, 38.1; Livy, 6.3.6–9, 9.14.15–16. No less an authority than Vespasian opines (according to Josephus, *BJ* 2.209) that "nothing is more redoubtable than despair." Early in book seven of *The Art of War*, Machiavelli recommends that fortresses be designed without inner citadels or places of retreat because these will tempt the besieged away from a desperate defense—yet he deftly avoids blaming Catarina Sforza for the loss of Forli.

63. It can be assumed that those Roman commanders who began circumvallation without extensive intimidation or a testing assault felt that enemy morale was high enough to withstand a desultory siege. Beginning to surround the city with a ditch and palisade during the intimidation phase was a message of Rome's serious intent and the clearest reminder of the zero-sum nature of the siege, so it could either break the morale of weak-desperation defenders who were pinning their hopes on the siege not being prosecuted or begin crushing the spirits of strong-desperation fighters who were to face the moral attrition of a long siege.

to intend massacre, thus impressing upon his own troops that they must prevail or die.[64]

Circumvallation, therefore, was a powerful message in the cultural context of siege warfare. Cutting the besieged off from the outside world was a retaliation for their refusal to fight in the open, and it sent the message that their consent was no longer relevant. This was a doubling down of the overarching moral extortion: after circumvallation, easy terms were no longer available. The realization that an assault could come at any moment might crack weakening morale. On the other hand, the mute demonstration of their loss of freedom might motivate the defenders to fight all the harder for liberty or death.[65]

It must be emphasized that circumvallation was a regular precursor to the siege assault and not an indication that the siege was intended to become a blockade. At Vellaunodunum, for instance, Caesar spent two days in circumvallation, although he states specifically that he intended to take the town quickly and by assault.[66] At other times an active siege did indeed lapse into a blockade, and a belated circumvallation can indicate this transition, especially if the commander in chief moves on and leaves the rest of the operation to a subordinate.[67] Yet to lump together "blockade and circumvallation" will, in many cases, obscure the aggressive nature of the Roman siege.[68]

THE SIEGE PROGRESSION: ASSAULT

> Dares, as if he stormed a city's bulwarks
> Or kept a mountain fortress under siege,
> Scanned thoroughly and shrewdly for a gap,
> And drove assaults from everywhere . . .[69]

---

64. App. *Pun.* 118. See also Onasander 32.5–7.

65. See chapter 6 for Titus' siege of Jerusalem, the most significant example of a delayed circumvallation against a desperate defense. See also App. *Mith.* 38.

66. *BG* 7.11. Davies (2006), 65, sees the circumvallation as prelude to assault as a Caesarian innovation. This is plausible, although the lack of detailed information about sieges in the generations preceding Caesar renders the assumption unprovable.

67. Hannibal did this on multiple occasions (App. *Hann.* 29, 33; see also Livy 23.30; Polyb. 7.1), as did Caesar (*BC* 1.36) and Sulla (App. *B Civ.* 1.89–90).

68. Gilliver (1999), 148. See also pages 77–79, below.

69. Vergil, Aeneid 5.439–442, trans. Ruden. Onasander, 42.6, uses a very similar analogy: "Just as a good wrestler, the general must make feints and threats at many points, worrying and deceiving his opponents, here and there, at many places, striving, by securing

Like Vergil's old and resourceful wrestler, the general had a wide range of assault options before him. Guiding his choice was the reliable inverse relationship between time and danger, the benefits of a quick siege weighed against the casualties caused by hurried preparations or repeated assaults.[70] The options can be grouped into three broad categories (although a certain amount of mixing and matching is unavoidable).

First, a general assault on the fortifications more or less as they stand. The engineering support for such an attack is minimal—at most consisting of artillery, ladders, or hand implements such as picks and crowbars, and, if necessary, large (but mobile) "sheds" or "mantlets."[71] Our second category avoids such direct confrontation in favor of surprise and trickery, including the sort of general stratagems that can be studied within the context of the progression. While many such assaults would rely upon the coup de main against a weak point in the defenses—often a gate—the besiegers could make their own weak point by tunneling into the city. The third type of assault is the longest, most costly, and most deadly, since extensive engineering overcomes the obstacle of fortifications only to funnel the climactic attack into a relatively narrow section of the defenses. Variously translated as siege mound, ramp, or embankment, the *agger* was the quintessential Roman siege work, a man-made hill that effectively eliminated the defenders' advantage of altitude. Its presence—or, alternatively, the use of siege towers and battering rams at a site approachable without a ramp—characterizes what I describe as the "heavy" or "heavily engineered" assault.[72] The long, dangerous process of building such works meant that sieges of this sort almost always ended in a massacre.

Our first category, the general assault, is carried out by infantry, either without any special equipment at all or with the aid of ladders, screens, and hand-tools. These occur frequently in Livy, and success is presented as being due to Roman confidence and combat motivation. Any insignificant

---

a firm hold on one part, to overturn the whole substance of the city." See also Plut. *Sull.* 12; Ariosto, *Orlando Furioso* 45.75.

70. See Livy 9.24.2, Josephus *BJ* 3.161ff.

71. It is impossible to know the precise character and dimension of such devices, as the technical terms evolve and are used with varying degrees of precision. For a sorting out of *vineae, testudines, musculi, plutei, crates,* and the like, see Davies (2006); Campbell (2006).

72. For a detailed analysis of the *agger*, see Davies (2006), 15, 97ff; see also Campbell (2005), 52–53. For those preferring a poetic evocation, Lucan's description of the raising of Caesar's ramp at Massilia, 3.394ff., is awesome.

town was expected to be carried "at the first rush"; any delay was a disappointment.[73] Romulea is taken by fearless troops incited by the promise of easy booty.

> Here, too, no siege works were constructed, no artillery employed, the moment the standards were brought up to the walls no resistance on the part of the defenders could keep the men back; they planted their scaling-ladders just where they happened to be, and swarmed on to the walls. The town was taken and sacked . . . and a vast amount of plunder secured.

So too was Ferentinum, immediately afterward, despite the fact that "the position had been made as strong as possible by nature and by art, and the walls were defended with the utmost energy."[74]

Assault by escalade (using scaling ladders) required little time, but significant combat motivation.[75] Soldiers ran forward, some carrying ladders, others hurling javelins or *pila* in the hopes of pinning down the defenders.[76] They were extremely vulnerable: "Some held their shields above their heads . . . others rushed forward with ladders on their shoulders . . . and all exposed their breasts to every kind of weapon" as they rushed across the killing zone toward the arrows and stones flying at them from the walls.[77] "The largest share of toil and danger," fell upon those who were the first to mount the ladders.[78] They were subject not only to the proverbial hail of missiles but, should they persevere, to the full attentions of the wall's defenders:

---

73. E.g., Livy 6.10.1–4, 9.26.2, 37.31.2–3.

74. Livy, 10.17.7–10, trans. Roberts.

75. Whitehead (2010), 122, on Apollodorus 176.4, suggests plausibly that ladders made in standard segments for easy assemblage may have been provided for Trajan's Dacian campaign. See chapter 4, note 80 for the calculation involved in a proper escalade.

76. There is one great image of such an assault in Roman figural art, scene 113 (Cichorius 84) of Trajan's column. That assault troops did not usually climb the ladder while carrying a sword in one hand and a severed head in the other seems a safe guess, and thus a reminder of how much leeway must be allowed for artistic license in the column's combat scenes.

77. Ammianus, 21.12.13, trans. Hamilton. Watson (1993b), 142, has thirteen general principles of siege warfare, of which the least impeachable is number four: "Infantry crossing the killing zone is the Queen's Move of siege warfare, the point at which the offense is most vulnerable."

78. Val. Max. 3.2.6b.

the Romans set ladders up against the porticoes (of the Temple). The Jews did not hurry to stop this, but attacked violently when they had climbed up. Some they pushed back and threw down, others they attacked and killed, many they cut down with their swords as they stepped off the ladders, before they could protect themselves with their shields, and a few ladders laden with soldiers were pushed sideways at the top and toppled—the Jews also suffered many casualties. Those who had carried standards fought fiercely for them, since their loss was disaster and a disgrace, yet eventually the standards were taken by the Jews, who slaughtered all who had mounted. The rest, intimidated by the fate of the fallen, retreated.[79]

A common tactic was to feint against dispersed sections of the wall in order to obscure the true object of the assault and spread out the defenders.[80] At Megara, a suburb built just outside the walls of Carthage, a small group waited until the garrison was distracted by a general attack on a different point of the defenses to scramble up a tower, cross by drop bridge to the adjacent wall, and seize the gate.[81]

A good example of the moderate tactical complexity of a general assault is Corbulo's attack on Volandum, in which slingers and artillerymen fired on all points of the wall to cover two assaults: one with ladders, and the other forming a *testudo* and tearing at the wall with hand-tools.[82] Covering fire was always an important ingredient of success. An assault under Germanicus of a simple earth rampart was driven back until slingers and *tormenta* could be brought up, but then swiftly succeeded.[83] In Gallic assaults on the Roman fortifications at Alesia, handwork and artillery also stand

---

79. *BJ* 6.222–6. trans. adapted from Thackeray.
80. E.g., Livy, 4.59.4–6, 36.22.7–9.
81. App. *Pun.* 117.
82. Tac. *Ann.* 13.39. The probability that Tacitus was working from Corbulo's *commentarii* (*Ann.* 15.16) makes it likely that these details are accurate. Scene 116 (Cichorius 87) of Trajan's column also seems to show the use of hand-tools against a wall during an assault, and scene 71 (Cichorius 51) shows a *testudo* assault on a less forbidding fortress.
83. Tac. *Ann.* 2.20. See also Josephus, *BJ* 5.492. The need for covering fire probably also explains the construction of siege towers before the assault of the pitifully walled Sarmatian settlement of Uspe, Tac. *Ann.* 12.16–17. See also Ammianus 20.7.6, as well as Josephus' evocative description of the volume of missile fire he faced at Jotapata (*BJ* 3.166–8), fire intended to cover the construction of an assault ramp—although Josephus' narrative of this siege is not reliable enough to situate any incident securely within one phase of our general progression.

out: "they began to fling down hurdles, to dislodge our men from the rampart with slings, arrows, and stones, and to carry out everything else proper to an assault."[84] The great dangers here were the certainty of heavy casualties in the front ranks and the necessity of having many reinforcements following close behind. If an assault reached the wall but was then turned back, the assault troops were likely to mix with support troops and become a panicked, crowded rout.[85]

Careful tactics and good timing were important, but the ability to succeed in a general assault rested on morale. In a good example from the German wars of the principate, pride was the prime factor driving the legionaries of Petilius Cerialis against the stone rampart of the hill town of Rigodulum. Roman confidence in their *virtus* and contempt for their enemies neutralized the tactical advantage of fortifications.

> These defences could not frighten a general of Rome. Petilius ordered his infantry to force a passage, and sent his cavalry up the rising ground, telling himself that any advantage such a ramshackle bunch of enemies derived from its position was more than outweighed by that which his own men could expect from their gallantry (*virtus*).[86]

Corbulo followed the same program, exhorting his troops by belittling their opponents, calling them faithless and cowardly fleers. Ammianus similarly opposes the rage-driven ardor of the assaulting Persians to the huge fortifications and imposing natural advantages of Bezabde. Josephus depicts a morally superior assault as a wave of men advancing together, fiercely and in unison—broken or scattered rushes are indicative of bad morale. Competitive rivalry among such high-spirited attacking troops can be particularly effective.[87] Such morale is the most valuable asset for an attacking commander, but, as seen in the escalade of the Temple porticoes, it is fragile.

---

84. Caesar, *BG* 7.81.
85. E.g. Ammianus 21.12.6.
86. Tac. *Hist.* 4.71. Trans. Wellesley.
87. Tac. *Ann.* 13.39; Ammianus 20.7.11; Josephus *BJ* 6.17. In addition to leading from the front, Alexander the Great depended upon just such competitive rivalry; see Arr. *Anab.* 2.27.6–7. Romans, especially aristocrats, were supposed to behave in the same way: see Val. Max. 3.2.6b, and pages 35–40, above.

The second category of siege assault—surprise attack and stratagem—is easily the most diverse.[88] The slow pace of a siege allowed plenty of scope for fooling a static enemy, and the Trojan horse surely lurked in the back of many Roman minds.[89] More relevant than the bold stratagem that would seize a city outright, however, were those that promised advantage in the psychological war of attrition: "For it is a common weakness of human nature that we are apt in strange and unfamiliar circumstances to be too confident or too terrified."[90] Vegetius mentions the effectiveness of timing assaults for periods of habitual inactivity, and suggests feigning abandonment of the siege and then returning for a surprise assault.[91] Onasander, more attentive to issues of morale than the gadget-happy Vegetius, is concerned with the usefulness of night actions to terrify the defender. Nighttime assaults are more frightening, and also more likely to result in confusion: if one or two attackers gain the wall at night, defenders may believe their city to be taken and flee.[92] Convincing some the defenders to betray the city, the possibility of which varied widely based on political circumstances, was disreputable, but often attempted.[93]

When there was little hope of treachery, Roman besiegers were more likely to use the various psychological gambits and small trickeries recommended in handbooks. Onasander suggests that a single trumpeter, climbing to a location whence his sudden peals would suggest a surprise attack, can accomplish the fall of a city, and Josephus reports that a significant portion of Jerusalem's defenses fell after a nighttime rush by only two dozen volunteers, one of them a trumpeter.[94] Sallust has a similar incident in which a secret path enables a trumpeter to climb into the rear of a Numidian fortress and panic the defenders.[95] More basic still was Lucullus' victory at the difficult siege of Amissus, achieved simply by attacking dur-

---

88. The compilers of ancient military stratagem are armchair warriors rather than veteran tacticians or observers, so their compendia of clever tricks are less useful for analyzing specific sieges than for getting a sense of the different directions a progression (or narrative) might take. See Whitehead (2008).

89. Certainly in Livy's: see pages 86–88.

90. Caesar, *BC* 2.4, trans. adapted from Loeb.

91. Veg. *Mil.* 4.26–8. His counter stratagems, some of which involve "keen-scented" dogs or the clamorous descendants of the Capitoline geese, do not inspire confidence.

92. Onasander, 42.1.

93. Goldsworthy (2000), 78, determines that "almost as many cities fell to treachery as to conventional means during the Punic Wars."

94. Onasander 42.17; Josephus, *BJ* 6.68.

95. Sall. *Iug.* 93–4.

ing the established time for the changing of the guard.[96] Caesar took the wall of Avaricum in a sneaky coup de main: after twenty-five days of work on a mound and towers, he took advantage of a heavy rain to suddenly rush the wall, terrifying and defeating the defenders.[97] That such tactics were less than completely glorious—that the victory they might win was of lesser quality—is clear in the dismissive characterization of the event that Caesar puts in the mouth of Vercingetorix: "The Romans had not conquered by courage (*virtus*) nor in pitched battle, but by stratagem and by knowledge of siege operations."[98]

While such opportunities might always present themselves to the bold general, the siege progression generally hardened as it extended, and a sudden reversion to a general assault after heavy engineering had been attempted was likely to indicate low morale among the attackers. To revert to the ratchet analogy, the gear wheel turned when the gates closed, and again after circumvallation and the first serious assault. As the long, slow construction of an *agger* drew toward completion, the wheel was grinding toward its heaviest "click." The defenders had committed to their defiance, and so the besiegers committed time, effort, and blood. Both sides were morally unbroken, so heavy engineering was brought to bear to reduce the tactical advantages of the defenders' fortifications.

The progression through these stages can be seen in greater detail in the longer siege narratives examined in the next four chapters. Too often, in briefer accounts, the historian or his sources elide nondecisive opening stages in order to describe the eye-catching machinery of the heavy assault, and we are left to sift a grab bag of tactics and techniques. Not every effort involved a siege mound: the fortifications could be compromised by undermining, by ramming to create a breach, by bringing up siege towers that reverse the advantage of altitude. Not surprisingly, then, the longer sieges involved many different methods, used both in sequence and simultaneously, in order to launch attacks at several different points.

Highly effective, especially against high masonry walls—but involving a difficult combination of expertise, strenuous and dangerous labor, and stealth—was undermining. If successful, a mine, after its supporting timbers had been fired to cause a cave-in, might bring down a large section of a wall. But mines might be detected and either flooded or attacked by

---

96. Plut. *Luc.* 19.2.
97. *BG* 7.27. See pages 130–36.
98. *BG* 7.29.

means of countermines, and were only chosen by Roman commanders when other tactics seemed not to avail.[99] As we have seen, walls could also be attacked at their base by soldiers wielding hand-tools—a tactic more akin to ramming assaults than mining operations. Common during the fourth-century wars with Persia, such attacks were also used at the Caesarian siege of Massilia and during the Jewish War. Gamala was taken, for instance, when a few soldiers leveraged out five stones by hand, toppling a tower and creating a breach.[100]

Such assaults were very dangerous. While battering troops might be protected from arrows and small stones by the heavy sheds or towers which suspended the rams, they would be the target of any mural artillery, surprise sally, or heavy missiles dropped or rolled from the walls. And the defenders would always try to burn wooden siege machines. If these attacks failed, countermeasures included lowering sacks filled with chaff and various methods of breaking off or grappling the head of the ram. The Persian garrison of Bezabde entangled a ram with lassoes and attempted to burn it with scalding pitch and other incendiary materials, while Archimedes earned lasting fame with his wall-mounted ship-grabbing machines.[101]

Going through the wall was difficult, given the tactical advantages of greater height; engineering a way over, then, was often worth the effort of equalizing that advantage. Relatively low walls too well-defended for a general assault by escalade could be approached by the *agger*, in the form of a broad embankment that would allow more effective suppressing fire and make a long stretch of the wall available for general assault. This was Caesar's favorite tactic in the low-tech, high-manpower, high-energy Gallic Wars. By working up to the wall behind screens and filling any defensive ditch, then building a mound to wall height, Caesar could neutralize the height of the walls and then overtop them with towers, firing down over any parapets in order to clear the walls for the assault.[102]

High walls or true hilltop fortifications (most famously Masada) could be approached by a long *agger*, constructed at a right angle to the wall.

---

99. Flooding: Vitr. *De arch* 10.16.11. See also Livy 38.5–7, James (2004). See also chapter 4, note 59; Davies (2006), 118, suggests that undermining fell into disuse during the principate.

100. Josephus, *BJ* 4.64, 6.24–28; Ammianus 20.6.3–7, 20.7.9–13.

101. Veg. *Mil.* 4.14; Josephus 3.222–6; Caesar *BG* 7.22; Ammianus 20.11.15. See also Gilliver (1999) 138–40. Archimedes: pages 107–9.

102. See pages 128–29. See also Davies (2006), 97, who advocates a distinction between the ramp, which approaches the wall, and the mound, which overtops it. But both forms, if actually distinct, were called *agger* by the Romans.

Several such ramps were built at Jerusalem, and the Persian capture of Dura, too, seems to have been by siege ramp.[103] The narrow assault would be supported, then, by a siege tower pushed up to the top of the ramp. Alternatively, cities with less imposing walls could be approached by one or several towers without the benefit of the *agger*, although the ground would need to be leveled and any ditches filled.

The siege tower always attracts the eye of the commentator: this is high technology in the most literal sense, a vivid statement of the will of the besieger to answer the challenge posed by those who shelter behind walls. Although we know roughly how they worked, the details of any specific siege tower are rarely clear. We have no good contemporary images, and archaeology cannot be much help in reconstructing a temporary wooden structure. Siege towers might be simple platforms intended only to allow missile troops to fire at the defenders, but they might also be elaborate, multilevel constructions featuring a ram, multiple artillery emplacements, and various screens, drawbridges, and other devices. Most were rolled up to the wall by brute manpower, although floating siege towers were a recurring feature of the Punic Wars and reappear in late antiquity. While the general assault was a Roman tour de force, the star of the heavy assault was still the Hellenistic helepolis, carrying artillery pieces, sheltering assault infantry, and mounting a huge battering ram.[104] There is more anecdotal evidence of such massive machines proving to be examples of self-defeating grandiosity (a familiar feature of military innovation) than testimony to their effectiveness, and prudent Roman commanders were usually content with towers that could provide covering fire or bring a ram to the wall.

Before turning our attention to the ram, which holds a crucial place in the culture of the heavy siege assault, let us take an opportunity to recapitulate the progression by discussing the lone visual narrative of a Roman siege. This is the siege of what is usually assumed to be Sarmizegethusa, the Dacian capital, depicted in scenes 113–24 of Trajan's column.[105] While the experience of trying to interpret a visual siege narrative (the text on which

---

103. Jerusalem: see chapter 6. Dura: James (2004).

104. See Ammianus 21.12. The Arch of Severus depicts a two-story siege tower with a battering ram and a boarding bridge. See also Gilliver (1999), 136–38.

105. Plates 83–94 in Cichorius, which are widely available online. There are other siege scenes on the column—including a Dacian assault on a Roman fort that depicts a rather charming hand-held, ram-headed battering ram (scene 32, Cichorius 24)—but only one extended narrative.

the reliefs were likely based is lost) makes one very grateful for the texts that do survive, knowledge of the siege progression can aid our understanding of the reliefs. The narrative begins with a depiction of the Roman camp and the failed initial escalade. The next scene (114) shows Trajan overlooking fortifications—a unique image of the general deciding the course of his siege—followed by a Dacian sally (115) and what looks like a renewed assault using hand-tools on the fortifications (116). Interpretation now becomes somewhat fraught: Roman soldiers are cutting wood (117) while Trajan receives suppliant Dacians (118). Whatever was said, they evidently did not agree to the emperor's terms, as dramatic scenes follow in which the defenders fire their own town and, in most interpretations, drink poison to avoid capture. Roman troops rush to the city, and in the last image of the sequence we see them carrying off plunder.[106]

Although no heavy assault of Sarmizegethusa took place, the extremity of the Dacian response makes sense: they have been defeated in the field, they refused to yield, and they contested the siege until heavy engineering began. They cannot expect mercy even from the wise and beneficent Trajan, so suicide becomes a reasonably attractive option—and the only one to which the Roman artists would be likely to grant, as they do, the appearance of nobility, a grudging barbarian *virtus*.[107]

Interestingly, the Roman facility with ramp and tower meant that the battering ram—the quintessential weapon of siege warfare from pharaonic Egypt to the High Middle Ages—has a relatively low profile. It was always an option, but given the difficulty of assaulting through a battered gate or a narrow breach, it was less a solution than a facilitator of the most deadly sort of siege assault.[108] In fact, there are so few references in the more reliable sources for our period to any breaching of the wall of a major fortification that it seems reasonable to suspect that the ubiquity of the ram is

---

106. I disagree with Richmond (1982), 40–42, and Rossi (1971) 190–99, who see representations of simultaneous action in different places. Coarelli (2000), 188–89 is closer to my view, namely that, after the failure of the light assault, Dacian leaders take advantage of the pause (indicated by the cutting of wood) to ask for terms before the heavy assault. The rest of the sequence—final assault, fire and suicide, surrender of survivors, and plundering—would then make sense.

107. Another famous image (scene 145, Cichorius 106) from the column depicts the suicide of Decebalus, the Dacian leader. On suicide see pages 225–27.

108. See, e.g., Polyb. 21.28; Livy 44.12.1–3; Josephus *BJ* 3.213–228—a dramatic, but oddly placed and decidedly not decisive ramming incident.

due more to its establishment in the literature than to the practice of siege warfare.[109]

But its rather blunt symbolic potential meant that the act of ramming acquired a synechdochal importance in siege lore. "The battering ram . . . was not just a device for creating breaches in walls; it seems to have had a greater significance in Roman warfare."[110] And so the sharpest division in the progression of the Roman siege is the use of the battering ram: both Caesar and Cicero refer to the widely held understanding that surrender was generally accepted before a ram was brought into action—a fact often reflected in the histories. Rome and its neighbors knew the convention that, while little enough might be guaranteed in the early stages of a siege, once the ram touched the walls those inside could no longer expect any mercy.[111]

Caesar, although he rarely afterwards used a ram, makes this plain in his ultimatum to the Atuatuci: "Caesar replied that he would save their state alive rather because it was his custom than for any desert on their part, if they surrendered before the battering ram touched the wall."[112]

---

109. Goldsworthy (2003), 194–95, asserts that ramming holes in walls (as opposed to using rams against gates or ramparts) was a frequent and effective tactic, but he mentions only Gamala and Jotapata, relatively small places defended by amateurs who, though highly motivated, were (comparatively) lacking in mastery of missile and ram-countermeasure defenses. Rams are more prominent in the Eastern wars of late antiquity (paradoxically, but suggestively, the less advanced fortifications in the west—see Caesar *BG* 7.23—resisted ramming better than stone walls did) but it still seems that their tactical importance is an inherited assumption with very little evidence to support it. See Whitehead (2010) on the conflation of scattered references in the modern conception of the Roman ram.

110. Gilliver (1999), 140.

111. The near completion of a mine marked the same sort of transition: see page 92. See also App. *B. Civ.* 4.72. In the Middle Ages, it was the firing of a battering engine or cannon; see Keen (1965), 120, note 4. In the highly technical sieges of the late seventeenth century, "once the third parallel had been constructed and the mines charged, the commander of the fortress would generally accept an offer of terms . . . certain in the guarantee that the population he had defended would be spared." Neill (1998), 507. See Pepper (2000), 574, for an interesting episode during the sixteenth-century renegotiation of custom and expediency in which breaching artillery's requirement for at least a small amount of tactical surprise found itself at cross-purposes with the herald's traditional announcement of imminent attacks.

112. *BG* 2.32. Since the Atuatuci are portrayed as a bunch of Gallic rubes—mocking the puny Romans for building a siege tower so far away from their walls and then falling on their faces in fear and suing for peace when it begins to move—this may be a bit of fun at their expense: Caesar, accused of being a special favorite of the gods, has portrayed as "his custom" what his audience knew to be standard procedure.

Cicero ratifies this standard of ancient warfare when he philosophically advocates mercy to captured defenders even after "the ram has hammered at their walls."[113] The approach of the ram, or the ram-bearing tower, then, was the last moment of intimidation. After battering began it was a fight to the death. The assault troops understood, too, that the siege would certainly involve two things: a desperate struggle to penetrate the fortifications and, afterwards, a sack.

Rome's enemies understood this "rule" of siege warfare as well, as a close reading of our best sources demonstrates. At Pirisabora, spirited defense turned to immediate surrender when a helepolis bearing a large ram was constructed. At Bezabde, Ammianus dramatizes the Persian reaction to a ram being brought into action—they are "stricken with horror"—thus emphasizing the importance of their decision to continue to resist, which they then do with "utter recklessness."[114] At Jerusalem, the first contact of a battering ram with the wall is the moment when the rebel factions "seeing themselves exposed to a common danger" drop their violent infighting and agree to a truce that will allow cooperation against the Romans. Much later on, Titus refers to his offers of leniency as "in deliberate forgetfulness of the laws of war."[115] There is no mistaking what those laws required.

> Thereupon Titus, indignant that men in the position of captives should proffer proposals to him as victors, ordered proclamation to be made to them neither to desert nor to hope for terms any longer, for he would spare none; but to fight with all their might and save themselves as best they could, because all his actions henceforth would be governed by the laws of war. He then gave his troops permission to burn and sack the city.[116]

Were Roman commanders really bound by these "laws"? Of course not: Titus is shown bending them, and from Publius Claudius Pulcher's drinking chickens to Nelson's blind eye, military commanders have always sacrificed laws, customs, basic human decency, direct orders, and religious necessity to expediency.[117] The "laws of siege warfare" are just a story—but

---

113. *Off.* 1.35. Of course, such a "law of war" could still be broken, or exaggerated for the rhetorical effect of claiming exceptional *clementia*. See note 27.
114. 24.2.19–21; 20.11.13–15.
115. *BJ* 5.277, 6.346. See also Luc. 2.505–7; App. *Hisp.* 48.
116. *BJ* 6.352–53.
117. For Titus at the siege of Jerusalem, a complicated situation, see chapter 6.

a story that shaped reality. Because well-known customs governed expectations they influenced both the course of combat and its ex post facto assessment. In this sense, the "laws" really did put constraints on the activities even of an all-powerful commander. Long sieges that involved heavy engineering often ended in brutal sacks and massacres, but extenuating circumstances could be used to justify bending the "rules."[118]

BLOCKADE

A final form of the siege is the blockade. This was never a desirable option: it was too passive and too time-consuming, and, given that it offered no chance for a soldier to cover himself with glory, rather un-Roman.[119] Still, a strongly defended site and/or strategic pressure could make a blockade unavoidable. Blockade might be chosen as early as the pre-contact stage, or after a failed attempt at intimidation. Although no great praise would be forthcoming, no opprobrium necessarily attached: having to blockade was an unfortunate position to be in, but an understandable necessity against a determined opponent.[120] Yet it was something of an embarrassment—an indication of moral defeat—for a siege that had progressed past the point of the general assault to peter out into a blockade.[121] The blockade as lapsed siege was more typical of barbarian enemies who lacked the skill to engineer an assault, but Roman commanders were occasionally pushed into blockading tactics by a determined defense.[122]

Whereas a true siege aimed at conquest by force, a blockade aimed, simply, to starve the defenders into submission. Once an army or a population was blockaded, demonstrations involving food and water replaced the physical skirmishing and intimidation of siege warfare in an attempt to effect quicker surrender. Livy gives us besieged Romans, taunted by their

---

118. For counter-customary leniency see App. *Ill.* 24; *Hisp.* 54, 73; see also chapter 8, pages 225–27, and note 48.

119. In that it provided ample time for philosophical reflection, the blockade was perhaps more Greek. See Pl. *Symp.* 220c-d.

120. For the two most famous instances of Roman blockade, see pages 113–15 and 137–41.

121. It is likely that many examples of this are elided in the Roman sources—but see Memnon 34.5 and Polyb. 8.34–6. See also Josephus' wobbly narrative of Jotapata (conducted by his future patron, Vespasian, while he himself commanded the defense) which involves both blockading tactics and repeated assaults by Romans "enflamed to fury by shame and regarding the lack of instant victory as tantamount to defeat," *BJ* 3.156.

122. Barbarians: e.g. *BG* 5.38ff. Romans: *BJ* 5.491–3; 501.

enemies, who prefer to throw bread at their besiegers to silence them, and starve.[123] Caesar's soldiers, blockading Pompey but themselves short of grain, made ersatz bread from a sort of root, and threw it to silence their adversaries' taunts—the moral strength indicated by possessing confidence despite such rations caused Pompey to order this information suppressed.[124] Similar bluster can be seen in a Gallic chieftain's insistence that the defenders of Alesia prepare for cannibalism, although the siege was yet young and there was hope of relief.[125]

Yet it is important to realize that this is a point of conflict between rational strategy and the dictates of (military) culture: whatever the logic of fortifying and waiting instead of marching out, such a posture lacks manly glory and may approach shamefulness. Thus it is not surprising that Caesar the propagandist has no qualms telling us that, when Vercingetorix fortified himself in Alesia and waited for reinforcements instead of fighting it out, Caesar refused to let the women and children of Alesia pass between the siege lines.[126] Blockade was a nasty tactic suited to those who cowered instead of fighting for their freedom. If the men were refusing battle, the ordinary rules of conduct were no longer operative, and the laws of siege warfare considered the starvation of their families to be perfectly legitimate.[127]

So, while a blockade might take place on the very same site as a siege, while it might operate within the same moral/cultural sphere as siege warfare, it is still more than mere sophistry to insist that it is fundamentally different from an active siege: as different as *deditio* and *expugnatio,* surrender and conquest by storm. A blockade has neither the hard turning of the gear wheel of stress and danger nor, in most circumstances, the same spinning release of the sack. Nor is it quibbling to insist on the attempt at determining the commander's instead of lazily diagnosing a blockade from the presence of works of circumvallation or making ex post facto assumptions based on a modern reading of the strategic context. Lines of circumvallation and the interdiction of supply and reinforcement may result in

---

123. Livy, 5.48.4.
124. Caesar, *BC* 3.48; Suet. *Iul.* 68.
125. Caesar, *BG,* 7.77.
126. *BG* 7.78.
127. Hence my placement of the blockade at the end of the progression: those who resisted a long blockade had no more rights than those who resisted a battering ram. Onasander, 42.23, who also places blockades at the end of his categorization of siege possibilities, recommends sending women and children into the blockaded city, to increase starvation and attack morale.

surrender, but they are also part of the physical and psychological arsenal that the besieging commander deploys against the defenders to weaken their resistance to an assault.[128]

These were the decisions that faced the commander of the besieging army. If there had been no opportunity for an immediate assault, if intimidation had failed to win capitulation, and no sort of general assault or stratagem had met with success, then he would find himself in a tight corner of the flowchart, nearly out of options. At this central moment in every serious siege, the Roman commander would have been considering—probably in a *consilium* consisting of friends, officers, and the army's specialists in artillery, mining, and construction—his heavy assault options. As the brief sketches of various techniques presented earlier perhaps demonstrate, this final stage is difficult to grasp without going into considerable detail. Much of the rest of this book will be concerned with studying the handful of siege accounts that can sustain such an inquiry, namely the narratives of Polybius, Livy, Caesar, Josephus, and Ammianus.

Despite great differences in the composition of the attacking armies, the characteristics of the defenders, the nature of the larger campaigns, and the physical attributes of the siege target, the siege progression—if it is not refined to the point of brittleness—holds up well. Roman siege warfare from the Second Punic War to the late fourth century was fought with the same basic set of assumptions and procedures. A firm grasp of the moral context of sieges—and of their *agger*-like progression, ever onward and upward in intensity—will enable a more subtle and more complete understanding of even the most comprehensive siege accounts.

---

128. Gilliver (1999), 147; (2007), 149. See also Rance (2007), 360.

FOUR

THE REPUBLIC

A siege is not an event so much as a process, its extension in time as essential as its fixedness in space. Roman siege warfare emerges into history only when a historian fashions a siege narrative, a story of particular actions transpiring against a backdrop of generic expectation. Moreover, we can only be confident in a historical reading of this story when we possess enough work by the same author to understand how he goes about working raw material—observed facts or written sources—into a story.[1] In one sense, then, Roman siege warfare begins in Livy, who sprinkles accounts of sieges through the early books of his history. But Livy's understanding of early Roman history is limited and cannot be considered historical in the conventional sense of being factually secure. To know what we are reading about we need a number of narratives by a writer knowledgeable about both the technical and cultural aspects of military affairs—which means, in practice, that the writer must be contemporary (or nearly so) with the events he describes.[2] Later we will find Caesar, Josephus, and

---

1. I am influenced here, loosely but not insignificantly, by White (1973). However, the goal throughout this book is to understand something of siege warfare as it was actually experienced by Roman armies. There are problematic gaps between historical narrative and historical event, but this should not mean that treating a literary text as if it can indeed represent reality (however imperfectly) is therefore pointless. This would be to throw the baby out just because the bathwater has grown cloudy with post-modern bath salts.

2. See pages 12–14.

Ammianus, but in the long centuries before Caesar we have only Polybius. Therefore, this chapter centers on a handful of the surviving siege narratives in his histories. Yet Livy is also useful, not least in that he sometimes works directly from lost sections of Polybius. Comparing the different choices of the two authors—one Greek and avowedly devoted to historical truth; the other Roman and, while also professing fealty to truth, more comfortable with the literary possibilities of historical narrative—can be illuminating.

Given the fragmentary nature of the sources, a comprehensive and balanced account of Roman siege warfare is not possible. Rather than attempting to leap from stone to protruding stone across the inundated areas of history, the goal here is to provide further support for the general arguments of chapter 3 while also equipping the reader to interpret the scores of other sieges mentioned in the sources. This is best accomplished by looking both at a few representative case studies and at the accounts of particularly significant or unusual sieges, in rough but not perfect chronological order.[3] The emphasis throughout will be on the literary handling of sieges. The physical and technological details will be discussed only when they are really necessary to the imaginative reconstruction of human experience.[4] We are aiming at a "truth" less exact than the most secure archaeological data—yet this sort of truth has the virtue of involving both mind and matter, and of describing movement in time and space, which are, after all, crucial factors in siege warfare.[5]

LIVY

While we can catch fleeting glimpses of actual siege processes in his early books, Livy's "prose epic" of early Rome depends upon a number of different now-lost sources. Yet Livy is a strong author, and the very fabrication of these narratives render them usable. It may be patchwork underneath, but Livy weaves freely around whatever bare events the annalistic tradition

---

3. I make only sparing use of Appian and Plutarch, and none of Cassius Dio—additional "facts" are counterproductive if we can't read the author well enough.

4. See pages 2–4.

5. Two complementary works, then, are Campbell (2005), an accessible and well-illustrated study of Roman sieges, with emphasis on the physical details of fortifications and machines but too great an assumption of historical continuity between and among the few well-attested sieges and their narrators; and Davies (2006), which provides a useful typology of siege works, based on excavations, but deals rather briskly with texts on unexcavated sieges.

or collective memory insisted upon, creating the whole cloth of the Roman siege story. Livy lived under Augustus—after, that is, Caesar's influential commentaries had been published, and centuries after many of the sieges occurred. His usefulness is less a matter of testimony to specific events than a demonstration of how sieges were understood, and how a popular historian might tell a siege story.[6]

There was very little true siege warfare in the early centuries of Roman expansion. The peoples and polities of ancient Italy simply lacked the logistical and technological ability—not only to construct towers and artillery but also to feed an army encamped for many days in the same place. Their town walls deterred raiding and were usually successful in forcing military decisions into the open field. When a siege did take place, it must have been a matter of a simple assault, stratagem, or, in rare cases, blockade. Livy's early sieges—more anecdotes than narratives—are highly stereotypical but usually plausible representations of historical reality, reflecting this tentative siege warfare rather than the clearly defined stages of the later warfare of refusal. Sallies, surrenders, and general assaults figure prominently, and few if any sieges involved sustained combat.[7]

Yet two of the ways in which Livy approaches his siege narratives, whether semi-historical or essentially fictive, are worth noting here, since each appears to demonstrate Livy's appreciation of an essential factor in the mature siege warfare of the late republic. First, Livy's sieges are moral affairs. The emphasis is placed consistently—indeed, almost unfailingly—on

---

6. For Livy see the commentaries of Ogilvie, Oakley, and Briscoe, as well as Kraus (1994); Kraus and Woodman (1997); Whitby (2007), 71; and Levene (2010). There is little space here for general discussion of Livy's sources and style, and none for close examination of his prose. For recent bibliography on Livy and siege warfare, see Roth (2006). Roth (2006), 57, following Walsh, Oakley, and Kraus, notes that, since Caesar is our first real military narrative in Latin, "it is difficult to judge, however, to what extent Livy is borrowing from Caesar or simply following a more general historical convention." The current chapter, then, puts the chronological cart before the narrative horse: first we read (history) and then we write (it). This is especially true of the early years, which figure prominently here, and about the uncertain historicity of which Livy is fairly forthcoming—see 6.1.2. About "facts," too, Livy errs, but carefully: later siege technologies make anachronistic appearances, although he does not precisely describe such technologies in the early going, presumably because he knows that they would be out of place. Roth (2006), 51; see e.g., 2.17.1, 2.25.5, 6.9.2.

7. See, e.g., 2.11.5, 2.16.6, 10.34, 10.43.5. Literary interaction (e.g., the preservation of annalistic style, Homeric allusion, brief embroideries on Hellenistic themes, or even the influence of Caesar) is more noticeable than any grappling with historical reality. See esp. Kraus and Woodman (1997), 67.

factors of morale and motivation, and it is these factors that decide military outcomes and define the narratives.[8] This is not to say that Livy ignored traditional elements such as topography and feats of engineering—after all, a siege without site description and a technology list would be like epic without invocation or *aristeia*. But these elements were not relied upon to tell the story. Instead, his sieges begin, shift dynamically, and end around issues of confidence and aggression.[9]

---

8. See, e.g., 2.64.6. The battle (it is not a siege) is won after the Roman commander tricks disheartened men into advancing by lying about a victory on the other wing. Livy's *impetu facto, dum se putant vincere vicere* can stand for both an oft-repeated trope and a basic approach to analyzing military affairs. An even more dramatic trick is pulled by a Q. Fabius, who inspires his men to desperate courage by declaring that he will burn their camp behind them. The ploy works, the Samnites are routed, and the inferiority of fortifications to actual fighting men is reaffirmed: *armis munimenta, non munimentis arma tuta esse debent* (9.23.7–17). It would not be an overstatement to say that Livy's combat narratives are only occasionally comprehensible and complete in tactical or operational terms, yet always coherent from a moral/motivational point of view, and that this represents both a literary *déformation historique* and a workable explanation of historical combat. See Levene (2010), chapter 4 and, especially, pages 283–300; I have, unfortunately, been unable to engage more fully here with this important discussion of Livian combat narratives.

9. One fault in Roth's (2006) very useful article is a lack of attention to Livy's use of morale. Roth reverses theme and variation when he attributes to Livy a "focus on the physicality of sieges," yet notices the lack of technological detail. Livy didn't know as much about siege machines as the other authors discussed in this study, but that is not the reason he avoided them (indeed, sometimes he bungles details—see note 57 below). Rather, Livy made short work of these generic must-haves in order to focus on moral issues. Roth's example of this physical focus, a description of Polyxenidas' siege of Colophon (37.26.4–13), which is indeed typical, has Livy listing the siege equipment as it is deployed. But instead of describing its use, Livy instead describes its moral impact on the Colophonians and explains the Roman officer's decisions as based on his sense of honor and his assessment of Polyxenidas' fighting spirit. Roth's contention that Livy's method of using of particular terms for siege equipment demonstrates his taking the viewpoint of the commander is unpersuasive, despite his relatively positive (and relatively persuasive) assessment of Livy's handling of technical vocabulary. Even if Livy gets the words right, the persistence through time of any connection between a specific object and the term describing it is nowhere as precise as historians generally assume. Can we look at the terms "gun" or "cannon" as used by historians, technical writers, and novelists over the past two centuries and identify the objects to which they refer with anything like the precision that actual military history would demand? Still, Roth is correct about Livy writing from the commander's point of view, and he makes the important point that Livy lacks any interest (so pronounced in Caesar and the later historians in this study) in naming the ordinary soldiers who perform heroic deeds. This is because Livy, especially in the earlier books of his history, is "doing epic" more than he is absorbing the politically tinged "all for one" atmosphere of Roman military writing. Since he wants his aristocratic heroes front and center but cannot (once he is done with Coriolanus, Camillus, Cossus and their ilk) have securely historical Roman

Livy is well aware of the fundamental sense of shame that characterized siege warfare—the notion that fighting from behind walls showed an unmanly fear of open conflict.[10] The postures of fighting forces relative to their city walls or camp defenses are thus indications of possible shame or fear, and these moral states have tactical consequences. Thus, Livy shows generals to be primarily concerned with taking the moral temperature of the siege, which is often a matter of dealing with cold terror or the hot flash of a sally. When a sally—a temporary assertion of wall-disdaining valor—is defeated, a counterattack is likely to be successful, and that success might so augment the fighting spirits (*anima*) of the soldiers that further successful sieges result.[11] When no sally is forthcoming, this tells the general that a town may be easily taken. In one story, Camillus begins a formal investment of Satricum, but when no sallies interrupt the work he diagnoses their low *anima* and orders an immediate assault by escalade. Tidily, the demoralized defenders immediately surrender.[12] Livy even shows super-motivated soldiers insisting on an immediate assault by escalade, forgoing the potential aid of siege works or artillery.[13]

The second major feature of Livy's siege narratives is his recognition that early Roman sieges fell into two generally distinct operational categories: static blockade or siege by assault. These categories can appear to blur when extensive siege works are involved, but Livy consistently treats them separately.[14] In a typical brief account of Roman campaigning we are told

---

generals storming walls like Hector or Rodomonte, he emphasizes instead their role not only as decision-making commanders but as leaders who win by skillfully managing and manipulating their soldiers' morale. See also Walsh (1961), 179, on Livy's selective compression of the siege of Gabii (1.53.4ff), and the siege of New Carthage, pages 99–107, below.

10. See pages 15–19.

11. E.g., 8.13.7–8; for a successful sally see, e.g., 7.7.2.

12. 6.8.9–10. Extreme valor in defense of the walls can even be eulogized as open-field-combat-worthy behavior; the defenders putting their faith *in armis et uirtute quam in moenibus* (37.32.5; see also 32.17.8). One might mischievously ask, then, why they didn't sally forth and put their battle-ready *virtus* to the test without the tactical advantage of those walls. The answer is only that the rhetoric of morale has created an awkward juxtaposition with the actual military narrative.

13. 10.17.7–8. Their general fires the men here with the promise of booty, and they sack the town after the assault. That the *tormenta* they disdain are anachronistic is neither here nor there—Livy's idea that highly motivated troops can win speed assaults on targets that would require heavy engineering to achieve a successful assault by less well-motivated troops is amply borne out by the broadest evidence.

14. The "jingle" *obsidioni atque oppugnationi* (36.10.8, see Kraus and Woodman 1997, 68) can appear to be a Livian rhetorical flourish—the fulsome doubling of military jargon—

that no towns were assaulted or blockaded, while in another area of operations the failure of a Roman assault was followed by digging in to begin a blockade.[15] Although details are few and untrustworthy, this seems to have been a likely course for an early Roman siege—if it could not be quickly assaulted it might languish into a blockade which, if not well supplied and assiduous, would not bring decision.[16] Later, during the first two Punic Wars, when Roman logistics were well developed but advanced siege engineering techniques were still unfamiliar, blockading, both as a strategy and an operational complement to active sieges, occurred more often.[17] In general, the later books of Livy show the complete siege progression in embryo, with the different types of assaults beginning to be distinguishable. Yet whenever the Roman army was in fine fettle it stormed any town that closed its gates, and one notice informs us that Rome once took thirty-one "cities" in fifty days, "every one by assault."[18] The assault was glorious and quick; entirely preferable to a blockade.

---

and at other points (e.g., 37.17.7, or [in epitome] 44.13.4) it is difficult to tell if Livy is using the words with any sense of careful distinction. However, in the longer narratives, Livy is generally consistent in representing the operational difference between the two (see, e.g., 25.26.2). The problem, not unique to Livy, is that the presence of works of circumvallation is often casually taken as the indicator of a static *obsidio* (and indeed, this comes to be the more general term for "siege," while *oppugnatio* can represent any assault on the tactical level, as well as a full-process siege by assault) when the distinction must rest rather on the harder-to-distinguish question of intent. Extensive siege works, however identical in form, may represent either a blockade or thorough preparation for an *oppugnatio*, as Livy well knew from Caesar. See Roth (2006), 56, and note 76. Good examples of the more nuanced usage can be found at 4.61.2–3, 21.8.1, and 26.4.1. Note also that, while used often to distinguish from surrender (*deditio*), the phrase *vi ceperunt*—*vi* being the operative term—describes an event indistinguishable from those described by *oppugno*-related words, i.e., *expugnatio*.

15. 5.12.5–6. The Gauls do the same at 5.43.2–4.
16. See, e.g., 10.9.8–9.
17. Especially during the First Punic War, as at Lilybaeum, where a vigorous siege eventually lapsed into a blockade. Polybius 1.48l0, after a rapid but vivid narrative, is explicit about the shift. Curiously, at Agrigentum, Rome seems to have had no interest in an active siege, although perhaps this is explained, Polybius, 1.17.6–1.19 (does not have good sources to work with), by the presence of another large Carthaginian army. The long blockade of Capua during the Second Punic War is also notable for the presence of an undefeated army (commanded by Hannibal) in the vicinity.
18. 9.45.17. Oakley (2005) III, 596–99, discusses the practice of listing and counting such military events, noting that this passage "has as good a chance as any of being based on authentic testimony."

The first decade of Livy presents one essential siege narrative: the siege of Veii. Significantly, it is pitched primarily as a story of persistence, a victory based on Roman tenacity in both blockade and assault. Livy dramatizes this idea of *perseverantia,* a natural Roman quality that becomes a moral/strategic asset when reputation alone can destroy enemy confidence.[19] This is a retrojection into the distant past of what did indeed characterize Roman siege warfare in the late republic and empire: whatever the operational approach, by whatever technological and tactical means, it was underwritten by Rome's extreme tenacity.

As Rome became a regional power, Veii, only a few miles upriver, was an inevitable obstacle. There was certainly a war and a Roman victory, probably concluding in the 390s BCE, so Livy's account is accurate in the broadest outline. But it is also heavily worked up: Livy stresses religious themes throughout his fifth book, and the account of this victorious war (in which Roman *pietas* enables victory when the gods abandon Veii) is paired with the Gallic sack of Rome (a punishment for subsequent Roman impiety and a heavy-handed turn of Nemesis' wheel). More important is a specific literary allusion: the siege of Veii, which Livy stretches into a ten-year affair, is a Troy story, with the Romans playing the role of the victorious Greeks.[20]

Once this *topos* is established, it should come as no surprise to readers ancient or modern that Veii eventually fell when a small number of soldiers emerged from a sacred space within the walls. But Livy's recounting of *perseverantia* and the progress of the siege is worth going into in some detail. No sooner does the narrative begin in earnest then we are told that Veii must be taken by blockade rather than assault, and that winter quarters will be necessary. While this recalls the hardships suffered by the besiegers at Troy, it is also a significant thematic linkage of siege warfare with the (later) professionalization of the Roman army—soldiers are now to be, for the first time, regularly paid.[21] Moreover, Claudius argues, the expense of maintaining the blockading force is necessary both to Rome's soldiers—

---

19. 5.6.8–9. *Perseverantia* can be read here as the guarantor of Roman *virtus:* if an assault should happen to fail, the enemy will know that a long siege, including continued assaults and a blockade, is to come.

20. See especially Kraus (1994). Ogilvie (1965), 626–30, provides a good introduction.

21. 5.2.1–3, 5.5.5–6. Claudius' speech includes more anachronisms, including double fortifications that would have reminded Livy's readers of Caesar's works at Alesia (on which see chapter 5). As Veii was indeed a difficult site, there is no reason to doubt the existence of blockading works and a fortified camp.

they must balance their *virtus* in the assault by learning the *disciplina* of the blockade—and to Rome's reputation as a power to be feared.[22] The story set, Livy then mixes authentic history with predictable siege narrative stuffing: sallies by the Veiientes, an Etruscan rising, personal and social divisions among the Romans. All of this helps him explain how siege works failed to reach the wall despite years of opportunity.[23] At this point, the religious theme becomes dominant—a new rite propitiates the gods, Delphi is appealed to—and the years stretch toward Trojan decision.

Livy's narrative of the climactic assault is centered on the famous figure of M. Furius Camillus and on the beginning of a mine, the two entering the narrative almost simultaneously. The portrayal of Camillus in Livy is sticky from the overlay of too many coats of heroic treatment and the prompt renovation of military discipline upon his arrival is a cliché—there is not much here that seems securely historical.[24] Yet the narrative still demonstrates Livy's understanding of that central dynamic of siege morale: that in a heavy assault, long, steady discipline is needed as much as the final burst of aggression.

The fall of Veii is vividly rendered. With picked men in the tunnel ready to leap out from within the temple of Juno, a seemingly foolhardy general assault on the walls is made by men fired by the promise of Veii's wealth. The tunnel infiltration may actually have happened (it has the benefit of old tradition in its favor, and mining—or exploiting existing tunnels in Veii's porous rock—was certainly possible), and a general assault as covering action was quite common. But when hell breaks loose in the city we find ourselves with one foot in history and one in myth. The Troy overtones are not only general—wealth and disaster, prodigies, a city abandoned by its gods, Camillus' wily use of stratagem and religion, the screaming of women and children as the killing begins—but as specific as

---

22. 5.6. Note the juxtaposition of *disciplina* at 5.6.1 and *virtus* at 5.6.6—Claudius then launches into the strategic *perseverantia* argument, although the distinction between a long (active) siege and a winter blockade is carefully maintained.

23. Livy 5.7–11. See also Ogilvie (1965), 641.

24. 5.19.9–11: the forbidding of skirmishing between the fortifications—the type scene, real and symbolic, of the mutual testing of combat motivation—enforces the temporary swinging of the pendulum from *virtus* toward *disciplina*. Camillus reflects elements of Sulla, Scipio, and Augustus (and Livy will make him recall Odysseus) but these allusions reinforce the emphasis on the commander's decisions, another common element of siege narratives. See Walsh (1961), 99; Levene (2010), 300ff. Restoring discipline: see, e.g., App. *Pun.* 115; Livy 44.33.5–9; or, much later, Tac. *Ann.* 11.18. See also Astin (1967), appendix II, nos. 33–41.

the Trojan Horse-like emergence of the Roman fighters from the tunnel and a variant story (which Livy holds at arm's length) involving a reminiscence of the palladium.[25] As Livy closes the episode he reminds us not only of the ten years and the greatness of Veii, but also of the role of fate. Interestingly, he implies that this was a sort of defeat for Rome, or at least the denial of a more preferential victory. Open force failed to take the city, but because the fall was destined to happen, it was taken by "works"— that is, the tunnel.[26]

The tunnel to the temple is a "fairy story" rather than history, but Livy's conclusion of the Veii episode does demonstrate that he understands—as any first-century Roman would—that siege warfare is defined by the manner of approach.[27] His treatment of better-known sieges in the later books of his history demonstrates this awareness, but even in brief notices he was careful to indicate the stages of siege warfare. Whatever story Livy is telling, he allows us to see relevant details of intimidation and negotiation and the basic form of any engineering or assaults.

For example, his brief account of L. Scipio's siege of Orongis nevertheless expresses pre-contact, contact, and multiple assault phases before describing the unusual circumstances of the town's actual fall: after encamping, Scipio sought a parley, then invested the town, then launched a testing assault (by escalade, with only one-third of his forces), then sent a larger force in a general assault.[28] Or there is Philip V's siege of Abydos in 200 BCE, offered by P. G. Walsh as an example of Livy's fondness for an episodic narrative. Livy relies on Polybius' account of this relatively minor siege, which did not involve Roman troops. While he compresses some aspects—leaving just a sentence or two for an account of the siege process and the later notice of surrender—he indulges in a comparatively lengthy treatment of the suicidal madness of the townspeople, who had sworn to die when the city was on the point of falling. Livy wants to tell a tragic story that will remind his readers of Saguntum, yet he still respects the siege narrative by including in his introduction every crucial indication of the siege's progress: a general assault had been deterred, a wall had been

---

25. 5.21–2. See also Kraus (1994), 272–73.
26. 5.22.8: *operibus tamen non vi expugnata est.*
27. Fairy story: Ogilvie (1965), 669. See also Kraus (1994), 272, for an apt allusion to Monty Python.
28. 28.3. This siege is thus militarily comprehensible even though most of the narrative is built to serve the larger (tragic) theme of the incident.

breached, and mines were poised to destroy the new wall behind the breach.[29] This combination—an accurate outline with component sections that may be dramatically expanded or compressed—is quite typical of Livy.[30]

POLYBIUS

Yet this typical Livian siege relies on a Polybian account that is far from typical of its author. Polybius, the most militarily dependable source for the siege warfare of the last centuries of the Roman republic, was born around 200 BCE, held political and military posts in Achaea as a young man, and spent many years as a (very privileged) Roman detainee. He witnessed sieges, was equipped to understand what he was seeing, and was well placed to research and interview both in Greece and at Rome. His friendship with Scipio Aemilianus, scion of two great Roman military families, would have provided both insight and access to sources.[31] Scholars also tend to locate his value in his style: Polybius wrote vigorous and relatively unadorned prose, often editorializing in order to criticize the verbose emotionalism of his Hellenistic predecessors and declare his own dedication to plain truth. He saw himself above all as a practical historian—

---

29. Livy 31.17–8, drawing on Polyb. 16.30–4. For Livy's handling of sack episodes see Walsh (1961), 178–79, and pages 191ff. for a general theory of Livy' siege narratives. McDonald (1957), 169, notes in his description of Livy's stylistic transformation of Polybius that "the stages of the action are clearly defined," as does Roth (2006), 66, note 121. See also Levene (2010), chapter 2.

30. Roth (2006), 60, points to Livy's lack of interest in the actual length of sieges: not only does he rarely give any count of elapsed time, but he even drops this information when his source provides it. I am mindful of Roth's warning that any particular theory would be strained to near-uselessness by forcing it onto every Livian siege narrative. My goal here is to show, by looking for the siege progression (which, after all, is essentially an elaboration of Roth's observation that "sieges themselves keep the set patterns"), that Livy leaves important details in place even when he compresses "events" to allow "literature" to expand. Appian is similar to Livy in terms of this confirmedly episodic narrative style: while the timing and the tactical details are hazy, he does show the general selecting his preferred techniques and then marks the transitions between major stages of the siege. See, e.g., *Mith.* 24–7.

31. See Polyb. 31.24. See also Walbank (1972), chapter 1, and (2002), which suggests that Polybius may have been a military advisor or consultant to the Romans. Regardless, he certainly wrote a (lost) work on tactics, and was thus well informed in many ways that demand our reliance on his interpretations. Still, complete accounts of the second-century sieges that he witnessed do not survive, and so the Polybian sieges discussed here are events that took place before his own lifetime—a marked difference from the truly contemporary history examined in the next three chapters.

letting the facts hang in the balance and speak for themselves (although, to remix the metaphors, he is constantly fussing with the scales and tends to talk over his own narrative).[32]

Yet, from another point of view, to accept Polybius' claims to narrative plainness at face value is to fall into a trap. The overburden of language, style, and emplotment do not lie so lightly on the facts beneath that the text can be strip-mined for real information rather than read as a narrative. Polybius makes a strong but rather forced case for himself as an exception, and despite his relative reliability on factual matters, he engages rhetorical techniques, writes speeches for his characters, and plainly considered the reception of his history.[33]

Polybius' siege narratives usually feature good explanations of the machinery and simple, stage-by-stage descriptions of how the operations con-

---

32. See Walbank (1972), 34–39, on "tragic history" and other targets of Polybius' scorn, 66ff on his "practical history," and 71–84 on his sources and methods. Pritchett (1969), 37, concludes that Polybius is the best (i.e., the most reliable) military historian of antiquity. McGing (2010), 11, is similarly positive, despite the rueful comment that "the single most characteristic feature of P's writing" is "his almost constant authorial intervention to explain, disagree, or ruminate discursively." (Of course, these ruminations are necessary to his personality and project, and one can't help but note that Polybius was unhappy in living so long before the discovery of the footnote.) McGing also offers a useful presentation of Polybius' theory and practice of historiography, especially in the well-known digression in book twelve. Marsden (1974), 294–95, finds Polybius to be "a veritable mine of information for the military man," remarking also that "[i]t may be a positive advantage that he did not include more interpretative sections, which might have contaminated the factual evidence rather than clarified it." Marsden, the great scholar of ancient artillery, had very technical interests, and it is his preference for objects over narrative that leads to the Whiggish declaration that Polybius "began the breakthrough into more advanced, even modern, military history." See also Walbank (2002), 24–25 for a list of military gadgets mentioned in consequence of Polybius' particular "interest in technical improvements."

33. Davidson (1991) rails against simplistic readings, stressing instead the importance of recognizing Polybius' interest less in events than in the impact they make on those who take them in. What he calls "the pathological level" I would recognize as an appreciation of the importance of morale in warfare—I agree with Davidson's assessment of Polybius' perceptions, although we differ on semantics. Yet there is no need to distinguish between "military" defeat and defeat of the ψυχή, since general military defeat that is not fundamentally moral (i.e., one side flees or otherwise acknowledges defeat) but rather consists in something material (every soldier on one side being struck down by a weapon?) doesn't really occur in the open edged-weapon confrontations of ancient battle. The categorical exception, of course, is a situation of "desperation," when those about to be defeated are trapped and can expect no mercy. This is the crucial moral distinction between siege and other warfare. See also chapter 2, note 5.

formed to the plans laid by the commanders.[34] Yet at Abydos we get a bare-bones description of the operational plan and are told that "this siege was not at all remarkable for the extent of the machinery employed, or the ingenuity displayed in those works on which besiegers and besieged are wont to exhaust all their invention and skill against each other." Instead, it is "the noble spirit and extraordinary gallantry" that we ought to pay attention to.[35] Polybius, like Livy, moves quickly through the siege in order to get to its conclusion: the strange scene of Philip backing away from the breached inner wall of the fallen city as its inhabitants murder each other.[36] This episode is much discussed, as something like the exception that proves the rule of Polybius' avoidance of emotion.[37] Yet Walbank has also argued that Polybius' "ruthless, hard, and realistic" mind was drawn to the story not, as was Livy's, by the horror and drama of it all, but rather by the special glory of this suicide pact.[38]

This is all well and good, but it ignores the fact that Polybius, like Livy, is still careful to sketch the outline of the siege, thus providing his readers

---

34. See, e.g., the careful attention to both operational detail and morale in the long siege of Lilybaeum, 1.42–5 and 48–9. There are, of course, limits to the self-serious rationalism of Polybius, but he is at pains to present himself as a reform movement of one, returning to the true (Thucydidean) path, with its focus on causality and the explication of recent political and military history. This, rather than any affection for epic inflection, is the reason that he writes from the point of view of the general, or the statesman. See especially Walbank (1972), 43, 56–58. See Marsden (1974), 291, on Polybius' "fundamentally accurate" description of siege machines. In a striking, but textually problematic fragment (29.12.7–8), Polybius, in railing against inferior historians, uses siege accounts as a typical example (that is, as a typical example of a type). "Such historians as I refer to, when they are describing in the course of their work the siege, say of Phanoteia, or Coroneia, or [Haliartus], are forced to display all the contrivances, bold strokes, and other features of the siege; and when they come to the capture of Tarentum, the sieges of Corinth, Sardis, Gaza, Bactra, and, above all, of Carthage, they must draw on their own resources to prolong the agony and heighten the picture, and are not at all satisfied with me for giving a more truthful relation of such events as they really occurred." Adapted from Shuckburgh, with Walbank (1979), 375.

35. 16.30.2–3. Trans. Shuckburgh.

36. 16.32–34.

37. Walbank (1972), 39, sees this episode as a succumbing to temptation, explained in part by larger thematic interests in τύχη and in Philip V, whose story is clearly emplotted as a tragedy—but he also explains it by reference to Polybius' moralizing interests. See also D'Huys (1987) 224–6, and McGing (2010), 73.

38. Walbank (1967), 542; (1972), 178. I find that Eckstein (1995), 51 ff., has preceded me in grumpily disagreeing with those scholars who see this siege narrative as indicative of Polybian cold-bloodedness, although his criticism of Walbank on this matter seems a bit unfair.

with the necessary context for an appreciation of the civic suicide drama. What does the siege progression tell us? First, there is Polybius' prefatory notice, which speaks to the expectation of his readers, announcing that *this* one is not about technology or a battle of wits. Next, Polybius notes the high morale of the defenders, which enabled the "courageous resistance" that drove back his ships with catapult missiles and fire. Polybius may be very interested in technology, but he consistently makes morale the ultimate cause of military success—even here, when it is a matter of accurate shooting from mural artillery rather than hand-to-hand combat.[39] There was then some sort of testing or general assault: Livy interprets Polybius' vague "siege operations on land" as an assault driven off by the same artillery, and we then hear that the wall has been undermined.[40] Livy's gloss (or interpolation) makes sense, and rather than taking this merely as clear evidence of Livy's source embroideries (which it is), we should seize upon it as a clue that Livy weaves his siege stories on the same frame, namely the siege progression. Philip was accustomed to mining, but he would surely have tested the morale of the defenders with an assault, and if there is a reference to mural artillery but none to any contact with the walls, it is logical for later commentators—in Augustan Rome or here and now—to guess that these operations included some sort of assault but no heavily engineered attempt on the walls.

When Philip turned to undermining, his sappers were quickly successful: the wall crumbles, and although the defenders had detected the mine and built an inner wall to seal off the breach, this wall too was soon undermined. Then—Polybius is careful to mark the sequence of events—the city sends ambassadors to parley with Philip. This is, again, exactly what should happen now: the pause before the breaching of the wall is the exact equivalent, in a mining-dominated siege, of the moment when the ram is in place and poised to strike—the last chance to negotiate.[41] The ambassadors propose a standard, if lenient, agreement, but Philip demands surrender without terms, and the ambassadors return knowing now that it

---

39. See Eckstein (1995), *passim,* and 168–70: "what is striking in *the Histories* is the tremendous fragility of soldiers' morale." Absolutely: but this should be seen as evidence of Polybius' excellence as a reporter on military realities, rather than of his ability to play up emotion as well as reason.

40. 16.30.5: τοῖς δὲ κατὰ γῆν ἔργοις. 31.17.1: *tormentis. . . adeuntis aditu arcebant.*

41. See also Polybius 5.4.6 and 5.100.6.

must be a fight to the death.[42] Both historians have given us a succinct account of events that is informed and enabled by the common understanding of the standard siege progression.

And now the real drama—the oath, the last desperate defense, the self-slaughter—can begin. It is a drama, however, defined by the warfare of refusal. Livy, it is true, reaches straightaway for tragic and epic coloring, writing of rage and madness and the rounding up of doomed women and children.[43] But for Polybius, the "nobility" of the Abydenes, their "the special eminence and unique glory" begins to make a certain contextual sense. There is indeed a ruthless rationality here: to accept that continued resistance will guarantee a vicious sack and thus to plan both to destroy the city's wealth and to preemptively kill the victims of rape, slavery, and slaughter by strangers is to fully embrace the special logic of siege warfare.[44] Again, the sequence of events is telling: they reject the terms, they make the solemn oath to destroy themselves, and then they end their countermining efforts.[45] Having chosen death, they allow the inner wall to be breached.

> As soon as the interior wall had fallen, the men, according to their oaths, sprang upon the ruins and fought the enemy with such desperate courage, that Philip, though he had kept sending the Macedonians to the front in relays till nightfall, at last abandoned the contest in despair of accomplishing the capture at all. For not only did the Abydenian forlorn hope take their stand upon the dead bodies of the fallen enemies, and maintain the battle with fury; nor was

---

42. For Polybius' ἐπιτρέπω (16.30.8) Livy uses *permitto* (31.17.4), which he elsewhere (36.28.1–5) connects to the "unconditional" surrender of *deditio*.

43. 31.17.45: *ab indignatione simul ac desperatione iram accendit . . . ad Saguntinam rabiem uersi*. The use of *desperatio*, though, is perhaps as precise as it is dramatic.

44. See chapter 3. Livy follows precisely Polybius' (16.31–3) details of the plan, with one addition: to throwing valuables into the harbor and killing the women and children he adds the burning of buildings. Walsh (1961), 194 points out that this makes Abydos more like Saguntum—but it also adds a "missing" element of the full *urbs direpta* catalogue. Cultural distance and "ruthlessness" are still hardly enough to allow for Polybius' admiration, but the same feeling is at least partially present in Livy: the references to "madness" and "crime" in his account are more apostrophe than analysis. After all, a central contention of this book is that siege warfare was in some sense beyond or outside of military "law," that it was a routinized or structured madness, behavior that could be predicted and thus not completely condemned yet still seemed "criminal."

45. 16.31.8.

it only that they fought gallantly with mere swords and spears; but when any of these weapons had been rendered useless, or had been knocked out of their hands, they grappled with the Macedonians, and either hurled them to the ground arms and all, or broke their sarissae, and stabbing their faces and exposed parts of their bodies with the broken ends, threw them into a complete panic. (16.33.1–3)

This "appallingly realistic . . . combat" is not stock description or impressionistic filler.[46] Livy, by contrast, omits any description of the fighting (he refers simply to "picked men" dying in front of the breach) and turns his account, at the last, into a victim's drama rather than a siege horror story.[47] I have used Shuckburgh's 1889 translation of Polybius, in large part because of his rendering of *hoi prokinduneuontes* (literally "those first into danger" or perhaps "those who bear the brunt of battle") as "forlorn hope." Strictly speaking, a forlorn hope is an ad hoc unit, composed entirely of volunteers, which leads the storming of a breach—the aim being to provoke a volley and reveal any hidden defenses. Few of the volunteers were expected to survive.[48] These are defenders, and there were no cannon to feed, but the rest of the sense is exactly right: they fight with no hope of survival, they fill a breach with their bodies, and by insisting upon close combat they force the enemy to match their desperate courage. The intimate violence of this passage may recall epic or "emotional" pseudo-history, but its primary purpose—its justification as history—is to emphasize the rationale behind the ratcheting tension of the warfare of refusal. Sacks are horrible because besiegers are more willing to conduct general assaults or toil

---

46. D'Huys (1987), 230.

47. 31.17.7 Walsh (1961), 193 notes his general "sympathy" for defenders and preference for describing their state of mind instead of their tactics, a "literary" flaw that typifies the way in which Livy is so much less useful (than Polybius) to military historians—yet the desperation of the defenders should be recognized as a fundamental (moral) aspect of the military situation; see chapter 2, note 5. See also 28.19.9–15.

48. Shuckburgh was born in 1843, only a generation after Britain's most famous forlorn hopes were shot to pieces in the breaches of several Spanish border fortresses. The tactical purpose of the forlorn hope was specific to the age of muzzle-loading guns, the idea being that the "real" assault party could begin their advance while the defenders were reloading after firing into the forlorn hope at point-blank range. Although there could be a rough analogy here with ancient mural artillery, the higher rate of fire of bows, spears, and slings meant that there would be little less danger for a second wave of assault troops. Incidentally, the resonance of this once-popular term is based on a false etymology: the "hope" is a Dutch *hoop*—"heap" in the sense of "group of men" and "forlorn" is merely *verloren,* or lost.

in mines than they are to die in a breach, grappled and stabbed with their own broken weapons by men who know they have nothing to lose.

Abydos, then, was "true" and "realistic" drama—but it was unusual. More typical of Polybian siege narratives is Ambracia, a tough little Greek hill city besieged by Roman armies in 189 BCE. Although the entire account has not survived, we do know that the site was forbidding enough—steep, well fortified, and approachable only from one direction—that the preliminary states of the siege progression were dispensed with.[49] After reconnoitering, the Roman commander (M. Fulvius Nobilior) began constructing both a fortified line (to cut off the city and protect his troops) and siege works that approached the city wall at five points.[50]

The siege then takes place in three major episodes. First, the Roman works reach the walls and there is a technological back and forth: Rome attacks the walls with rams and the battlements with scythe-like implements on poles, while the defenders counter with counterweighted cranes to drop weights on the rams and grappling hooks that yank the scythes over the battlements, breaking the poles in the process. Polybius, as usual, brackets the physical with the moral. Seeing the scale and energy of the Roman attack, the defenders are "terribly alarmed," but their ability to successfully counter the devices actually at work on their wall results in increased confidence—they sally against the siege works.[51] Both accounts then pause to describe events elsewhere. Stage one of the siege is over, but the crucial information has been communicated: rams are in use, morale is high on both sides, and either side might yet prevail.[52]

---

49. 21.25–8. The comparison below is complicated by the fact that Livy's narrative (38.3–9) appears to be based on Polybius, but on a much more complete text of Polybius than that which survives (and perhaps on Ennius as well). It seems certain, for example, that Polybius (see, e.g., 1.12.4 or 1.42.1) began as usual by describing the topography, and that Livy (38.4.1–5) preserved this description. See Briscoe (2008), 2. That the technical section of a longer siege narrative was preserved is a testament to the early date of the gadgetary turn. See page 3, above. That there was no initial sally from the defenders (21.26.3–4) is more likely, given subsequent events, to indicate that they were biding their time than that they were in a state of low morale.

50. Not, *contra* Kern (1999), 276, a circumvallation, since the natural obstacles of cliff and river were expected to contribute to the blockade—Livy is careful to admit this distinction, here. For the topography and scholarly dispute over the five locations, see Briscoe (2008), 39; Walbank (1979) 4–5.

51. 21.27.3: ἐκπληκτικὴν συνέβαινε γίνεσθαι τοῖς ἔνδον.

52. Polybius 21.27.1–6; Livy 38.5.1–5. Livy's cutaway to the whereabouts of Nicanor co-

Next, 500 Aetolian soldiers join the defenders (passing through a weak point in the Roman lines) with a plan for a nocturnal sally to be coordinated with other forces outside the city. The defenders duly sally in force, but the external army fails to materialize, and although their attack causes many casualties and burns part of the Roman works, it is presented as a failure, given what might have been accomplished if the Romans had been simultaneously attacked in the rear.[53] Livy adds a notice that the defenders, feeling betrayed, now "confined themselves to fighting in comparative safety from the walls and towers."[54] At this point, Livy again cuts away to external events and one of our Polybian fragments ends. Even when the passage of actual time is not closely marked, the narrative observes and enacts the major progressions of the siege.

When the narratives resume, we are at the desperation stage. The several breaches are defended both by makeshift counter-walls and by the armored bodies of the defenders themselves, and Roman assaults cannot break through.[55] Fulvius therefore ordered the mining operations, which have always attracted interest in these accounts: the defenders dig a trench behind their wall and use sheets of bronze to locate the Roman digging (through vibration); they then countermine and break into the Roman tunnel and, after subterranean skirmishing, construct a sort of smoke projector to drive the Romans from the tunnel. The technical ingenuity here is the centerpiece and the climax of Polybius' account, the story of a siege fought to a stalemate by equally matched opponents.[56]

Livy follows Polybius closely here, but he struggles with the Greek, and thus the differences between the two texts, while illustrative, should be handled with care. Livy omits the bronze sheets (probably because he does not understand their use) and seems to misunderstand the purpose of the tunneling.[57] In Polybius, it is fairly clear that the mine is intended to break

---

incides exactly with the end of one fragmentary excerpt from Polybius. Livy's more dramatic account of the fear and confidence of the besieged is characteristic, but it is also possible that Polybius may originally have included more information about morale.

53. Livy 38.5–6; Polybius 21.27.7–9.

54. 38.6.9, trans. Roberts.

55. Polybius 21.28.2. Livy 38.7.5, which recalls the breach defenders of Abydos: *armati ruinis superstantes instar munimenti erant.* See also 32.17.7–8; 32.23.7–9; and note 32.

56. Polybius 21.28.3–18. See Walbank (1979), 126–27 for discussion of the bronze implements. The fragment, happily, includes a few words shifting the scene immediately after Rome abandons the mine—Polybius too cut away before returning to describe events after the siege. For another description of many implements of siege warfare see 9.41–42.4, which is, unfortunately, isolated and paraphrased.

57. Livy (38.7.6–13) also mistakes "shields" for doors, but he otherwise embroiders only

the tactical deadlock around the small breaches by bringing down a large section of the wall at once, but Livy seems to think that the tunnel is intended to surface within the town, allowing for the infiltration of Roman troops.[58]

So Livy does not quite understand what is going on, yet he is able to contextualize it more clearly, especially for Roman readers. Mines (of either type) were not a favored tactic because they were only possible in certain situations and because they took too long. Yet to give up frontal assaults and settle for a mine is to trade "open force" for a "secret tunnel." The adjectival emphasis clearly conveys disapproval. Thus we can guess at a third reason why Roman siege warfare rarely involved mining: unless it was the first heavy engineering option, its lateness and (necessary) furtiveness implied the failure of Roman force.[59] Polybius' morally muted battle of the technologists is subtly shaded, by Livy, into a story of Roman embarrassment and failure. A very necessary shading, for the news that a surrender is negotiated—after the rams, after fighting in the breaches and the mine—comes as a slightly smaller shock in Livy than in Polybius. Polybius seems to be discussing business as usual in the late Hellenistic world, while Livy knows that (despite terms very favorable to Rome) the end of such a long siege in anything less than a storm and sack would be unacceptable.[60]

---

to suggest—plausibly—that the miners fought initially with their tools and were replaced by different men armed with proper weapons. I have too much sympathy with Livy's plight—the Greek here is thorny!—to dwell upon his "howlers" here (on which see Walsh 1958), at least until after my own have been enumerated. For kindlier verdicts on Livy's fumbles see Briscoe (2008), 44–45; or McDonald (1957), 161.

58. If I am right in reading Livy's assumption (although he may be in doubt and thus intentionally vague), then he must be wrong; these are indeed the two potential uses of any "mining" operations, but despite the dramatic potential (already exploited at Veii and in other essentially fictional sieges) of soldiers leaping from a tunnel, it would not be worth the effort unless a nearby gate could quickly be opened, which was not the case at Ambracia. Rather, the mine here is a tactical microcosm of the Messines attack of 1917, when a large-scale undermining of enemy works was planned to supersede the failure of multiple local efforts to achieve a breakthrough.

59. 38.7.6: *Itaque cum aperta ui parum procederet consuli res, cuniculum occultum uineis ante contecto loco agere instituit.* The same is implied in Livy's concluding remarks on Veii, on which see pages 87–89. There are only a handful of Roman sieges that involve offensive mines. If one discounts Veii as unhistorical (Davies 2006, 117–18 is too sanguine about the historicity of Livy's mines) then not until Julian's invasion of Persia in 363 CE (see pages 201–3, below) do Roman troops actually dig their way into an enemy city. The evidence for successful undermining is hardly greater, and we are left with only a few isolated "special cases." Other than as a defensive tactic (i.e., undermining of siege ramps), mining should be relegated to the footnotes of Roman military history.

60. Polybius 21.29–30; Livy 38.8–9.

And yet perhaps Ambracia was sacked, despite the fact that it surrendered and agreed to treaty terms. Although we begin to stray too far into technical obscurities, the bloodless listing of indemnities that immediately follows the siege account (Livy notes the capitulation but claims that there was no destruction beyond the confiscations spelled out in the treaty) may conceal the harsher reality.[61] Before his return to Rome and eventual triumph, Fulvius was accused by a rival Roman political faction of having wrongfully besieged and sacked Ambracia. Ambraciot ambassadors were brought to Rome and claimed to have been "blockaded and assaulted . . . and sacked," and the senate voted them restitution, but delayed decision on the matter of the booty taken by Fulvius. This is significant: the senate accepted the (apparently false) accusation that the war had been unjust, but they stuck on the issue of whether the city had in fact been taken by force. Fulvius' enemy then forced through a motion stating that "that there was no evidence that Ambracia had been taken by storm." When Fulvius returned to Rome, Livy gives us a short version of the speech he made in his defense, in which he carefully avoids claiming that the city was in fact taken by storm and makes no mention of the negotiations that brought about its capitulation. Instead, he rests his argument on the elaboration and intensity of the siege: he mentions the siege works and tunneling and claims that there were fifteen days of combat before a final battle left 3,000 of the enemy dead.[62] His silence about the actual capitulation must mean two things: that the failure of the assaults to carry the city outright is indeed an embarrassment and that he is, nevertheless, legally justified. The terms of the surrender—capitulation occurring only after a fully engineered siege had breached the walls—must have been understood to equate to capture by force/by assault. The Ambraciots surrendered in order to avoid a massacre, but they still suffered an ex post facto sack, enriching Fulvius and his troops.[63] Polybius' technological stalemate is, in Livy, a

---

61. Polybius 21.30.1–9; Livy 38.9.6–13. Livy follows Polybius but his subsequent discussion of later political arguments derives from another source.

62. Livy 38.43–44; 39.4. 38.43.4: *obsessos deinde et oppugnatos se . . . direptione urbis*. 38.44.6: *Ambraciam ui captam esse non uideri*. Roberts' translation of *oppugnatos* as "carried by storm" is thus significantly wrong—if the city had suffered *expugnatio* then there would have been *vis* and no complaint could be made about the sack (Sage, in the Loeb, has the lovely and accurate "beleaguered and besieged").

63. Livy's introduction of "fifteen days" and the mention of a siege mound (*agger*), neither of which were included in Polybius or in book 38, point to the use of some annalistic record which may preserve the substance of Fulvius' justification of his actions. It

military/moral compromise. The all but successful extended siege must end in a sack, but Fulvius settles for the material form of a sack without the violence, saving some face even as the people of Ambracia save their lives.

CARTHAGO NOVA

New Carthage (modern Cartagena), the major Carthaginian base in Spain, was targeted by the young Publius Cornelius Scipio at the beginning of the campaign of 209 BCE. The brief, famous siege that resulted brings further into focus the tension between control and chaos in both Polybius and Livy. The natural structure of siege and siege narrative run hand in-hand with the writer's desire to foreground the commander and his decisions—but assaults are chaotic affairs, difficult to submit to causal explanation. Unlike the sieges detailed earlier, this was a major event in Roman military history: it helped to turn the tide of the Second Punic War and it was the first major step in the career of Scipio, who would go on to beat Hannibal, conquer Carthage, take the cognomen "Africanus," be considered *A Greater Than Napoleon,* and otherwise exemplify generalship. He was also the adoptive grandfather of Scipio Aemilianus, the final conqueror of Carthage (at the end of the Third Punic War) and the patron of Polybius. Not surprisingly, then, we understand the military context of this siege quite

---

may also be an anachronism: while Rome evidently began occasionally using the *agger* as an assault ramp (with or without rolling towers) during the Punic Wars, it did not become the tactic of choice until Caesar. Campbell (2006), 132 puts the transition from the "storming escalade, unsupported by heavy machinery" to the assault-with-mound at around this period. He and Davies (2006) may be too confident of the consistency with which words such as *agger, pluteus,* and *vinea* were applied, by different authors, to specific objects. As for Ambracia, scholarly interest has, characteristically, focused on *ius ad bellum* and the confusing information on the various treaties, rather than the *ius in bello* of the conventions of siege warfare. See Briscoe (2008), 218–20, and 48–50. Briscoe, 48, notes that "(i)t seems that a city which made a *deditio* after a siege is regarded as *vi capta.*" As this was generally the case only after the heavily engineered siege had been reached, it is strange not to see the famous "ram laws" (see pages 74–77, above) introduced at this point. There is an interesting parallel in the sack of Tarentum in 209, when the Romans are admitted into the town by a traitor, yet a massacre takes place. In Plutarch's account (*Fab.* 22.4–6), Fabius Maximus cynically orders his men to assault over the walls in order to legitimize massacre and plunder and hide the less reputable fact of taking the town by treachery. Livy (27.16.1–8) allows for three possibilities: the killing may have been due to hatred, or a mistake, or *ad proditionis famam ut ui potius atque armis captum Tarentum uideretur exstinguendam.*

well—Polybius visited the city years later and also draws on eyewitness testimony. And yet such a commander (and such a relationship to the writer) can exert an overlarge influence on the shaping of the narrative. Scipio must be handled with care.[64]

The attack on New Carthage was a bold stroke. Most sieges occur at the end of a campaign, but Scipio aimed to take the lightly held city before the three Carthaginian armies in Spain had even taken the field. A long siege was out of the question, and some sort of light assault was necessary. But the city was formidable: situated between the Mediterranean and a lagoon, its high walls were normally approachable only along a narrow isthmus. Scipio, however, had a plan, and with the divulging of this plan the Polybian story of the siege begins—unusually—even before the Romans arrived at the city. The siege can be quickly summarized: after a direct attack on the landward side was repulsed, Scipio sent a detachment to wade through the lagoon, surprising the defenders and enabling a coordinated assault to carry the city.

Polybius, rejecting the claims of earlier writers, is at pains to show that this victory is due not to Scipio's fortune but rather to his careful and clever planning.[65] He cites several sources in order to demonstrate that Scipio knew in advance that the water level in the lagoon could be counted upon to drop at a certain time. Is this then the "rationalization" of a miraculous

---

64. Napoleon: Liddell Hart (1930). Scullard (1970) is still to be recommended for a study of Scipio in context. Polybius' sources, in addition to the testimony of Gaius Laelius, who served as Scipio's lieutenant during the campaign (and would have been an old man when he spoke to Polybius) and whatever Scipio family tradition he may have been privy to, probably included Fabius Pictor and Silenus. See especially Walbank (1967), 191ff. Eckstein (1995), 9ff., argues that "the pro-Aemilian and pro-Scipionic *Tendenz*... should not be exaggerated." But while he does criticize relatively minor relatives, Polybius is full of fulsome praise for the two foremost Scipios.

65. 10.9.2: not to τύχη; that is, but rather πρόνοια. Polybius' ongoing spat with earlier historians and his use of τύχη (which does, elsewhere, help explain Scipio's successes) are both much discussed in the scholarly literature. See Walbank (1967), 191ff., and 204, and (1957), 22ff. Despite Scipio's dominance of the narrative, Polybius does not let things get out of hand—it is more a matter of reading carefully than, as with Josephus' portrayal of Titus, of primly averting our eyes whenever the hero erupts into the narrative. See also McGing (2010), 7–11, 38ff. Eckstein (1995), chapters 2 and 6, emphasizes Polybius' commitment to Scipio as a model of intelligent and self-controlled generalship, but argues against over-interpreting this deemphasizing of personal heroism as evidence of a ruthlessly unsentimental or Machiavellian streak. In particular, he sees the New Carthage narrative as constructed to show "the polarity of order and organization on one side, and disorder, chaos, and defeat on the other" (page 180). Curiously, however, Eckstein (forgivably) avoids the lagoon controversy and misreads the failure of the first attack, on which see immediately below.

story—a biblical mashup of the Sea of Reeds and the siege of Jericho? Probably not. Many scholars have waded into the controversy and provided some explanation of the lagoon's apparent drop in water level, and it is best to conclude that Polybius is basically right: the surprise attack was planned in advance, and the water level dropped at the right time.[66] It was a neat trick—an excellent example of a tactical category in which sudden approach from a topographically unlikely direction succeeds because the defense has been concentrated on the easier approaches—but it was not miraculous.[67] Polybius is keen to emphasize the cleverness and the operational control of his hero.

---

66. The problem hinges upon 10.8.7 and 10.10.12: that the lagoon recedes every evening, and that this is taken advantage of by fishermen who cross the channel to the sea. Walbank (1967) notes that the lagoon may be crossable even without this mysterious ebb, which may or may not be tidal (he does not equate "ebb" and "tide" "without second thoughts" as Lillo et al. 1988, 478 allege). Tides are, however, insignificant in the Mediterranean and very weak at Cartagena. Scullard (1970), 55–57, follows Livy's addition (26.45.8) of a sudden wind (and adds a nice digression on wind-aided isthmus crossing, both biblical and historical). The Scipionic wind, *pace* Kern (1999), 270, who follows Scullard's acceptance of Livy, is rightly rejected by Lillo et al., since it cannot fit the "rational" argument that Scipio planned the timing of the assault. Their suggestion of sluice gates, operated by local fisherman, that allowed the water level to be dropped—generally at evening, hence the mistaken reading of somewhat regular "tides," but also on cue—is convincing, despite Hoyos (1992), who has sluice gates but not fishermen. But the palm goes to Lowe (2000), who carefully scrutinizes the geography of the site, brings in additional scholarly literature, and comments extensively on the ancient fishing industry. In short, Scipio's attack took advantage of sluice gates, normally used in industrial salt production, to lower the water level for the final coordinated attack. It is also the case, as Lowe reminds us (as does Scullard, thirty years earlier), that Polybius describes the lagoon as being ordinarily fordable in multiple places. Thus nowhere is it clear that the water-level drop is essential to the success of the assault: we may have here yet another example of a nifty bit of technology looming far too large in the historical conversation.

67. Difficult sieges are rather often resolved by just such a sudden attack on a point of "natural strength" that, in being therefore unguarded (or at least insufficiently defended), has become a point of relative tactical weakness. It seems to be both a little-recognized commonality of siege warfare and a favorite historians' trope, combining the elements of surprise, counterintuitiveness, and the juxtaposition of physical obstacles and human activity. McGing (2010), 103, and Davidson (1991), 17–18 have noticed the repeated examples in Polybius, which also speak to the Polybian habit of demonstrating military expertise based on a fuller appreciation of tactics in its psychological context. That is, the besiegers' assessment of the fortifications must take into account the defenders' assessment, and can often locate points of overconfidence as "counterintuitive" points of actual weakness. See, e.g., 3.18.3, 4.70–1, 7.15.2–5, and 8.13.9. This nugget of ancient military wisdom has proved so irresistible to so many writers that it was long ago transformed into trope—it could grow up to be a charming article someday. See, e.g., App. *Pun.* 113; Livy 24.46.1–2, 28.19.18–20.4, 8.53; Onasander 42.15–6; Herodotus 1.84.2–4; Plut. *Sull.* 14; Xen. *Cyr.* 7.2.3; Sall. *Iug.* 93; Arr. *Anab.* 2.26 and 4.18.4–19.4; and, in the medieval Japanese *Taiheki*, McCullough (1976), 176.

But that's not all there is to the story. First, we should note the persistence of conventional structure. Arrival is followed by entrenchment and the review of topography.[68] Polybius then shifts to an emphasis on morale. We get the interesting tidbit that Scipio only fortified his camp on the far side of the isthmus, leaving the side toward the city unprotected. Since Scipio's army vastly outnumbered the Carthaginian defenders (even when supplemented by townsmen) this serves as an unusual negative example of intimidation through construction, a statement of confidence that dares the defenders to sally.[69] The exhortation follows, and the plot thickens. Our clever general predictably promises rewards and refers to the *corona muralis,* but our rationalist historian also has him explain that the assault plan came to him in a dream sent by "Poseidon." This was certainly already part of the Scipio legend when it came to Polybius, who not only retains it but voices approval: "This shrewd combination of accurate calculation with the promise of gold crowns and the assurance of the help of Providence created great enthusiasm among the young soldiers and raised their spirits." Whatever Scipio may have believed, he is clearly both playing on the beliefs of his soldiers in order to spur the combat motivation of the assault troops and helping to fashion his own legend.[70]

The mention of Poseidon, of course, sets up the miraculous lagoon, and Livy will have Scipio reference Neptune just before that assault.[71] But first, an opportunity presented itself: when the Romans left their camp they were met by a sally from the city, taking up the challenge implied by their lack of inner fortifications, and a fierce contest—described in notably cliché fashion—developed. But Rome soon prevailed (perhaps in part because, as Polybius suggests, they were better able to reinforce freely from their unfortified camp) and chased the Carthaginian-led force back toward the city, nearly entering on their heels.[72] Since ladders had already been prepared, a general assault now developed, and Scipio, protected by shield

---

68. 10.9–10.

69. Thus, technically, we have (outer) lines of circumvallation without (inner) lines of contravallation—see chapter 3, note 57. 10.11.3: Polybius gives intimidation as one possible explanation—tactical freedom being the other. On intimidation through construction, see chapter 3, pages 58–59, and note 42.

70. 10.11.8, trans. Scott-Kilvert. See also Livy 26.19.5–8. See Scullard and Walbank, *op. cit.* for (necessarily uncertain) discussion of the religiosity of Scipio.

71. Livy 26.45.9.

72. 10.12. Scullard (1970), 60–61, interprets Scipio's intention, probably correctly, as a testing assault that, once met with the sally, became a serious general assault.

bearers, moved into the range of missile fire to show himself to his troops.[73] Polybius provides here a perfect description of the general as moral leader, inspiring reckless courage and presenting himself as a witness for prospective heroes of the escalade.

Yet the assault failed, apparently for physical rather than moral reasons. While the "fury and zeal of the Romans"[74] is sufficient, the height of the walls presents unforeseen tactical difficulties. Ladders break under the weight of multiple climbers, while soldiers become "dizzy" at the top of the unbroken ladders.[75] These rather strange problems are mentioned in the same breath as a most common difficulty of an escalade—that large objects thrown from the walls are killing men on the ladders. Despite all of this, men still quickly take the places of those who fall (from) above them. Polybius, who at other points in his work is at pains to emphasize Roman discipline generally and the benefits of tactical subdivision in particular, here strips the escalade down to a matter of Scipio as leader and the aggression of his most highly motivated troops.[76] As I argued in chapter 3, this persistent, voluntary risk taking in the face of (apparently) high casualties is both difficult to achieve and fundamental to the success of any siege assault. Polybius, elsewhere, recognizes the Roman emphasis on stimulating vol-

---

73. 10.13.1–3. Marsden (1969), 78–79, citing Livy's (26.47.5–6) count of 476 artillery pieces later found within the city, describes New Carthage as "plainly the main Carthaginian arsenal in Spain" (on which it did not deign to rain). Given that there were only 1,000 experienced troops in the city, no more than a small fraction of these could have been in operation—but enough to make Scipio, however favored of Neptune, take such a precaution.

74. 10.13.10: τὴν ἐπιφορὰν καὶ τὴν ὁρμὴν τῶν Ῥωμαίων. Eckstein (1995), 180–81, omits mention of this (perfectly normal) aspect of any siege assault, instead finding "the orderliness of what was merely a Roman maneuver." This is wrong, and, in treating the Roman soldiers as automata capable of assaulting a defended wall without benefit of emotion, Eckstein both misunderstands the nature of combat and gives short shrift to the inspirational leadership of Scipio.

75. 10.13.8–10. The verb in question is the unusual σκοτάω, which Polybius does not elsewhere associate specifically with heights. Walbank and Scullard are both silent about this very odd claim, and it is tempting to suggest that Polybius may be intentionally vague, leaving the reader to wonder whether this is really a physical symptom—ladder-induced vertigo—or a moral/motivational failing at the point of the attack.

76. On Roman military organization, 6.19ff.; for centurions—absent from this scene although they are the crucial subordinate unit commanders at this and most other points in Roman military history—(mis)represented as being steadfast rather than aggressively courageous, 6.24.9. Polybius wants the centurions to be stolid, but he clearly recognizes the importance of desperate courage, on which see 5.100, and chapter 2, note 5.

untary risk-taking by hope of reward, as his Scipio has done.[77] Yet in the next sentence Scipio calls off the attack because it is now late in the day and "the soldiers were fatigued."

Something odd is going on here. The tactical explanation would be fairly simple: if a number of ladders are out of commission, an escalade's chance of success will diminish rapidly as the defenders focus their efforts on the few remaining points on the wall where attackers may yet appear. This explanation would not cover Scipio with glory, as he should have prepared enough (and strong enough) ladders, and it would be out of place in a narrative constructed around the idea of Scipio's cleverness. Nor would Scipio have given up on the attack as long as a few ladders and a few willing men remained: the cost in casualties would be relatively light (with only a few men engaged at a time) and the seizure of even a small section of wall might lead swiftly to the collapse of resistance among recently routed troops. Surely, then, a better guess at what happened would be that the most suicidally brave had become casualties by this point and the pace of volunteer replacement at the foot of the ladders was flagging—and that this is what caused Scipio to realize that the chance of success was vanishingly slim. But Polybius has clearly stated the opposite. Now, there is an overriding operational explanation, of course: Scipio has the lagoon attack ready as a plan b, and the morning involved either an intimidation attempt or a testing assault that developed into a general assault after the sally had been defeated.[78]

But why does the assault fail? The moral narrative picks up, as we would expect it to, with the notice that the morale of the defenders is raised by their victory. And the renewal of the frontal assault (as cover for the 500 men moving through the lagoon—only now is the lateness of the day connected to the ebb in the lagoon) is also presented as a moral gambit: since the morale of the defenders was predicated on their having achieved a victory, the renewed attack is calculated to puncture their swollen confidence. So Scipio has allowed an assault to go on as long as his men were willing, then almost immediately launched a counterattack (with more ladders!) designed to dishearten the defenders and allow the "outflanking" by the lagoon party. Physical fatigue cannot have been the real reason for the withdrawal.

---

77. 6.39.4–5; Scipio's speech of the previous day, 10.11.6–8, mentions both the "official" *corona muralis* and the rewarding of voluntary risk taking.

78. So Walbank (1967), 194: "probably designed to exhaust the enemy rather than to capture the city by direct assault."

Livy's account, which follows Polybius but offers many elaborations, is more tactically comprehensible. He provides details of the Carthaginian dispositions and describes the landing of troops on the seaward side of the town during the first attack, and he also makes reference to the high volume of missile fire from the city. More importantly, he presents the first assault as an ad hoc attack ordered only when Scipio notices that, after the failed sally, the demoralized defenders are not manning the walls. The explanation of the Roman failure also follows Polybius, even including the epidemic of vertigo, with one exception: Livy is explicit that some of the ladders are not tall enough. Is Livy interpreting or drawing on another source? He claims that the broken ladders were the taller, weaker ones that actually could reach the top of the wall, which suggests interpretation. Regardless, Livy's tale makes more sense, and, if we accept it, we find Polybius hoisted on his own petard.[79] Twice in the extant portions of his histories Polybius harps upon the importance of properly measuring ladders before an assault—indeed, ladder measuring is nearly metonymical for prudent generalship.[80] If Polybius really wished to center the narrative of the siege on the rational control of Scipio, he was rather careless to leave this evidence of poor advance planning.

Returning to Livy, it is significant that he is morally more consistent than Polybius: he emphasizes the primary significance of Scipio's presence as a "witness and spectator" of his men's actions, and he dramatizes their competition to mount the ladders. He also makes the defenders' success, which raises their morale, the reason for the recall, rather than the physical exhaustion of the assault troops. Since it is difficult to see how the static defenders of a rampart could manifest such "boldness," it seems safe to assume that Livy imagines the pace of the wall assault to be slowing when Scipio decides to call it off. Each of these differences in some way detracts attention from Scipio's intellectual control of the enterprise. Livy's Scipio

---

79. 26.44–6. Livy also seems to imply, at 46.1, that the landward approach is subject to enfilade from the walls, although whether this is an invention or some underappreciated aspect of the topography and fortifications is hard to say. Kern (1999), 269–71, chooses to imagine "sambucas" being involved in the attack, on the assumption that there was no other way for the assault troops to get from ship to shore to wall—an egregious instance of the fascination with siege technology distorting an ancient narrative—but his emphasis on Scipio's "psychological" strokes against the city is correct.

80. 9.18.5–9, 5.98. See Walbank (1972), 88, on Polybius' penchant for professional pedantry. See also McGing (2010), 39–40. Polybius may be missing the point (and perhaps deliberately) that a Roman aristocratic general may choose to concentrate on moral or operational issues, leaving such calculations to lower-status Roman professionals—or *graeculi*.

is a skillful leader, even when his tactical decisions do not meet with success. Here things are soon under control again and victory comes quickly; at the later and lesser siege of "Iliturgi," Scipio's response to the repulse of his assaults is to threaten to lead the next one himself, coming close to the walls before his men stop him and, thus freshly motivated, renew their assault and capture the city.[81] Livy's equanimity regarding proximate examples of cerebral generalship and rousing moral leadership is probably appropriate—each certainly had its place.

In the end, the sources are clear that the 500 men sent through the lagoon met no resistance and were able to enter the city while its defenders were busy repulsing the second assault on the landward and seaward walls. If Polybius' narrative has been problematic to this point, his description of the subsequent massacre and sack (in which Scipio maintains complete control of his troops) is so unbelievable that it retrospectively taints the rest of the story.[82] Polybius, usually more astute in these matters than Livy, has distorted the narrative by overdetermining its twin conclusions (the clever combined assault and the oxymoronic orderly sack). In doing so, he injected far too much Scipionic certitude into the early portions of the account.[83] Scipio, as an intelligent Roman commander, would have hoped for success by intimidation and gambled, wisely, on an opportunistic general assault. He would have worked his way through the "flowchart" of assault options, however quickly the siege progressed. Only in hindsight is the lagoon plan a stroke of destiny rather than an audacious maneuver to be tried after an initial assault fails. And only because it is subject to this heavy-handed theme of Scipionic control is the failure of the first assault so oddly rendered.[84] Scipio

---

81. 28.19. "Iliturgi" is likely a mistake for Ilorci, another Spanish town. The incident is highly dramatized, but the principle—the beloved commander shaming/motivating his troops by exposing himself to greater danger—was to become a tried and true gambit of Roman leaders. See *BG* 2.25; pages 166 and 198–99, for similar acts by Titus and Julian.

82. For the sack of New Carthage, see pages 208–9.

83. Ironically, Polybius (11.2.4–7) notes elsewhere that the ability to imagine failure as well as success when considering a military operation is a rare and essential quality in a great general. See also Scullard (1970), 60.

84. Given Polybius' finicky concern with ladders and wall heights elsewhere, it is very strange to allow this mistake in preparation to be so visible in the narrative. The failure to explain or editorialize is perhaps interpretable as an indication of Polybian embarrassment—are the dizzy men and broken ladders the smoking gun of a guilty conscientiousness, evidence of Scipionic failure that, thus preserved but ignored, loom larger than they should? Perhaps not.

as paragon makes for a good object lesson in generalship, but it veils our sight of the siege narrative.[85]

SYRACUSE

The siege of Syracuse, undertaken a few years before the siege of New Carthage, hits two of our narrative archetypes so hard that it is something like a most anthologized poem of Roman republican warfare: memorable, but not representative. Many casual students of the ancient world know the siege through two stories about the mathematician Archimedes: that he built artillery and grappling machines (although not, alas, super-hot death rays) and that he was killed during the sack while intent upon a calculation.[86] The siege was both long and complex, but Polybius' account survives only as an opening assault—written as a new sort of hero parable—and one additional fragment. Livy's more complete account is embedded in a larger strategic narrative, but it, too, during the portions describing active siege operations, gives a starring role to Archimedes. Elsewhere, Livy also emphasizes the decisions of the Roman commander, the structure of the siege progression, and the highlights of technology and morale.[87]

---

85. Sacks (1981), 126–31, argues that books eight and nine constitute a didactic "special section of Polybius' history" centered on "military science"—not an independent excursus but rather a set piece on Hannibal and Scipio which uses narrative history to teach generalship. This is a move away from "true history" toward an extended handbook exemplum, another reason why the complexities of the event are not adequately treated in the narrative. See also Eckstein (1995), 161ff.

86. Thus did the Romans ever deal with the unsettlingly thoughtful—but there are many versions of this story, on which see Jaeger (2008), 77ff. See Plut. *Marc.* 14–24 for another version of the entire siege, including three variations on the killing of Archimedes. The heat-ray story does not appear until Lucian (*Hippias* 2), that pioneer in "speculative fiction." The sack of Syracuse will be discussed in chapter 8.

87. The complexity of the siege, with different parts of the city falling at different times, foreshadows the siege of Jerusalem; on which see chapter 6. Although Syracuse took longer (over two years, beginning in early 213) there was, after the initial assaults, a long period of blockade. All agree that Polybius, who would have had access to Roman participants, had a good source. We have a complete narrative of the early part of the siege from Polybius, 8.5–9 (in the revised numbering system used by Walbank; 8.3–7 in some other texts), but otherwise only a brief notice of the capture of Epipolae (8.37) survives. It is difficult to tell how the intervening periods would have been covered, but a description of the final stages was surely written. Livy's narrative of these two busy years in the Second Punic War cuts away from Syracuse several times, but the coverage is complete, probably draws on the lost sections of Polybius, and therefore is our best source for the eventual capture of the city. I

Polybius informs us that "in some cases the genius of one man is far more effective than superiority in numbers." And so we get two themes for the price of one: the siege as technical sparring match and the siege as a backdrop for individual greatness. The emphasis on Archimedes' genius is so heavy that Polybius abridges or abandons fundamental elements of the siege narrative.[88] We get a very sketchy description of Syracuse's topography and defenses, and very little on the thinking of the Roman commanders (including M. Claudius Marcellus, a general hardly less great than Scipio). Of the combined land-sea assault, Polybius paints a sort of synchronic mural, on which we see each technological element of the attack and defense laid out side by side, but without any description of specific actions or movement through time.

Instead, we get relatively detailed descriptions of the machines, which then contend with each other while the human operators seem to shrink in size and significance.[89] The Romans employ conventional light engineering techniques from the landward side (evidently there was not much in the way of intimidation or testing assaults), but approach by sea with huge boarding bridges (called *sambucae* after a sort of harp that they resembled) mounted on lashed-together ships. Archimedes defeats the assault with not one countermeasure but many: various sizes of stone- and bolt-shooting artillery, then a counterweight crane to smash the *sambucae* by dropping boulders on them. There is no casualty report but rather the notice that being thus under fire throughout the long approach to the wall (instead of being able to pass quickly through the missile zone and then engage) is demoralizing. The Romans withdraw, then attack at night only to discover that they are in even greater danger from previously concealed weapons, including not only smaller pieces firing through arrow slits but also by a sort of grappling crane that is able to grab and hoist a ship, then drop it back to break or founder.[90] Despite the ingenuity and apparent ef-

---

will ignore the larger political and strategic contexts of the operation and concentrate on the two assaults that can be read in both authors.

88. 8.3.3/8.5.3, trans. Scott-Kilvert. It is interesting that the "lone genius" figure appears so infrequently in siege literature, probably because the general as tactical savant fits more naturally with the actual practice of working through the progression's "flowchart." The only comparable figure may be Vauban, who dominated the siege-rife warfare of late seventeenth-century Western Europe.

89. Polybius' ancient influence may be felt, through a long chain of transmission, in certain styles of twentieth-century popular military history, which also tend to celebrate machines and forget the humanity of their operators and victims.

90. 8.4.4–6/8.6.4–6. It is fruitless to try to reconstruct machines from such descrip-

fectiveness of this machine, it seems likely that the placing of many small bolt shooters low in the wall or in outworks at the foot of the wall was the most tactically significant aspect of the defense. In the briefer résumé of the attacks on the landward side, it is again the mixture of artillery that seems crucial, while a man-grabbing crane is an attention-grabbing sideshow.

Polybius is not a subtle writer, but there is a particularly wearisome quality to his emphasis on Archimedes, even if the turning of Roman morale and the importance of the tactical dispersion of the defensive artillery (although this is credited to Archimedes) peek through. Archimedes perplexes Marcellus; Marcellus makes a self-effacing joke about his ships being Archimedes' playthings (this reverses, with all the subtlety of a *sambuca*-crushing crane, the usual trope of the defenders being at the mercy of the besieging general's array of tactics and techniques); each innovation is reintroduced in the few lines describing the landward assault; finally, the theme is triply restated in accompanying the Roman decision to move from siege to blockade.[91] Other than the joke and brief attention to their machines, both the Roman generals and their troops are virtually absent from the narrative of their own assault.

Livy's account is more complete, beginning with the negotiation phase. There were hopes that the pro-Carthaginian regime in Syracuse could be suborned or convinced to join Rome, but the Syracusan leadership demonstrated confidence by meeting the Roman envoy outside of the gates with a threatening refusal to cooperate. Roman confidence was high too, however, because they had recently stormed Leontini at the first assault and because the huge circumference of Syracuse's walls would be difficult to defend. After this brief notice of the stage of the progression and the moral situation, Livy follows Polybius relatively faithfully through the first assault: the plurals fall away as Archimedes rises above the contest and his machines frustrate the Romans. Still, Livy is pacing himself for the longer account: there is less repetition of Archimedes' genius, and Marcellus and the experience of his men garner some attention, even amid the machines.[92]

---

tions, but some have counterparts in the surviving technical treatises. See Marsden (1969), 108–9 and (1971); Campbell (2003), 33–34; as well as Walbank (1967), 71–77.

91. 8.7.7–8/8.9.7–8. Triply: "the genius of one man . . . if one old man of Syracuse were removed . . . the ability of Archimedes." Trans. Scott-Kilvert.

92. Livy 24.33–34. The changes in the descriptions of the machines are not very significant, although Walsh (1961), 158, 192, connects the omission of several, including the *sam-*

When the narrative of the siege picks up again the following year, it is Marcellus, or rather Marcellus and the army, who take the leading role. Livy is careful to note that both assault and blockade have failed, since Carthaginian ships have been able to resupply the city. Thus, while the "power and courage of the general and the army" will take the city, they will do so only after Marcellus is constrained to choose the unsatisfactory third way of treachery, sending Syracusans with the Roman army to conspire with men on the inside.[93] Nothing comes of the plot, but a subsequent parley allows a Roman, evidently one of those uncelebrated officers who possessed siege-specific skills, to reassess the height of the wall. Then a deserter tells of a coming festival that will leave the defenders drunk. Thus both the timing and placement of the Roman assault rest on ill-gotten intelligence, although Livy is rather fastidious to emphasize this. Polybius— the last fragment of his account picks up here—is interested in the method of height estimation but is not as concerned about the manner in which the information was obtained. Two ladders are specially prepared.[94]

We are very fortunate to have Polybius' text here, so that we can read carefully his description of how Marcellus arranged the assault party: "he spoke openly to those who were fit to make the first ascent and to face the greatest danger, holding out to them promises of brilliant rewards." In other words, Marcellus approaches his known-to-be-daring men, but he elicits volunteers rather than either choosing a particular unit or picking the soldiers himself—a point that is underscored when he picks the men who will carry and support the attack and the units that will stand by to be admitted if the assault party can open a gate, and when he repeats the promise of rewards just before the assault is launched.[95] Although this is a stealth operation rather than true force, the element of heroic volunteerism is emphasized.

---

bucae, with Livy's greater love of emotion and "lack of interest in such technical apparatus." Characteristically, Livy also omits Polybius' reference to the five days of preparation for the attack. Marcellus' effective handling of the Sicilian campaign, which was highly active throughout much of the blockade of Syracuse, is a major part of Livy's larger narrative.

93. 25.23.2: *ui ac uirtute ducis exercitusque.*

94. Livy 25.23.8ff, Polybius 9.37.1–13. This is a rare example in Polybius of a wall segment being chosen for assault because it is lower (i.e., more vulnerable) rather than high or naturally forbidding and thus unguarded. The fact that the defenders are more likely to be drunk because they are drinking on short rations nicely (and unusually) brings together the effect of the blockade with the specific considerations of an assault. Drunk defenders occur elsewhere as both literary *topos* and (alleged) historical explanation—see Verg. *Aen.* 2.265; Pseudo-Zachariah 7.26b.

95. 8.37.4. Trans. adapted from Shuckburgh.

Livy, although following closely, reads Roman hierarchy into the story at the expense of this emphasis on combat motivation—he has Marcellus delegate tribunes who then choose likely centurions and soldiers. It is interesting that Polybius, who elsewhere idealizes Roman discipline, represents the assault as a volunteer mission, while Livy, otherwise prone to heroics, imagines the chain of command to be in place. Perhaps Livy wants to emphasize Marcellus' *virtus* in choosing the plan, but he also seems to fall into the trap (which snares all but the most preternaturally aware historians at one time or another) of interpreting decisions with foreknowledge of their outcome: he writes as if this is not a dangerous gamble but rather a perfectly executed coup de main. Which it did turn out to be: the assault party mounts the wall, kills the defenders, opens a gate, and admits the other troops, who quickly spread out over the heights of Epipolae, taking control of most of the sprawling city. What Livy forgot is that the assault might have resulted in a fight on the wall or the extermination of the assault party before they could open the gate. It didn't happen that way, but Polybius, whose Marcellus speaks of the danger of the first assault, remembers the possibility. Livy's Marcellus is concerned only with finding men fit for the "boldness" and importance of the enterprise.[96]

The siege, with the stalemate thus broken but several independently fortified areas of the city still able to hold out, devolved into a blockade that included both new negotiations and a few limited actions. The political complexity of the situation prevented any clean resolution, and, while the final stages involved another combination of "treachery" and surprise assaults, there was no heavy engineering. There is little, then, to be gained from a close reading of the rest of the siege, although the sack of Syracuse is discussed in chapter 8.[97]

After Syracuse and Polybius' early second-century sieges, we come to a gap in the narrative history of the Roman siege. Although Scipio's invasion of Africa and defeat of Hannibal was one of the great climaxes of Roman history, it featured no successful sieges, and the accounts we have

---

96. 25.23.15.

97. 25.24.8–31.11. Politics: as a rich Hellenistic city that had ties to both Carthage and Rome and a strategically crucial ally, Syracuse was more or less exempt from the stern rules of the warfare of refusal. In addition, the presence of Syracusan "deserters" with Rome, whose interests had to be protected; of Roman deserters within Syracuse, who would be put to death no matter how the siege was resolved; and of the rest of the population, caught in between both those groups as well as between the Roman and Carthaginian empires, meant that no general ultimata could be applied. These sorts of cases—revolts and civil wars as well as the rare inter-imperial city-state—require special treatment that falls beyond the scope of this book.

of them are unsatisfactory. In fact, the vagaries of military history and textual survival leave us without a really good siege narrative until Caesar's *Commentaries*.

THE LATE REPUBLIC

Even the final destruction of Rome's great rival does not fill the void of the century and a half between the Second Punic War and the wars of Caesar. The long siege of Carthage (149–146) BCE was similar in many ways to the siege of Syracuse: there were several failed assaults on a large and formidable city followed by long periods of blockade that were rendered ineffective due to resupply from the sea. When a more effective general—Polybius' very own Scipio Aemilianus—arrived, he undertook extensive earthworks to finally cut the city off and then mounted a heavily engineered assault that seized a quay and closed the harbor. The following spring, he took the city by storm and another famous sack ensued.[98] Yet the accounts of Livy and Polybius—who was an eyewitness—are almost completely lost, and we are dependent for these details on the inconsistent Appian.[99] Writing in

---

98. App. *Pun.* 90–132. Campbell (2006), 113, claims that the siege can "neatly encapsulate Roman siegecraft of the period." But this is only for lack of better evidence, and involves much guesswork. A general assault is still a "favoured tactic," but the lack of supporting artillery may well have been common in the second century. Nor are the attempts at escalade before the full assault—with, if Appian can be trusted not to anachronize, the full tower-and-siege-ramp treatment that was as yet unusual—evidence of incompetence, but rather of a working-through of the typical progression (e.g., what seems to be a testing assault at *Pun.* 97). Similarly, we cannot say whether Scipio's decision to build extensive works—because he still captured the city with a heavy assault without waiting for starvation to complete its work, this looks very much like normal imperial practice—should be considered a family habit (Campbell 2006, 114), a forward-looking innovation, or merely a choice suited to the situation at hand. It is tempting to read the assault on Megara as an exemplary set piece of inspirational leadership and volunteer aggression, but we cannot trust its operational context (on which see Astin (1967), 341, tracing the debate as far as Kromayer, as to whether this represents a brilliant Scipionic stroke or a blunder) enough to understand it as part of the siege narrative.

99. Appian is a good read, but also sloppy with details and literarily inconsistent—resembling, in some ways, the later practice of historical fiction more than he does his fellow ancient historians. He is also less thematically dependable than the stronger sources, and so his siege accounts do not bear up to close scrutiny. His Carthage features, for instance, hair-powered catapults (a possibility, but not on the scale he suggests); battering rams that require crews of 6,000 men; and several tactically inexplicable actions, some of which involve the heavy hand of fate. A good example of Appian is the account at *Ill.* 19–20, where Augustus himself takes on the role of the hero general fighting to inspire his

the second century CE, Appian used Polybius, probably extensively, and we might guess from what we have that Polybius celebrated the achievements of Scipio to the point of imperiling the coherence of his narrative. The praise in Appian is extreme, yet Scipio's deeds often seem to make little sense. This is bad history, but Appian does provide a nice justification of his approach when he imagines the reaction of the equally hero-smitten citizens of Rome to the end of the war:

> They talked about the height of the walls, and the size of the stones, and the fires that so often destroyed the engines. They pictured to each other the whole war, as though it were just taking place under their own eyes, suiting the action to the word; and they seemed to see Scipio on the ladders, on shipboard, at the gates, in the battles, and darting hither and thither.[100]

The citizens of Rome should have known better, but, not having access to good contemporary history, they filled in the picture sketched by report and eyewitness testimony with an overdose of the epic imagination.

Interestingly, the other well-known siege conducted by Scipio Aemilianus is a story located near the opposite end of several spectra: although a victory, it is more an embarrassment for Rome than a triumph; there is a conspicuous absence of combat heroism on the Roman side; and Appian (we are again largely dependent on his account) echoes Livy's sympathies for the doomed defenders rather than the ruthless Roman conquerors. This is the siege of Numantia, a hill town of relatively minor importance that had recently defeated and repeatedly defied Rome.[101] Hence, the siege was a grand strategic, or rather a moral, exception from the beginning. When Scipio arrived before the walls of Numantia, there was no question of encouraging any surrender—there could be no terms, only capitulation or destruction.[102]

---

troops, charging personally across an unstable assault bridge. It is a perfect potted siege, with each aspect of the story in the place one would expect to find it—but it is too fictionalized to fit comfortably within any traditional definition of "history."

100. App. *Pun.* 134. Trans. White.

101. Several different generals in the years before Scipio had bungled, and the embarrassments included a failed escalade, broken treaties, and even a shameful nighttime withdrawal. See Campbell (2006), 122.

102. App. *Hisp.* 87ff. Appian is presumed to have drawn on Polybius here, as well as on other sources. See Astin (1967), 141, for a good assessment of why the other contemporary

Naturally, this changed the operational nature of the siege, which famously began with a complete circumvallation involving extensive defenses, towers, and artillery emplacements.[103] This is often interpreted both as a measure of prudence and a foreshadowing of initial circumvallation as the rule of imperial siegecraft—and both ideas are at least plausible. It may also have been true that the Roman armies were too demoralized to prosecute an aggressive siege and needed such walls, but whatever the validity of these theories the crucial point is that since the total destruction of Numantia was required, the distinction between blockade and siege was irrelevant. The practicality of the works was not important, only the message that the defenders had no hope.

The oddity of the situation was marked by Appian. Scipio, who had avoided battle since arriving in Spain the previous year and had refused to meet the Numantines when they came out to fight before their walls, "was the first general, as I think, to throw a wall around a city which did not shun battle in the open field."[104] The explanation may be a complete distrust of his own troops, as Appian suggests, but it is also the fact that beating a bunch of Celtiberian tribesmen wouldn't wipe away the shame of having been defeated by them. When Appian makes Scipio say that he will not bother fighting "desperate men" in the open, he means that he has decided upon their refusal: even before the circumvallation has begun, the Numantines are already dead men. The unprecedented circumvallation doesn't point to an early commitment to blockade and starvation, but rather to Scipio's belief that open warfare is unacceptable, since a military victory is not the goal.[105] The only goal is to destroy the town—

Roman war in Spain—the "Viriatic War"—could, by contrast, be pragmatically assessed and terminated by treaty.

103. The description is matched only by Caesar at Alesia, *BG* 7.72–3, although the situation that led to the heavy circumvallation could hardly be more different.

104. App. *Hisp.* 91, trans. White. As Campbell (2006), 127, (2005), 10, notes, this is also an odd claim given that Scipio had walled off Carthage only a little over a decade earlier. But Campbell's explanation—that perhaps Appian is aware that Carthage was cut off without walls actually enclosing every foot of the perimeter—probably attributes to Appian a modern (or Polybian) punctiliousness that he lacks. The walling-off of Carthage was a mid-operational adjustment made by Scipio for essentially tactical purposes, and thus not terribly notable for its completeness. At Numantia, the point was the complete redress of past defeats—the walls represent a moral rather than an operational "last resort," and the Catonian echoes of the emphasis on the necessity of total destruction ring false.

105. This is Appian's reasonable assumption—that starvation must be the goal—but it does not make the best sense given the emphasis on the settled intent to completely destroy

revenge rather than rectification—and blockade is the surest way to accomplish it.

Appian's siege struggles against the total absence of the usual narrative progression.[106] Scipio is silent and his troops are immobile, except in repelling Numantine attacks on the circumvallation. Scrambling, Appian devises something of a reversal of roles: the Numantines behave as besiegers, making reasonable speeches and valorous assaults, including a special operation with a portable bridge that succeeds in getting messengers over the siege walls. But this experiment is quickly dropped. When the town begins to run short on food, Appian turns to the tropes of desperation and starvation: the Numantines resort to cannibalism before surrendering, and their courage and tragic love of freedom is celebrated. Scipio is again praised for his unwillingness to throw away Roman lives in pointless fighting against desperate men. In the end, the Numantines are granted a symbolic victory: Scipio allows them, having surrendered unconditionally, a day's respite in which to kill themselves, and most do so. It is worth noting that this blockade/siege, while unusual from the point of view of offensive operations, nonetheless embraces the common historiographical themes of being besieged. We are left with a horrifying description of the survivors: "Their bodies were foul, their hair and nails long, and they were smeared with dirt. They smelt most horribly, and the clothes they wore were likewise squalid . . . At the same time there was something fearful to the beholders in the expression of their eyes—an expression of anger, grief, toil, and the consciousness of having eaten human flesh."[107]

The decades before Caesar provide a few isolated siege accounts. Sallust, whose account of the late second-century war with Jugurtha was written roughly seventy-five years after the events it describes, gives militarily im-

---

the town. Moreover, the Roman troops could hardly be expected to fight well in a siege that was explicitly devoid of glory for the victors.

106. As do modern, archaeologically inclined accounts. See Campbell (2006), 122–28, with extensive commentary on the early twentieth-century excavations of Adolf Schulten. As interesting as the Roman works are, they do not match well with Appian's description (which is, for all its faults, an attempt to describe what happened) and Campbell's hope (2005), 17, that "archaeology and literature combine to illuminate each other" at Numantia does not seem to be borne out in his own treatment of the siege (e.g., 2005, 10/2006, 128). See, rather, Dobson (2008).

107. App. *Hisp.* 97, trans. White.

precise and rhetorically predictable accounts of several sieges.[108] Of some interest is his account of Marius—the great general who, we are told, had come to the notice of Scipio Aemilianus when he was a young soldier at Numantia—conducting a campaign to subdue the towns and fortresses of an arid section of North Africa in 107 BCE.[109] Moving quickly, Marius takes some of these small fortified targets by "fear," others by force, and others by "rewards."[110] In other words, the standard array of approaches—pre-contact inducements, intimidation, and assault—are still in use. But this was a sort of *chevauchée* or ravaging strategy: we are told that Marius sought to draw Jugurtha out to defend these places, but failed. He then took the town of Capsa, after a forced march, by coup de main, surprising its defenders as they opened the gates in the morning.[111] Finally, Marius besieges a hill-top fort containing Jugurtha's treasures, and is nearly defeated by the difficulty of the place, which can only be approached from one side. The story (there is no way to confirm the historicity of this highly literary treatment) then gives us two tidbits that we would like to recognize as important facts as well as irresistible literary touchstones. First, that the failed assault on the fortress causes disproportionate casualties among the "best," or most aggressive, men, and thus crushes overall combat motivation. Second, that whenever defenders are highly confident in the physical impregnability of their fortress, someone—in this case, a Ligurian auxiliary possessed of a hankering for snails and a climber's irresistible attraction to a lonely mountain—is going to sneak up behind them.[112]

We know virtually nothing about the sieges of the Italian wars of the early first century, and have only glimpses of some of the sieges of the Mithridatic wars. Appian's account of Mithridates' siege of Rhodes is a notable gadget story—technological hubris is represented in the failure of a gigantic ship-mounted *sambuca*—that is structured, nonetheless, around swings in morale and motivation.[113] Appian also describes Sulla's siege of

---

108. Sallust, despite a stint as Roman governor in North Africa, seems to lack basic military knowledge and (also) omits crucial details. His siege stories do show a general observance of the importance of exhortation, reward, and other aspects of morale, but are generally brief and sloppy about operational detail. See, for example, *Iug.* 21–3, 57 (a nice image of the intimidation phase), or 76 (a good example of baroque embellishment on a classical siege theme).
109. Plut. *Mar.* 3.2; Sall. *Iug.*, 89–94.
110. *Iug.* 89.2: *partim vi, alia metu aut praemia.*
111. *Iug.* 91.
112. *Iug.* 92.9: *optimus quisque cadere aut sauciari, ceteris metus augeri.* On impregnability, see note 67.
113. App. *Mith.* 26.

Athens, a complex and confusing account that includes the separate siege of the Piraeus. Once again, both technology and morale figure heavily. After an initial escalade against the walls of the Piraeus had failed, Sulla built towers and a siege mound, which were burnt in a sally.[114] The combined siege includes not only towers, but battering operations, undermining, combat within the mines and countermines, and a fierce, multiple-breach assault, all intermingled with standard descriptions of starvation and suffering.[115] Once again, it is a shame that we can't depend upon the author to understand and convey operational context, as his description of the final moral collapse of the defenders of the Piraeus is an excellent example of the moral nature of siege assaults. After Sulla's "bravest soldiers" have seized some of the wall, he fires a mine that suddenly creates another breach:

> This great and unexpected crash demoralized the forces guarding the walls everywhere, as each one expected that the ground would sink under him next. Fear and loss of confidence kept them turning this way and that way, so that they offered only a feeble resistance to the enemy.[116]

Although Polybius and Livy each has his own way of stating theme and variation, together they demonstrate the early solidity of a standard sort of siege narrative, a loose matrix of assumptions and understandings, of capabilities and preferences, that dominated both the practice and depiction of the siege warfare of the Roman republic. If we have learned to read for the interplay of technology and morale, and to handle with care the depiction of the besieging commander, we will be well prepared for the following three chapters. We have also seen that the more elaborate treatments of sieges tend to become fascinated with the sufferings of the besieged and struggle to integrate this story with the narrative of increasing aggression that characterizes the experience of the besiegers. For this reason, the following chapters focus on the siege progression, and discussion of the sack is postponed to the final chapter.

---

114. App. *Mith.* 30–7.

115. Appian's unusual use of μηνοειδής as a *terminus technicus* (aptly translated by White as "lunette") suggests that he is using a source with which we are otherwise unfamiliar. But if this source had detailed knowledge of the siege progression it is subsumed in Appian's narrative and, dramatic (and seemingly progression-appropriate) as many of the incidents are, it's impossible to understand this siege as a whole.

116. App. *Mith.* 36, trans. White.

A general summary the actual conduct of sieges cannot be precise. It is surely right to say that Rome was, in general, unusually aggressive: Roman generals were certainly less likely than their Hellenistic or Medieval European counterparts to wait for a breach. Assault was nearly always preferred to blockade, which was considered unfortunate even when improved logistics began to make it more feasible. Roman technical expertise increased over the centuries (but surely not evenly—we should not be tempted to draw straight lines between the scarce data points), and, while the speed assault or lightly engineered assault were almost always preferred tactical choices, the general of the first century BCE was much more likely to be able to efficiently choose heavy assaults supported by siege towers, ramps, and numerous artillery. It is fair to say that the panoply of the mature heavy assault had been developed but not yet fully exploited, either in terms of tactical efficiency or in being securely propelled by the fearsome Roman willingness to prefer extensive, dangerous labor to defeat. Caesar would do this, and the imperial army would maintain something of his level of ability and efficiency.

The formal progression outlined in chapter 3 belongs, therefore, more fully to the Caesarian and imperial siege. Yet we have seen here how its various stages (and, most importantly, the dynamic of refusal and escalation) can often be observed, even if consistent progress through each stage is rarely in evidence. The heavy emphasis on the role of the besieging commander that we find in Livy and Polybius is, therefore, appropriate.[117] The course of a siege is determined by his choices—this is obvious enough. But these choices do not originate in the general's genius. Rather, they derive from a common process that would best be visualized as a flowchart or decision tree. I have hoped to demonstrate that each decision to move along this path can only be made in consideration of the special moral challenges that it will pose to assault troops. Polybius, the allegedly ruthless historian of controlled generalship and technological and tactical efficiency, has shown us how these elements are crucial to the successful navigation of the siege progression—but neither does he stint on the stories of hero generals and brilliant mathematicians, desperate valor and sudden dizzy spells.

---

117. So too Kern (1999), 278, and Campbell (2006), 103: "The choice of strategy perhaps depended as much upon the commanding officer's temperament as upon the available resources and the lie of the land."

FIVE

SIEGE WARFARE IN CAESAR'S COMMENTARIES

Throughout the last decade and a half of his life, Julius Caesar made war almost unceasingly. Although he was unusually successful in forcing—and winning—open-field battles, Caesar also directed something like seventeen sieges in person. He campaigned against the tribes of Gaul, Germany, and Britain from 58 to 51 BCE, and then moved into the civil war that lasted until the summer of 45. We can follow the course of these campaigns better than those of perhaps any other ancient war, largely because Caesar took the trouble to write ten books of "commentaries," describing his own actions for the delectation of his supporters (and opponents) at Rome.[1]

Caesar being Caesar—one of the greatest Roman generals and a skillful writer to boot—these commentaries have been much read for millennia, and latterly became the starting point for an enormous philological and archaeological effort aimed at verifying the movements of Caesar's armies, especially in Gaul.[2] Over the past two centuries, the commentaries have

---

1. These are supplemented by four books written by Caesar's followers. Aulus Hirtius wrote the eighth book of the *Gallic Wars* and probably also the *Alexandrian War,* while unknown soldier writers of lesser skill wrote books on the wars in Africa and Spain.

2. The excavations of Colonel Stoffel, sponsored by Napoleon III and published in 1866, established the sites of several of the sieges that will be discussed here. T. Rice Holmes (1899) is still useful, but see Reddé (2001), (2003), (2008); and Griffin (2009) for slightly more up-to-date studies.

been read as pristine and unvarnished truth, as a malicious pack of self-serving lies, and many things in between. Happily, as the memory of Caesar as a universal elementary Latin text fades, there has been a resurgence in scholarly interest in Caesar's writings, and perhaps a certain consensus on what we might call his truthiness. He subtly magnified his own role, glorified his soldiers, and justified his actions to a wide readership at Rome—opponents and critics as well as the equestrians and army officers who were his (literate) political base. More generally, he spun traditional moralizing yarns: good Gauls to be protected and bad Gauls (and Germans) to be resisted, obediently brave Romans and recklessly brave Romans, treacherous ambushes and valiant battles.[3] Significantly, Caesar was not much interested in artfully shaping his narrative to emphasize didactic or dramatic themes, as Polybius and Livy did. He tells stories of action, one campaign per book, moving briskly and coming to the moments of high drama in good time. Other than immediate political spin and persistent self-aggrandizement, the only consistent imposition on the historical events is his habit of marking the twists and turns of fortune.

Fortunately, the subtleties of Caesarian truthiness and the morass of Roman politics need not concern us here. Given that thousands of men at Rome had first or secondhand knowledge of the campaigns, it would have been neither desirable to falsify basic events nor possible to do so without protest: we can trust the basic descriptions of events. The commentaries are thus a reasonably accurate reflection of events—possibly based on notes taken the same day as the event described—so "their warrant of truth, then, is not so much objectivity or even unusual honesty, but practical necessity."[4] Yet, given the importance of the commander's decisions and the valor of his best fighters, we must be wary of Caesar's tendency to exaggerate both his intellectual control over events and the valor of his centurions.[5] The commentaries are thus an excellent example of a literary pro-

---

3. See especially Levick (1998); Kraus (2009); and Raaflaub, ed., (forthcoming). Truthiness: "The Wørd," *Colbert Report*, Comedy Central, October 17, 2005. See also Riggsby (2006), and Powell (1998).

4. Riggsby (2006), 150. The evidence for note-taking at the time of the actual events is circumstantial, but fairly strong. For more on the genre see Riggsby, pages 133–50; and Kraus (2005), (2009), 160–68.

5. Often at the expense of the senatorial and equestrian officers who ranked in between, but were usually less politically desirable as supporting players. This distortion is of some significance for battle narratives but little for sieges, since Caesar did indeed make the big decisions, while his chosen tactics were usually implemented by technical experts or by the centurions who so often led assaults.

duction that moves freely without ever leaving the narrow path sketched by the constraints of historical reality.[6]

Caesar's reputation as a general has also suffered both a measure of decline and a recent leveling off. After centuries as a paragon of speed and decisiveness, twentieth-century commentators began to call attention to his recklessness and his large tally of strategic blunders.[7] The recent balance tends to accept that Caesar was indeed reckless, but not unforgivably so. Caesar did manifest a "tendency to seize the initiative and then hold it by maintaining a constant offensive [which] created an impression of force often far greater than the reality of the Roman military strength available at that time."[8] More simply put, he "took the offensive and was always spoiling for a fight," a propensity which is very much on display in his sieges.[9] This relentlessness, as well as the use of aggression to both intimidate on the strategic level and seize the operational initiative in the campaign at hand, was in fact typical of Roman generalship. Caesar was extraordinarily energetic, he was famous for moving quickly,[10] and he seems to have been an exceptional motivator of men, but his military success was achieved "in ways typical of Roman aristocrats . . . by being uniquely outstanding in terms of extremely conventional categories."[11] This is true too of his siegecraft: his legions, grown confident and efficient during their long years in Gaul, became a tool strong enough to apply with terrible force the many techniques of the Roman siege progression, developed over the two previous centuries but never, perhaps, driven as far as often as under Caesar.

Writing as he was for Romans, Caesar never stops to explain exactly how this tool worked. But he often plays to his readers with brief digressions on particularly impressive achievements. Much of what we know about Ro-

---

6. See also Rosenstein (2009), 85–86: the *Gallic Wars* are "scarcely objective accounts of the events they describe," yet "what gives confidence that such an enterprise is not wholly without validity is the knowledge that Caesar was not writing in a vacuum but for an audience of Roman readers who had very clear notions of what generals should do and how they should comport themselves on campaign." So too Kraus (2009), 165: "the hard core of his narrative—topographical details aside—seems reliable," and the *Gallic Wars* are "a coherent, plausible literary representation of experience."
7. E.g., Fuller (1969), 318–24.
8. Goldsworthy (1998), 197.
9. *B Afr.* 35.
10. Suet. *Iul* 57. But see also, 58, for the balance of aggression and caution.
11. Riggsby (2006), 207.

man field fortification comes from his description of his massive investment of Alesia, and he stops elsewhere to describe walls, bridges, and a siege ramp. Yet Caesar shows no sustained interest in military technology, and his accounts of tactics are matter-of-fact. Instead, he consistently highlights combat motivation: "no ancient writer who had actually seen a battle gives psychology a larger role in his battle descriptions than Caesar." Rather than anticipating the military historians who focus entirely on tactical movement over terrain, Caesar sees this as a mere preface to the essential narrative, which is "the action of *virtus* upon *virtus*."[12] Caesar uses *virtus* primarily to describe laudable courage on the part of his troops, but he also establishes several pointed dichotomies in which a contest of *virtus* is coded as proper and appropriate while its opposite—any less direct or slightly passive form of conflict—is tainted with a shameful unmanliness. *Virtus* can be opposed to terrain or tactics, to technology or stratagem. In each opposition, the implication is that forsaking an advantage gained by other means allows for a more satisfying direct contest of *virtus*. This is the same logic that shapes siege warfare: our technology will neutralize the advantages they have given themselves—shamefully, unmanfully—by refusing to fight in the open; once things are equal, Roman *virtus* will triumph.

It has become popular to liken Caesar the writer to a film director, swinging his textual "camera" across the battlefield either thematically, from tactics to motivation and *virtus*, or tactically, from event to event.[13] Here again the siege context clarifies: the "camera," like that of a 1920s film, is fixed, unable even to pan from side to side. Therefore, each new "shot" is in fact a new scene. There is usually a single physical set—the ramp, the tower, or the breach—which determines the problem of fortification, and siege engineering separates tactics from morale. Just as Caesar sees position and terrain as problems to be solved so that tactical equality may be reached and a proper battle of *virtus* joined, the siege process is an escalation of methods—the immediate assault, circumvallation, the general assault, heavy engineering—that stops when the tactical advantage of the defenders—their fortifications—has been neutralized. The siege is now a fair fight, which combat motivation may decide. If the men are willing and the wall is low, the siege process ends quickly and the assault—a con-

---

12. Lendon (1999), 296, 319–20. See especially the account of Pharsalus at *BC* 3.90–2, and Pompey's "irrational" disregard of morale. *Contra:* Riggsby (2006). I am largely persuaded by Lendon's take on Caesar, and likewise privilege the text over imposed or imagined external "realities."

13. Kagan (2006), 115. See also Lendon (1999), 317.

centrated form of combat but essentially similar, on the individual level, to open-field battle—takes place. If not, then, once the siege ramp, towers, and ladders match the height of the wall, it is time to fight. There are many sieges in Caesar, but in order to see this process in action we must choose quality over quantity, reading carefully through two major sieges of 52 BCE: the tense early campaign siege of Avaricum (Bourges) and Alesia, the climactic siege that wasn't.[14]

CAESAR AND THE SIEGE PROGRESSION

In order to best appreciate the high drama of 52 we should first acquire a general sense of Caesar's way of writing siege warfare, as well as his use (as commander) of the siege progression. This we can do by making a brief study of the minor sieges of the Gallic Wars and the siege operations of the Civil Wars, after which we will return to the great revolt of 52.

At no point in the *Gallic Wars* does Caesar approach the urban center of a new adversary early in a campaign. After the posturing phase at the beginning of the wars, he considers himself to be fighting a war of conquest against confirmed resisters, and so there is little pre-contact negotiating. A study of the Caesarian siege progression should thus begin with the contact stage and the choice between an immediate assault or a deployment toward siege preparation.[15]

Caesar several times describes an assault as *ex itinere*—meaning "straight from the line of march," without camping or making other preparations.[16] Interestingly, the first such instance describes a Gallic attack, and indeed, Caesar uses *ex itinere*—an unusual deviation from the more conservative Roman habit of camping before an attack—as a shorthand description of

---

14. There are several interesting sieges in the *Civil Wars,* but none would serve well the purpose of illustrating Caesar's use of the progression. The complexity of the political calculus generally deforms the normal context of refusal and threat, and the one operationally clear siege described at length—Massilia—is made problematic by the fact that Caesar, who was absent, describes it without his usual sensitivity to the emotional atmosphere of the siege. See Kraus (2007), 373–76.

15. During the civil wars, negotiations with divided or wavering communities were fairly common, and many towns forestalled potential sieges by sending envoys to meet Caesar and declare their allegiance.

16. See the footnote to *BG* 2.6 in the Loeb, and Liebenam (1909), although his *gewaltsamen Angriff* loses its impact by eventually including all tactics short of either blockade or the heavily engineered siege (*den förmlichen Angriff mit belagerungswerkzeugen*).

Gallic assault capabilities. His Roman readers well understood that prudence demanded camping and then testing the morale of the garrison before committing any forces to an assault, unless the commander knew the fortifications to be inadequate or the defenders to be very weak or demoralized. Hence, when Caesar describes the Belgae attacking the town of Bibrax[17] *ex itinere,* he indicates not only that it was done quickly but that it lacked preparation, entrenchment, or engineering support. Unlike the Romans, the Gauls have only one way of assaulting a city.

The Gauls' assault method is the same as that of the Belgae: when, after having drawn a large number of men around the whole of the fortifications, stones have begun to be cast against the wall on all sides, and the wall has been stripped of its defenders, [then], forming a *testudo,* they advance to the gates and undermine the wall.[18]

Caesar is able to save the town (of his allies, the Remi), discouraging the besiegers merely by sending in a force of missile troops during the night.

When Caesar reports a Roman assault *ex itinere,* he is careful to justify this expedient, which would prove costly if the defenders fought well. The assault *ex itinere* on Noviodunum (*BG* 2.12) fails—a bad miscalculation that Caesar blames, naturally, on poor intelligence: "he had heard that it was empty of defenders." The ensuing description of retrenchment via entrenchment confirms that an assault *ex itinere* was an affair of missiles, swords, shields, and hand-tools only. Another failed *ex itinere* is conducted by the young Publius Crassus (*BG* 3.21), although, since the attempt was made in the immediate aftermath of a rout, Caesar hints that he can be forgiven for assuming that the Sotiates would be demoralized. It is likely that many more successful assaults of this nature were in fact carried out, but on places of such little importance and with such little resistance that there was no need to record the event in the published commentaries.[19]

But these are exceptions. Almost every Caesarian siege began with the

---

17. *BG* 2.6. On the uncertain identity of this place see Holmes (1899), 394–96.

18. *BG* 2.6, trans. adapted from Edwards. See also *BG* 5.39. The Gauls are so ineffectual that Caesar, when hard-pressed and thus willing to admit to using a stratagem, compresses his camp and feigns low morale in order to lure such an assault by a much larger Gallic force (*BG* 5.51, 57). The Germans were no more skilled; see *BG* 6.41.

19. Many small places, such as the *oppidum Parthinorum* which Caesar takes by storm while pursuing Pompey's army, fell so quickly that they hardly constituted a siege. Caesar describes this *expugnatio* as *in* (rather than *ex*) *itinere* (*BC* 3.41).

construction of a camp. This was standard operating procedure, but Caesar is nevertheless careful to include the notice of camp construction in his narrative. It is a useful place marker for the Roman reader, indicating the transition from open campaign to siege.[20]

Occasionally, Caesar makes use of the pre-engagement intimidation phase, most notably at Metropolis in Thessaly: the townspeople, having heard that Pompey had been victorious, shut their gates to Caesar. The same had just been done by the people of Gomphi, and they had suffered assault, sack, and massacre. Caesar intimidated Metropolis into surrender by the simple expedient of parading prisoners from Gomphi and allowing them to describe their fate to their countrymen. Two other examples of an intimidation surrender constitute a sort of comedic subgenre in which ignorant Gauls surrender to the magical powers of Roman siege engineering. While Caesar mocks the ignorant Gauls, these accounts show that the labor and technology on display in the preparation for a formal siege were Rome's best form of intimidation. And if intimidation failed, the works were ready to be put to use.[21]

Once the camp was built, the engagement could begin, and Caesar, who generally disdained skirmishing, chose either to attempt a testing assault or to begin the "siege proper," normally by means of further entrenchments or circumvallation. A brief note on Caesar's Latin is necessary here. The noun *oppugnatio* (as well as its related verb) refers first to "an assault." Yet, since the entire siege process is fundamentally a mechanism for enabling direct assault, *oppugnatio* can also mean, by simple tactical synecdoche, "a siege."[22] While assaults can also take place outside of the siege context, the word is closely associated with the siege throughout the commentaries, and the verb almost always takes "town" or "camp" as its object.[23]

---

20. Even in the desperately hurried campaign of 52, Caesar tells us of his camps at Cenabum and Noviodunum; the notice of circumvallation at Vellaunodunum supersedes the camping notice, since a complete circumvallation included the construction of multiple camps for the besieging army (*BG* 7.11–13). The plain language of the *Bellum Hispaniense* makes clear the aggressive character of the siege camp: it is "a camp over against the town" (*BHisp.* 34; see also 5).

21. Metropolis: BC 3.81. See also B Alex. 30, where Caesar fails to "overawe" his adversary. Two other examples: see page 59, above.

22. *oppugnatio*=entire siege: e.g., *BG* 7.11, 7.17. *oppugnatio*=siege assault/goal of siege engineering: 7.11 (second usage), 7.19.

23. An *oppugnatio* is not a battlefield maneuver—it does not take place *in acie*. Only when the distinctions blur, as in the war of position amidst field fortifications around Dyr-

The first sort of *oppugnatio*, often, was an assault intended to gauge the relative morale of the two forces. If the attackers found surprisingly little resistance, they might take the target; otherwise, a foundation for moral ascendancy could be laid through successful skirmishing.[24] While such a testing assault may have existed in the liminal zone before the punitive "rules" of siege warfare came into effect, circumvallation initiated the full-blown siege.[25] This not only protected the besieging army and its works but also made a moral point: Caesar intended to remain until his target was taken and destroyed. Circumvallation marks major events. The term is used once (*BC* 3.43) of the field fortifications around Dyrrachium, and four times during the siege-heavy seventh book of the *Gallic Wars*. At Vellaunodunum (7.11), an *oppidum* of the Senones, Caesar moves immediately from the decision to besiege to a two-day investment by circumvallation. This act was enough to intimidate the town to surrender on the third day. At Avaricum (7.17), too, Caesar skips straight to a heavily engineered siege, and he explains what his knowledgeable readers would recognize as the omission of a step in the standard procedure: he did not build lines of circumvallation because the extremely difficult nature of the ground both effectively prevented it and provided equivalent obstruction/protection. At Gergovia (7.44), the Gauls sally to prevent true circumvallation, and Caesar is eventually defeated, while at Alesia (7.68) a cavalry victory during the approach march allows Caesar to begin circumvallation while the Gauls are demoralized, thus gaining an important early advantage. The only time that Caesar hesitates to surround a difficult target with fortifications is when, during the first stage of the open conflict with Pompey, he besieges

---

rachium (reminiscent more of late nineteenth- and early twentieth-century warfare than of other ancient conflicts, and called pointedly by Caesar *novum genus belli*, *BC* 3.50), do we find a siege-like *oppugnatio* (*BC* 3.73). The term more often invoked as the equivalent of the English "siege"—*obsidio*—is used by Caesar to mean "blockade" (e.g., *BG* 7.32). The significant factor in this distinction is the inclusion of the sense of "direct attack": *oppugnatio* includes this sense—even if in its larger sense it may encompass calculations of resource denial—but *obsidio* excludes it.

24. Caesar provides one clear example of each. In Britain, he praises the strength of a British *oppidum*, but "nevertheless" assaults from two sides and wins a quick victory when the enemy flees (*BG* 5.21). The fact that a two-pronged assault was made indicates that the army redeployed (i.e., that this was not an assault *ex itinere*); yet not even screens are mentioned, so it would seem that there was no engineering preparation at all. At Alesia (*BG* 7.70) Caesar launches a testing assault which entices the defenders to sally forth, resulting in a skirmish before the walls. This was won by his troops, greatly increasing their confidence.

25. See pages 63–65.

Corfinium (*BC* 1.16–19). Caesar arrives and camps, but only later decides against a speedy, lightly engineered assault and extends his fortifications, waiting for reinforcements. When these arrive, Caesar builds a second camp and extends his fortifications around the town (the verb here is *circummunio*) in order to add the threat of blockade (*obsidio*) to that of assault.[26] This awkward movement through the progression is easily explained by the shifting loyalties of a nascent civil war: Caesar hoped to stimulate faction and dissent within the town and probably intended only to pressure the Pompeians and not to assault. Indeed, the town expels its Pompeian commander and defects after only seven days.

Despite the fact that circumvallation increased the likelihood of either blockade or heavy assault, skirmishing and testing assaults did not necessarily then cease. Caesar skirmished his troops constantly during the siege-like warfare around Dyrrachium (*BC* 3.84), "daily increasing the army's confidence."[27] At Alexandria (*B Alex.* 15), the naval fighting in the great harbor served as the floating equivalent of skirmishes between city walls and siege works. Both sides watched the contest eagerly from their rooftops, amplifying the importance of an unimportant victory—multiplied by the number of witnesses it became proof of good fortune.

Circumvallation also proposed a choice of assault methods, and Caesar almost always chose either a general assault or the construction of siege mounds. His general assault consisted either of a quick attempt to storm the walls (involving ladders if necessary, but otherwise tactically identical to the assault *ex itinere*) or the more deliberate light assault behind shields and screens and under covering fire.[28] These are pretty fine distinctions, and the sources normally lack the detail to push categorization any farther—but Caesar knew of what he wrote. The contested landing on Pharos Island (*B Alex.* 17–18) is not described as an *oppugnatio*, despite the inherent difficulty of an amphibious assault against a defended beach and despite his specific emphasis on the difficulty of the beach terrain and the problem of plunging fire from nearby buildings. Yet, when his troops rout the defenders, we are told that they cannot follow up by storming the nearby buildings (their "continuous line of high towers takes the place of a

---

26. Caesar generally uses *circummunio* as a synonym of *circumvallo*, preferring the former to describe field fortifications, as at *BC* 1.81, 1.84, 3.66, 3.97. Of an *oppidum*, *BG* 2.30, and of a city (Utica), *BC* 2.36. It seems unlikely that the distinction is based on whether an actual rampart (*vallum*), or different type of ramparts, are used.

27. See also *BG* 7.80.

28. See *B Alex.* 30–31.

wall") because "our men were not equipped with ladders, screens, or the rest of the stuff necessary for an assault."

The taking of Gomphi involved a typical lightly engineered assault.

> Caesar, having made an entrenched camp, ordered ladders and mantlets for a hasty siege to be made and hurdles to be got ready. When these measures had been taken he exhorted his troops and explained to them how useful it would be for the purpose of alleviating the general scarcity to get possession of a well-filled and opulent town, and at the same time to strike terror into the remaining communities by the example of this town, and that this should be done quickly before reinforcements should come together. And so, experiencing the utmost zeal on the part of his troops, he began to besiege the town, which had very high walls, on the very day of his arrival after the ninth hour, and took it by storm before sunset, and gave it over to his men for plunder.[29]

The "hasty assault" is here characterized by not pausing to invest the town and by storming the town without benefit of siege towers. That the exhortation involves a careful explanation to his men of the moral and operational significance of a quick, deadly storm is characteristic of Caesar's skillful leadership. Yet the pressing operational concerns do not explain why Caesar was able to choose the mass assault over the more time-consuming heavily engineered siege—which "very high walls" would normally demand. The essential explanation is in Caesar's motivational advantage: he has gauged the morale of his troops and detected "singular enthusiasm."

Without such an advantage, Caesar's options would have been to bypass the city or to prepare a heavy assault. In a similar moment of decision, Hirtius depicts Caesar before a German camp, thinking through the siege progression to come without benefit even of PowerPoint slides that might remind him of the siege "flowchart" (*BG* 8.11). The natural and man-made strength of the fortification is such that "it could not be assaulted without an expensive action," so towers and siege works were required, but Caesar lacks the troops even to accomplish the necessary prerequisite—circumvallation—and hence sends for reinforcements.

The two essential elements of the Caesarian heavily engineered assault,

---

29. *BC* 3.80. See also *BG* 7.11.

then, were the *agger* and the *turris*—normally translated as "mound" or "siege ramp" and "siege tower." The *agger* allowed the wall to be approached, either by storm troops or for battering purposes, and it increased the total elevation of the tower(s).[30] The siege tower allowed troops to assault the top of the wall without being exposed on ladders, it provided a platform for artillery and missile troops to fire into the target fortification, and it sometimes carried a battering ram on its lowest story.[31] A tower took time to construct and a large ramp required weeks of labor. At the siege of Massilia, the engineering involved not only two *aggeres* and two *turres,* but also the extemporizing of a six-story brick artillery tower (*BC* 2.1–11). When these works were burnt during a sally (a third *agger* was subsequently built, faced with fireproof brick), Caesar speaks of months of work lost (*BC* 2.14–15).[32] These efforts could be supplemented by attempts to damage the walls by hand.[33] An active defense might involve the building of defensive towers and undermining the *agger*.[34] Because of such efforts by the defenders, siege works were built only "with great effort and continual fighting," which was both morally and physically draining.[35] The conventional sense of "investment" resounds: the time and the moral capital of the troops' motivation were unrecoverable, and to get so far and to fail was a shameful mistake—potentially a disaster.[36]

The heavy siege climaxed with the *virtus* on *virtus* clash of fighting men.

30. For the *agger,* see Holmes (1899), 594–601. See also Davies (2006), 99, and chapter 3, note 72. There were two somewhat distinct types of *agger:* one built perpendicular to the wall for the purpose of bringing up a single tower and effecting a breach (including those mentioned at *BG* 2.30–1 and 8.40, and *BC* 2.11,15), the other effectively parallel, providing a broad frontage from which to assault the wall. The works at Noviodunum (*BG* 2.12) and Avaricum were somewhat hybrid, permitting an assault between two towers, which provided flanking covering fire for the assault and threatened the wall itself. Caesar nowhere gives details of ordinary towers (the towers at Massilia are described, *BC* 2.8–11, because they were exceptional), so it is impossible to know whether they were mounted with artillery or equipped with drawbridges, as Vegetius (4.21) imagines.

31. Skirmishing from towers: *BC* 1.26. Towers and (detachable) rams: *B Alex.* 1–3. Plunging fire from towers: *BG* 8.41. See also *BHisp.* 19, Ammianus 19.7.5.

32. The siege of Massilia is a special case, both because of Caesar's absence and because the civil war conditions—specifically the notice (*BC* 2.13) that he instructed Trebonius to avoid taking the city by storm—distort the more typical moral calculus. See note 14.

33. See, e.g., *BC* 2.10–11.

34. See Avaricum, discussed in the next session, as well as *BG* 3.21, 7.22.

35. *BG* 8.41, trans. Edwards.

36. Caesar never made this mistake, although Avaricum and Alesia, discussed in more detail below, were close calls. Note the tone of the report on the raising of the siege of Acylla, which had already been prosecuted with "great siegeworks," *B Afr.* 43.

All the labor built toward the moment of the assault, typically "the time that the towers approached the wall," or "when the *agger* had almost touched the wall" (*BG* 7.18, 7.24). Caesar uses this moment as a place marker in his narrative of Avaricum: the works are advanced almost to the walls, he then fills the reader in on the other events of the siege, and only then does he return to narrate the assault.

Such tactics took time, but they were active: to wait passively for surrender (i.e., a true blockade) was to admit an inability to control the situation.[37] Caesar hated this, and was only occasionally forced to blockade, as at Uxellodunum, an *oppidum* located so precipitously that siege towers could not overtop its walls (*BG* 8.40). Yet he still found a way to use active tactics to (indirectly) achieve the desired end, building an *agger* and tower to cut off its access to water, thus forcing surrender.

Caesar's behavior as a siege commander fits well with the scholarly assessments of his battlefield generalship: he was an able practitioner of common Roman techniques, he was unusually energetic and aggressive in their application, and he was faster than most—although his operational hurry was often a consequence of strategic and grand-strategic overreach. There is another way in which Caesar was typically Roman but more so: he excelled at exploiting the peculiar intersection of siege warfare and combat motivation. He was acutely sensitive to the morale of his troops, he was a highly skilled motivator, and he writes more clearly than any other source about the crucial role of combat motivation in siege assaults. A closer look at two of his major sieges will clarify Caesar's contribution to our understanding of these issues.

THE CAMPAIGN OF 52 BCE AND THE SIEGE OF AVARICUM

Caesar's campaign of 52 was a difficult one, but in strategic terms the task was fairly simple: to crush the new, unified resistance offered by many of the Gallic tribes. The revolt began, in Caesar's telling, after a Gallic council of war and an assault on Cenabum (Orléans), where Roman traders were killed and their belongings plundered. Caesar quickly appropriated this event (or retroactively appropriated it for narrative purposes) as the propa-

---

37. *Obsessio* is also used of the restriction of operational movement (e.g., *BG* 3.24, 5.40), while *obsidio* carries a heavy emphasis on hunger. See Caesar's careful explanations at *BC* 3.47. Interestingly, Hirtius, despite the activity of the operations around Alesia, refers to that siege as *obsessio Alesiae* (8.14, see also 8.34), while Caesar does not.

gandistic linchpin of the campaign—not only as a claim of justification for the war, but also as groundwork for the combat motivation of his soldiers.[38] Caesar draws a sharp, straight line from that event to the coming campaign's nemesis—Vercingetorix of the Arverni—despite the fact that he was not involved in the decision to attack Cenabum, nor related to its perpetrators (7.3–4). The real danger of this revolt is indicated by the speed with which Caesar responded, forcing his way through snowbound passes and rushing to reach certain peoples before Vercingetorix could solicit or compel their aid in rebellion. After punishing and restoring to submission a few rebel towns, including Cenabum (which was sacked), saving the friendly Boii from the rebels, and besting Vercingetorix in a cavalry skirmish before Noviodunum, Caesar moved to take Avaricum, intending to use it as a headquarters for further pacification actions (7.6–13).

At this point, however, the nature of the campaign changed dramatically, and Caesar gives full credit for this new dispensation to his adversary in chief (7.14–15). Realizing the superiority of the Romans in open battle and siege warfare, Vercingetorix determined decided on strategic withdrawal, combining scorched-earth operations with guerrilla tactics. He also took the unusual step of destroying all settlements that he thought unable to hold out against a Roman siege. Vercingetorix evidently had much support among the Gauls: those not hiding he expected to campaign with him, even as he destroyed their homes in the service of strategy. Yet as long as certain cities were held by the Gauls, the strategy was incomplete, and the remaining strongholds provided Caesar with a triple opportunity: he could attack at the same time a valuable rebel asset, the morale of the rebel forces, and the credibility of their commander (who had judged the place to be safe from a Roman siege and could now be accused of disregard for his allies). Morale was the most important of the three.

As always, Caesar's operational speed was as demoralizing to the enemy as it was strategically effective. Confidence was especially important for soldiers resisting foreign conquest or rebelling against foreign domination. Wise commanders have always known that the best way to destroy enemy morale is to counter their expectations by attacking where they thought

---

38. Roman tradition demanded *iniuria* as a prerequisite for just war, and stretching this point by taking on the *iniuria* done to private citizens or to allied peoples were well-established precedents. The events at Cenabum, which Caesar amplified from *interfectio* (7.3) to *caedes* (7.42), are twice cited as an explanation for his soldiers' behavior. First, to explain their dedicated perseverance in the difficult siege of Avaricum (7.17), and second, to excuse their slaughtering of Gallic women and children during the sack (7.28).

themselves to be completely safe. An unexpected or "impossible" attack may be risky, but it has the virtue, like an athlete who sets the bar high at the very beginning of a competition and clears it, of seeming like many victories rolled into one. So, Caesar countered Vercingetorix's Fabian strategy by marching straight for Avaricum—one of the few strongly fortified Gallic towns. Avaricum was highly defensible because the surrounding swamps and river rendered it approachable only on a narrow southern frontage (7.15, 7.17).[39]

Caesar began to prepare a heavy assault: the strength of the site and the high morale of the defenders—they were in the first flush of rebellion and defending "almost the fairest city in all Gaul" (7.15)—precluded a speed assault. Caesar will soon, and rather pointedly, digress from the narrative of this, the first truly difficult siege of the Gallic Wars, in order to explain how the walls of Avaricum, built in the manner ever after known as *murus gallicus*, resist both battery and being pulled apart by grappling hooks (7.23).[40] The digression on a technical military matter is a typical Caesarian gambit, and here it serves to mark a transition within the siege progression: Caesar is expressing the fact that he has not been forced to mount a heavily engineered assault until now, as well as preparing a defense for any criticisms about the length of the siege.[41]

---

39. See Riggsby (2006), 24–41. Campbell (2006), 145–47, emphasizes the importance of a "gully" on this side, making an *agger* (more) necessary. On counter-tactical-intuition assants, see chapter 4, note 67.

40. This passage is a good example of why the practice of treating text "as event" is not well suited to Caesar's commentaries. Whatever the merits of approaching the *BG* as a self-contained text, Riggsby's (2006), 73–80, analysis of Caesar's account of Avaricum is hamstrung by the lack of consideration of physical reality. First, the position of Avaricum and the strength of its walls have been verified by archaeology and were not plausibly falsifiable by Caesar. Basic facts of military technology and the composition of Gallic fortifications would also have been widely known to contemporary Romans. Perhaps the details of a particular battle could be lied about, but technological achievements and striking vignettes cannot have been inventions—Caesar did not write to risk ridicule. The quotation marks in Riggsby's opinion that Caesar's notice of growing Gallic proficiency in siege warfare "may well reflect a 'real' historical trend" do indeed scare.

41. See Kraus (2009), 173. The placement of this digression, *pace* Riggsby, has little to do with any improvement in Gallic technical abilities and much to do with Caesar's interest in marking not only a place in the siege progression but our place as readers—knowledgeable, perhaps, but not necessarily in possession of the real soldier's knowledge of Gaul. Note also that the impressive wall wasn't breached and so, just like the impressive tower at Massilia (which though tactically successful was "defeated" by Massilot "treachery"), does not play a role in any final conquest. Caesar is choosing, somewhat quixotically, to make a textual mountain out of a historical molehill, and this transmutation causes the reader to miss the

First, though, there is the story of the difficulty of the siege. Suffering privation, skirmishing constantly, and once breaking off to march through the night against Vercingetorix and threaten a battle that did not materialize (7.18–19), Caesar's men pushed the *agger* upwards for twenty-five days, until it was 330 Roman feet wide and some eighty feet high. It rained constantly and it was cold; they were on short rations and the labor of cutting and hauling trees to form the frame of the *agger,* then filling the frame with earth and rubble, was backbreaking. But Caesar exhorted each legion, no doubt encouraging rivalry by making the construction work a competition. He also played upon the pride of his men. They knew the meaning of the investment in siege works: "they would regard it in the nature of a disgrace if they relinquished the siege they had begun" (7.17, 24).

Caesar even reports that the men sent their officers to beg him not to think of raising the siege because of their hardship. Whether or not the troops were as upset about the massacre at Cenabum as Caesar would have us believe, it is easy to understand that the very men who were suffering the dangers and labors of the siege, and who had in most cases fought the Gauls for years, would hold with the cultural value that saw a failed siege as deeply shameful. This steadfastness became part of the shared lore of the legions, and Caesar refers to it years later (*BC* 3.47), stoking the morale of the starving troops at Dyrrachium by reminding them of how well they withstood the privations of the siege of Avaricum.

But Gallic morale was also running high. Caesar pays Vercingetorix the compliment of writing up an extended scene in which the Gallic leader masterfully manipulates his fractious army (7.20–21), parading slaves posing as starving and demoralized Roman prisoners and thus inducing a strong force (10,000 men, Caesar claims) to volunteer to reinforce the garrison at Avaricum. Here is an adversary formidable enough to test Caesar, whose stature will both excuse the length of the campaign and add glory to its successful outcome. Following this ministration to their motivation, the defenders of Avaricum are active and ingenious, first countermining the *agger* and setting fire to its supports, then raising towers of their own. This frustrates Roman attempts to undermine the wall with counterattacks and various missiles (7.22, 24).

The crisis point that Caesar has foreshadowed (the *agger* is almost to the wall) arrives when a counterattack is launched by the defenders in the

---

fact that we are missing some important pieces of actual military-historical causality. See also Kraus (2007), 373–75, and Dodington (1980), 9, 65–75.

middle of the night. The *agger* is set alight from beneath, while two sallies attempt to destroy the towers. These evidently failed, but the burning of the screens that flanked the two towers (standing on either end of the *agger*) gave the Gauls a chance to approach without having to contend with a possible countercharge of Roman infantry. Focusing on this crisis, Caesar produces the dramatic apogee of the entire siege: the attempts of a succession of Gallic heroes, standing exposed in a gateway, to fling enough incendiary material onto one of the towers to burn it down. At least four in a row were killed by the high-velocity missiles of a *scorpio*, which was almost certainly mounted in the targeted tower. Once the fire in the *agger* had been extinguished, the legionaries were able to drive the Gauls back into the city, and the crisis passed (7.24–5).

Caesar's highlighting of this incident is a fairly common technique of military historiography, but it is more than simply an adornment of the narrative with a striking vignette. Rather, Caesar features the firethrowers in order to shape the confusing reality of the siege into a sensible explanation of the two crucial elements. The Gauls showed tremendous aggressive morale and they failed, shot down by Roman high technology in the form of a torsion-powered artillery piece that outranges their muscle-powered attack. The two great advantages of Rome are invoked together, here: technology and *virtus*. The failure of the Gallic heroes (7.25) is linked with, and balanced by, the success of the ensuing Roman assault (7.26–8). The Gauls show ingenuity in using fire and tactical feints to clear the tower of its defenders, and they show valor, but Roman technology triumphs and sets the stage for Roman combat motivation.[42] The way in which Caesar presents these events provides crucial evidence for the debate over the balance of direct historical report and authorial shaping—but first the narrative of Avaricum should be brought to a conclusion.

After the failed sallies, Gallic morale collapsed. The defenders sought to leave the town the next night, and were prevented by the women of the

---

42. H. J. Edwards, an Englishman who translated the *BG* for the 1917 Loeb edition, presumably working in England about 1916, glosses the *scorpio* in a footnote to *BG* 7.25 (page 417) as "a kind of small catapult, the Roman machine-gun." Had he written months later, after the first successful mass use of machine-gun-equipped tanks at Cambrai in 1917, he would have been able to extend his analogy, recognizing in the siege tower a source of mobile firepower that overcame the advantages of static defense. In this passage the siege tower is rendered potentially helpless in the same way that tanks can be—by stripping away its screen of infantry and subjecting it to close-range incendiary attack.

town alerting the Romans to the fact that they were about to be abandoned (7.26).[43] Once again, a dramatic incident is introduced by Caesar because it explains his next manipulation of the siege progression. The collapsing morale, as well as a fortuitous heavy rain (which reduced visibility and led the depressed defenders to let their guard down), convinced Caesar not to wait for further heavy engineering but instead to attempt a mass assault. This is not a deviation or a retrogression: the breadth of the *agger* indicates that mass assault had always been intended.

Caesar exhorted the troops and turned the assault into an explicit contest, promising special "rewards" to those who were first on the wall (7.27).[44] This surprise assault by highly motivated troops was successful, and after brief resistance within the town the Gallic troops were routed and the sack began. This included the massacre of women and children, as well as presumably all of the military-age males (other than the 800 that Caesar says escaped). Although this was normal behavior in the wake of a long and difficult siege, Caesar invokes revenge for the murder of Romans at Cenabum as a motive for his troops' bloodlust (7.28).[45]

To what extent has Caesar replaced the facts of the failed Gallic sally and the successful Roman assault with an artful fiction?[46] The narrative

---

43. This is one of the singular examples in Caesar of the inverted morality of siege warfare. The Gallic women in effect conspire with the Romans because they understand more clearly (in Caesar's maudlin description of the incident) that escape is impossible, that the siege cannot but end in a sack, and that they will escape great suffering only if the siege is raised. See chapter 8 for further discussion of the sack.

44. See pages 29–35.

45. This is not terribly plausible. Would soldiers, during a rainy night after a perilous assault after nearly a month of dangerous labor, dwell on the murder of a few Roman traders when they had their own dead comrades to avenge? See, by way of comparison, *BC* 2.13. Honor and shame were at stake, and the violent release of the stress of prolonged siege labor was naturally directed at the "perpetrators" of the siege.

46. Kagan (2006) does not discuss the siege of Avaricum, and could not of course respond to Riggsby (2006), yet her arguments can be deployed here against Riggsby's ascetic withdrawal from extratextual reality. Riggsby (2006), 91, misunderstands an important aspect of military *virtus*: the repeated references in the commentaries to officers witnessing the *virtus* of their men is not evidence for a "disciplinary" or "hierarchical" aspect of *virtus*. Rather, it is the most important intersection of combat motivation and leadership: commanders witness so that they can reward their men, as Caesar has just informed us (7.27). Given the high profile of *virtus* in Roman culture it should be studied intertextually in order to be fully understood—but not without reference to its origin in what can be efficiently described only as "real life." See BG 1.52, 3.14, 7.62, 7.80, 8.42; and pages 37–40. Working with this misunderstanding of *virtus*, Riggsby, 98, inverts the significance of the Gallic incendiary attack on the Roman tower: "Moreover, though perhaps suicidal, the

turns on two aspects of combat—motivation and technology—but these were the crucial facets of siege warfare, and Caesar would have strained to place the emphasis elsewhere. Yet his narrative also centers on two specific events: the failed incendiary attack on the tower and the climactic assault of the town. Only the second was a necessary focal point: the heroic incendiary flinging is but one small part of a well-planned counterattack that also included mass sallies and the much more dangerous igniting of the *agger*. Caesar stops and highlights that event for two reasons: because it shows the last moment at which Gallic *virtus* matched Roman *virtus*, and because Roman technology can be selectively portrayed (this is the only instance in which Caesar mentions the *scorpio*) as the agent of the turning point.[47]

This is a sort of collective *aristeia*—a story of doomed valor by the worthy enemy. It has been selected from among other plausible tactical centerpieces (there is less attention to the firefighting in the *agger*) because it was the most visible and most striking of the activities that comprised the large Gallic counterattack: a man alone, framed in a gateway, lit by his own fire, shot down from afar. Caesar's narrative dramatizes by emphasizing important aspects of the actual events. Siege technology enabled the wall to be approached, Gallic morale was high until after the counterattack/sally failed to overcome Roman technology, and then Roman aggression (held in check only by the fortifications and Vercingetorix's decision to refuse open battle) secured the victory.

ALESIA

After the sack of Avaricum Caesar rested his army for several days. He then split his force, sending Labienus north with four legions, while he marched south with six legions in pursuit of Vercingetorix, catching up to him at the foot of Gergovia, a strongly situated *oppidum*. Caesar gambled on an elaborate tactical ruse (involving muleteers posing as cavalry) and rushed to seize an important hill. His troops, due to an excess of zeal, not only

---

Gallic assault was certainly controlled. Exactly one person was setting fires at a time . . . the Gauls are now acting with the discipline and submission to authority characteristic of Roman soldiers. This keeps them focused on the common good, rather than individual glory." It is not the misreading of the Gallic activity per se, but the misreading of "the narrator's" intention that is most problematic: Caesar is emphasizing not that they appeared in sequence but that they kept trying to achieve a heroic act despite the near-certainty of death.
47. See also 7.29.

took the hill but carried on up to the very walls of the *oppidum* itself. Thus, when the Gallic forces who had been working on the other side of the plateau reached the fighting, they found the Romans exhausted and were able to pin them against the town walls. A rout ensued—the worst Roman defeat of the Gallic wars—and 46 centurions and 700 soldiers were killed (7.32–51).

Caesar withdrew to the territory of friendly tribes, temporarily conceding defeat. After a period in which both armies were reinforced, Vercingetorix followed and attacked Caesar on the march, somewhere near Dijon. This hastily described encounter battle was won by Caesar, thanks largely to a group of German cavalry that had just arrived. Vercingetorix fell back on the stronghold of Alesia, with Caesar in pursuit (7.67–8).

Upon arrival, Caesar found that Alesia, located on a high plateau protected by encircling hills and two streams, was so strong that it was "inexpugnable except with the help of a blockade." Caesar shows his awareness, again, of high Roman expectations for aggression in siege warfare. His "inexpugnable" comment involves three factors: not only the physical strength of the site but the size and combativeness of Vercingetorix's force and the small size of his own army. Caesar is badly outnumbered, and his enemy, as evidenced by their willingness to skirmish beyond their works, is confident.[48] Caesar's troops immediately began to build what would become a line of contravallation eleven miles in length, punctuated by twenty-three forts and supported by several large camps (7.69–70).[49]

This was very unusual. Even without reminders about relative troop strength, Caesar's notice of Alesia's imposing topography—much emphasized by the lengthy description of his elaborate siege works (7.72–4)[50]—is

---

48. See *BG* 7.71, 7.75–7. See also Kagan (2006), 137 for a discussion of the troop strengths at Alesia.

49. The extensive guesswork by Napoléon III that followed the mid-nineteenth-century excavations at Alesia has been corrected in several respects by late twentieth-century archaeologists and by the evidence of aerial photography, but the original excavators did succeed in identifying the location of the lines of contravallation and circumvallation and confirming that Caesar's account is accurate in the essentials. See Reddé (2001), (2008), and (2003), 165–85 for a discussion of the problematic influence of text on archaeology, and vice versa.

50. These function together much in the same way as the explanation of the *murus gallicus* digression at Avaricum. Yet "inexpugnable except by blockade" could very well be an ex post facto judgment. Had the various tribes not rallied to Vercingetorix and brought a huge army to relieve the siege, Caesar may have proceeded from circumvallation to a heavily engineered assault on the Gallic camp, and perhaps even on the *oppidum* itself. The strength of the site, however, balanced with the presence of so many trapped mouths to feed, would have put an active siege on a close-to-impossible timetable: the blockade tactic

a plea to remember the inferiority of his forces.[51] Caesar's Roman audience would have been struck by the aggressiveness of the decision to prosecute the siege. The aggressiveness, that is, of forcing the issue at Alesia at all. The strategic situation altered the moral tenor of the progression: this was no war of conquest but a mass revolt. Caesar was deep in what was now enemy territory, with a Gallic relief army forming in his rear. To invest time in circumvallation,[52] normally a conservative tactical decision, here represented a huge gamble, risking the total destruction of his army in order to prosecute the siege. The immediate blockade and the overriding strategic situation drives home an important point: Caesar's target was not really the city of Alesia, but rather the Gallic army and, as the leader of the revolt, Vercingetorix himself.[53] It should follow from this fact (although most historians have ignored the implication) that this action was not a siege in the traditional sense but rather a complex operation involving serial "blockades" of one army and then another.[54]

The nature of siege warfare is conditioned by the broad cultural consensus that refusing battle is a shameful act.[55] Neither side at Alesia refused battle. Vercingetorix is trapped, but he intends to fight Caesar's encirclement. Moreover, his direct conflict with Caesar is only part of the larger war between Caesar and the Gallic alliance, and as such is operationally linked to movements of the relief army. In fact, Caesar himself is shortly blockaded: having constructed a second line of fortifications facing outward, his army is now itself surrounded (7.74), and the only *oppugnatio* that takes place at Alesia is the subsequent assault on the lines of circumvallation by the relieving army (7.81).[56]

There are several days of fighting before the relieving army is routed

---

was necessarily Caesar's best option.

51. The speculations and excavations of, among others, an emperor, a duke, a colonel, and several Oxbridgians are discussed in Holmes (1899), 786–91. See also Keppie (1984) and Campbell (2005). The famous works have been partially reconstructed at an archaeological park near the site.

52. I.e., contravallation. See chapter 3, note 58.

53. Caesar's offensive actions are directed at the camps of the Gallic army, not the *oppidum*, which remained largely irrelevant to the battle of positions below it.

54. Although most historians discuss the "siege" of Alesia, Kagan (2006), 136; Dodington (1980), 55; and Rosenstein (2009), 97 do all refer to Alesia as a "battle."

55. See chapter 1, particularly pages 15–19.

56. Caesar thus occupies a rough ring, his opponents within and without the area of the ring, which is bounded by his two sets of fortifications. This "ring" is topologically identical not only to a doughnut but also a coffee cup and any other fortification besieged, on two sides, from two separate and noncontiguous locations. On which see Riggsby (2006), 41.

and the garrison of Alesia compelled to surrender. The type of combat that fills this time is generally equivalent to the mass or lightly engineered assault, although cavalry sallies are also prominent. In addition, each side is perhaps a month from starvation (7.71, 74). But these siege characteristics obscure the fact that the operations around Alesia were in fact a prolonged battle, or perhaps a campaign in miniature.[57] There is no refusal here, instead the jockeying for position and considerations of timing that mark mature tactics in a decisive operation. Caesar gambled on bringing Vercingetorix to battle, but once he witnessed the position around Alesia, he knew that he would need to blockade in order to force this. When the huge relieving army arrived, Caesar's initial operational gamble had failed. If the Gauls had not attacked him, his only viable option would have been a difficult breakout followed by a probably disastrous long retreat through hostile territory pursued by two armies—instead, he blockaded himself in the outer ring of defenses. Despite the lack of any plausible Roman relief army, Gallic martial pride and the plight of the army trapped in Alesia forced them to attack, which in turn provided Caesar with a final opportunity.

The curious cutaway digression to the Gallic council in Alesia (7.77) has been discussed from many points of view, but its significance is clear. The "nefarious" speech of Critognatus, who heaps scorn on those who would sally, seeing in this the false *virtus* of those too weak to endure a blockade, concludes with the suggestion that the defenders prepare to eat their noncombatants. The speech is, of course, an entertainment, a little frisson belonging to the bad old tradition of pseudo-ethnographic, proto-colonialist reportage. The cannibalism distracts the reader from Caesar's more pressing reasons for interrupting the battle narrative with an odd bit of ostensible hearsay. Critognatus is made to sound like a crazed zealot because his advice is strategically correct: their only chance is to wait for the relieving army and hope to crush Caesar between the two forces.[58] The realization that this is sound strategy should lead the reader to question the meaning of the alleged Gallic refusal to fight. Really, there is no shame here: one component of a large force has allowed itself to be trapped at Alesia and is merely stalling. However, Caesar's next act—he refuses to let

---

57. The only similar operation in the late republic or empire about which we are informed is Caesar's similar blockade and assault struggle with Pompey around Dyrrachium, *BC* 3.42–73—the next best comparanda are probably early modern.

58. The narrative strategy of painting trapped and resisting defenders as fanatical zealots will also be used by Josephus.

noncombatants pass through his lines in order to escape potential starvation or massacre within (7.78)—is the sort of potential atrocity that only the harsh rules of siege warfare condone. Caesar needed, at this point in the narrative, to rely on the fact that he was indeed blockading Alesia, even though this incidence of siege warfare was really only an operational accident, the prelude to a decisive battle, fought with mutual consent despite the presence of the extensive Roman works.

The Gallic relief force arrived soon after this Gallic council (like so many siege narrators, Caesar is vague on the passage of time). The next morning the huge new army launched a daylong assault on Caesar's outer fortifications and were eventually driven off by a sally from the German cavalry (7.80). The Gauls spent the following day preparing the materials necessary for a lightly engineered assault. This second attempt was coordinated with a sally from the inner army and launched suddenly at midnight, but Caesar's extensive fortifications held (7.81–2). A final attempt at midday involved a sneak attack on one of the Caesarian camps, a general assault by the relief army, and a sally by Vercingetorix that took the form of a lightly engineered assault against the lines of contravallation. Caesar depicts this as the necessary climax of the fighting, despite the fact that the thirty days of provisions do not seem to have been exhausted (7.83–7). We should suspect that the climactic presentation of the assault involves some retrospection on Caesar's part, but the battle was clearly desperate and confused. There were several irruptions into the Roman works, and Caesar was prevented by the fact that his forces were closed within a ring of double fortifications from gaining any overall vantage point that would allow him to exercise his usual level of control.

Caesar's leadership in the final fight is that of the commander in battle, rather than at a siege: he does not act as a static witness of the valor of his troops, since he can see only a few of them at a time, nor does he expose himself to distant missile fire, exhort his men, or promise rewards. Instead, he circulates until a critical moment and then appears—highly visible in his red cloak—as a token of inspiration and as a rallying point. Followed by his cavalry escort/reserve, his presence attracts the attention of the enemy and enables a characteristic act of decisive motivation on the part of his troops: they drop their *pila* and "go to swords." This is the sudden turning point of battle, campaign, and war, and within the space of a few words Caesar is reporting captives and booty (7.88). One further paragraph covers the surrender of Vercingetorix, and the book's final words explain the garrisoning of Gaul and Caesar's removal into winter quarters.

Caesar argues that he was outnumbered: thus he can be forgiven his extensive fortifications. His narrative of the construction of those formidable double lines distractingly focuses on their high-tech ability to wound the enemy (concealed stakes in pits, etc.), as if Caesar's will could make even fortifications take the offensive. Caesar's narrative does include standard scenes of assaults (exchanges of missiles figure prominently) on his fortified troops, but it focuses more on the use of the fortifications as the jumping-off point for offensive action.

This is a smoke screen of Caesarian artfulness, but the Alesia narrative still comprises an effective defense against any charge of defensiveness. Caesar offers two rationales. First, that the Gauls in Alesia refused to fight (or to accept the verdict of the battle near Dijon and surrender in the open), dishonorably forcing him to blockade their redoubt. Thus no taint of refusal clings to that outer line of fortification: Caesar is honoring a prior commitment to crush Vercingetorix, and this excuses the force multiplier of a line of circumvallation, which Roman military culture usually disdains as impeding proper motivation. Second, that his position—stationary, and behind fortifications—constitutes not being besieged, but rather a successful, battle-enabling stratagem. Using Vercingetorix's army as bait, he has lured a larger, overconfident army to a decisive contest. The fortifications only help to even his disadvantage in what is still a victory of *virtus*.

Both explanations are essentially fair, but incomplete: the Battle of Alesia was the chancy outcome of a contest that was stalemated on the operational and strategic levels. Caesar got the decisive battle he needed, and the Gallic chiefs were able to fight it with advantages of position and numbers that seemed to outweigh the disadvantage of having to assault Caesar's fortifications. It looked like a siege and was fought like a siege, but in the end it was a consensual battle in which extensive field fortifications played an unusual role—a strange foreshadowing of a much later conflict that dug extensively into the earth of northern France.

SIX

JOSEPHUS AND THE SIEGE OF JERUSALEM

A Roman army under another Caesar—the title bestowed on Titus as son of the reigning emperor Vespasian—laid siege to Jerusalem in the spring of 70 CE. It took nearly four months of hard fighting for it to reach, capture, and destroy the temple, and a further month elapsed before the entire city was taken. Tens of thousands of starving survivors were killed in the sack, and much of the city burnt. This siege was the climactic operation of the suppression of the Jewish revolt, which had begun in 66 CE. While the final stamping out of the revolt would take several years, it was clear that almost all resistance would cease once the holy city of the Jews was captured.[1] This was probably the longest and most difficult of all the sieges waged by Roman troops during the imperial period, and it was almost certainly the most destructive: this was no war of conquest or pacification, but the vengeful suppression of a stiff-necked people who, despite their long experience as Roman subjects, had chosen revolt and driven out the local garrisons. The siege of Jerusalem is also the subject of the lengthiest and most extravagant surviving description of an ancient military operation.[2]

---

1. Josephus describes several other sieges in *The Jewish War*, but due both to its almost unmanageable complexity and to limitations of space, this chapter focuses exclusively on the narrative of the siege of Jerusalem.

2. See Lendon (2005), 256; Goldsworthy (1999), 198. Longest: Millar (2005), 101. A siege of Byzantium under Septimius Severus lasted for several years, but ended only in

Jerusalem, a large city set in difficult, hilly terrain, was protected by several different walls and fortifications, which had the effect of dividing the city into several defensible subsections—few cities were as strongly fortified.[3] It was defended by thousands of experienced fighters, although they too were divided amongst themselves.[4] Few cities, either, were as fundamental to the culture of their people, and few other sieges could have begun with so large a proportion of the defenders already determined to fight to the death. To take the city, Titus had at his disposal an army comprising four entire legions, picked vexillations from two others, and tens of thousands of auxiliary and allied troops.[5]

The siege was complex in addition to being arduous. Because four discrete sections of the city were assaulted and consolidated in turn, attacking troops were kept continuously under the pressures of siege combat even after they had worked their way to the heavy assault and successfully stormed a target fortification. This made the operation as much an agglomeration of four consecutive sieges as one exceptionally long one. In taking Jerusalem, the Roman army progressed through some of the same stages of the siege as many as four times. This repetition provides a unique opportunity to assess the patterns of siege warfare, but it also shows the flexibility—or looseness—of the siege progression.

JOSEPHUS AND THE WRITING OF HISTORY

Our knowledge of this siege depends almost entirely on Josephus,[6] a Jew of priestly, upper-class background and the former commander of the Jewish forces in the Galilee. Having been captured, spared, and granted Flavian patronage, he turned apologist and propagandist. His account of the war, written in seven books, is laden with rhetorical flourishes, moralizing

---

starvation (Herodian 3.6.9) and had clearly been a passive blockade for some time.

3. While steep valleys protected the southern and eastern approaches, a broad frontage of wall could still be assaulted and no body of water prevented access or obstructed circumvallation. Tac. *Hist.* 5.11, notes that the walls would have sufficed to protect even a flat site.

4. Josephus counts 23,400 combatant defenders—a reasonable number, to which several tens of thousands of noncombatants must be added. See also Price (1992), appendix 3, on the fundamental unreliability of numbers—Price prefers 35,000 defenders; but see chapter 1, note 23.

5. Millar (2005), 101.

6. Tacitus' *Histories,* the relevant books being lost, provide only a few hints, likewise the brief glimpses of the siege in Suetonius and Cassius Dio. See Rajak (2002), 105.

digressions, and blatant misrepresentations.[7] This is not as problematic as it might seem. First, the sheer volume of Josephus' embellishments and the heavy-handedness of his propaganda permit the careful historian to peel away layers of political bias and genre distortion and uncover the dependable facts below. Second, Josephus shifts gears with startling abruptness, lurching, for instance, from tense combat narrative to overwrought tragedy (6.193) and back again (6.220). These shifts provide clear lines of demarcation between historically reliable passages and embellishments.[8] Third, sharp dissonance between a specific incident and any of the weighty themes that so burden his history signals historicity: if Josephus reports something that contradicts or sits awkwardly with one of his hobbyhorses, then it is very likely to have actually taken place.[9] Finally, Josephus' eagerness to present vignettes of heroism, barbarism, and nemesis as literary adornments to the narrative actually results in the preservation of minor events of the siege that would otherwise be passed over in his attention to the grand drama of Jewish impiety and the inevitability of Roman victory. The rather more stately bending of history to the frame of the imposed theme that we see in Livy, for instance, probably leaves behind many more interesting scraps of source material on the workshop floor.

So, while we need not doubt likely incidents reported without much elaboration, we must treat with special suspicion those details that are built into the edifice of one of Josephus' two grand themes: the glory and perfection of Titus and the question of responsibility for the destruction of the temple. These two themes converge as Josephus takes great pains to demonstrate that Titus did his utmost to prevent it—yet it remains clear from the surrounding narrative that this was not the case.[10] This is not to say

---

7. For the recent rehabilitation of Josephus see especially Rajak (2002). See also Price (1992), 180–82, using "internal controls," and corroborating of Josephus' outline of events. All translations in this chapter are based on the Loeb (Thackeray 1928), unless otherwise noted.

8. Indeed, the clumsiness of Josephus' propaganda is almost enough to make one suspect that he intends to signal his use of two different genres (see Parente, 2005) in order to allow his readers to separate it from an underlying account.

9. To take one general example among many, Josephus wishes to represent the "zealot" defenders as raving madmen. Thus, when he is forced to acknowledge their clever tactics and effective fighting, we can be confident that he is grudgingly reporting the truth.

10. Hence the contortions involving attempts to elicit surrender, discussed in more depth below. See, e.g., *BJ* 1.28, 5.289, 317, 348, 372; 6.95. See also what appear to be simple slips, *BJ* 7.1; *AJ* 20.250. See Parente (2005), 64–69; Barnes (2005). The opposite tradition, apparently deriving from Tacitus, is preserved by Sulpicius Severus, *Chronica* 2.30.3, but is just as tainted by partisanship and religiously motivated demonization. See Rajak (2002),

that Titus intended, or insisted upon, the temple's destruction—only that its significance to Titus' calculations as commander of the siege was nothing like the all overshadowing concern of Josephus' account. Instead, it seems clear that, whatever Titus' early intentions, he would have been unable to save the temple: given the length and bitter intensity of the siege, assault would lead to an unpreventable sack. But it suited his purpose as an imperial propagandist to invent Titus' concern for the temple and to portray the raging Roman soldiers as agents of divine vengeance.

Josephus' treatment of Titus borrows from several traditions and claims at least as many historical and intertextual contexts. Titus is the model Roman aristocrat—an exemplary figure who muscles other exempla to the margins of the text. He is a military boy wonder, fearless in the fray. And he is the model prince: brave, calm, and shrewd.[11] Each of these characterizations borrowed from reality, and each was exaggerated. The numerous atrocities perpetrated by the Roman troops under Titus' command and his repeated willingness to order massacres and executions are accompanied by a pseudo-philosophical commentary on justice, and balanced by flimsy assertions of Titus' clemency, or intentions thereto. Just as Josephus covers destruction with *clementia,* he counterbalances obvious mistakes in generalship with an emphasis on Titus' personal courage and willingness to trust the honor of his adversaries. This is nonsense, of course: whatever else he was, Titus was a young commander constrained by political expediency, military culture, and the pressures of an unprecedented siege. Yet by reading between the lines of Josephus' dramatic episodes and by untwining his twisted facts,[12] the outline of the progression of the siege of Jerusalem can be discovered.

JOSEPHUS AS A MILITARY HISTORIAN

Josephus has not been a popular source for scholars of the Roman army. Some of the reasons for this are understandable—he wrote in Greek, he was not a Roman, and he perjured himself with regularity. There is also

---

206–11; this single question does not greatly compromise the rest of Josephus' account of the siege.

11. See generally Rajak (2002), 205–12; Yavetz (1975). See also Gichon (1986), 294–95 and pages 89–90, 99–100, above, for Polybius' similar habit of committing relatively large infelicities when describing the behavior of members of his patron family.

12. Parente (2005), 59–60. Yavetz (1975), 420, suggests that to separate truth and fiction we must simply "find out the argument which suited Josephus best and hence disclose why and in which direction he twisted some basic facts."

the more subtle problem of his Hellenistic tendencies—notably the focus on the royal person and the lack, compared to the Latin narratives, of dramatized interactions between the commander and troops. His propagandistic obsessions leave a relatively small role for the soldiers who prosecuted the siege. Yet whenever promontories of identifiable description poke through the mists of drama and rhetoric this becomes a valuable narrative. The crucial information is all there: assaults, counterattacks, negotiations, the rage and violence of the soldiers. Josephus' dates and topography are reliable, and he was clearly working both from autopsy and from good notes.[13]

Josephus follows his Greek models in setting the scene with a careful description of the physical realities of the siege and the nature of Jerusalem's defenses (5.136–257). That his combat narratives are driven by rage, fear, and sudden twists of fate—and not by tactics—does not render them untruthful, or even all that difficult to handle. Josephus is free of the worst habits of classicizing historians, and does not ordinarily privilege topos over event. Whatever the distorting effects of his biases, he shows no inclination toward overpraising the Roman troops or whitewashing their behavior.[14]

Even the fact that the military narrative is often overshadowed by the tendency for sensational or pathetic history is not necessarily a bad thing. Given the moral context of a vicious and prolonged siege, it actually has much to recommend it: we generally know where and when an action takes place because Josephus could not falsify such information even if he wanted to—nor could he present a clear repulse as a victory. A dramatic narrative of close combat is no less accurate than a formal, tactical account, which would have little to say about the sub-tactical clash of small groups of fighters. Indeed, it should not come as a surprise to discover that a moralizing historian can be full of interesting insights about morale. If we move carefully around the rhetorical and thematic distortions, we find the best descriptions of the realities of close combat during the principate.

These descriptions are, after his detailed description of the entire progress of the siege, Josephus' most important contribution to military history. They reveal, despite his own attempts to explain away this conclusion, a surprising fact: the Jewish defenders of Jerusalem regularly outfought

---

13. See Price (1992), 191; and note 15. I follow Price in his assumptions that "most Roman movements and actions, except when directly related to a specific theme, are recorded as accurately as possible" and that Josephus was able to draw on *commentarii* (on which see chapter 5, note 4) for military details. See also Josephus *Vit.* 358.

14. See Price (1992), 193; Goldsworthy (1999), 199.

their Roman enemies in hand-to-hand combat. While scholars have noted the surprising effectiveness of the ad hoc Jewish forces against picked Roman legionaries and auxiliaries, a better understanding of how the siege context influenced these combats will cast more light on the situation.[15]

Throughout the *Jewish War,* the Jews consistently prevailed in close combat, despite their inferior equipment. Because the modern military lexicon associates speed, informal organization, and a refusal to openly face the enemy on a field of battle with guerrilla warfare, some writers have precisely inverted the significance of the Jewish fighting style against the Romans.[16] The only hope of success in the war had been to defeat the Roman army directly, and now that the issue was being sought at Jerusalem, the only chance of survival was to maintain the moral initiative, driving off the Roman army instead of awaiting the inevitable outcome. This demanded not guerrilla tactics but rather direct confrontation. The operational disadvantage of being besieged conferred, to highly motivated defenders, the tactical advantage of being able to choose the moment to sally and seek intense combat.

Josephus' descriptions of these fights are closer in style to Caesar than to Polybius or Thucydides, his usual models. Tactical movements set the scene, but confusion reigns after the fighting begins and the Jewish charge is described in moral terms. Early in the war the overconfident Roman speed assault on the Galilean town of Jotapata failed when the defenders "burst unexpectedly on the Romans . . . and kindled by the thought of the danger threatening their native city . . . quickly routed their opponents (3.112–3)." When the Romans arrived at Jerusalem, Jewish fighters "tore across the ravine with blood-curdling yells and fell upon the enemy (5.75)." A Roman legion in the process of entrenching is scattered, and Josephus tries to conceal their failure to hold their ground by explaining that "men . . . proficient in fighting in ordered ranks and by word of command" are confounded by "disordered warfare." He describes Titus' arrival as single-handedly stopping the rout (5.78–83).[17] But of course disorder against disorder will only allow any moral advantage free play—it is still clear that Jewish reckless courage is not being matched. Once re-formed, the Roman legionaries are able to

---

15. E.g., Goldsworthy (1996), 203–5; and Price (1992), appendix 12. Price is a very useful guide to the task of separating the layers of Josephan rhetoric from the underlying facts, but he underrates the moral advantages of desperation. See also Gichon (1986), 292; Goldsworthy (1999).

16. E.g., Furneaux (1973), 102.

17. Scene 97 (Cichorius 71) of Trajan's column depicts a similar royal rescue.

wound the exhausted and under-armored Jews. This same scene of skilled, heavily armed legionaries unable to compete with the reckless courage of the Jewish defenders occurred several times during the siege of Jotapata, and it will reoccur many times during the siege of Jerusalem, whenever legionaries or auxiliaries have to meet the desperate sallies of the rebels without support from missile troops or cavalry.

Lastly, there is the question of Josephus' qualifications as a source—his expertise and the accuracy of the information that underlies his narrative. Here he scores high marks: not only was he present in the entourage of Titus throughout the siege of Jerusalem, but he had personally led the defense of Jotapata against Vespasian.[18] He was certainly capable of providing highly accurate depictions of a siege, and, once these are rescued from the surrounding polemics, his account of the assault on Jerusalem is a most informative account of Roman siege warfare.

THE SIEGE PROGRESSION AT JERUSALEM

The siege of Jerusalem fell into four stages, each ending when a wall was successfully stormed and a section of the city captured. Inscribed upon the greater arc of the siege progression that stretches from Titus' arrival to the final sack, then, are the shorter arcs of four partial sieges. The first two involved the taking of the "third wall" (5.301–2), after heavy engineering but without a contested final assault, and the capture, loss, and recapture of an area of the city within the "second wall" (5.347).[19] A pause in operations was followed by the construction of siege works against the Antonia fortress, which bordered the temple (5.356). This advancement along the progression—a quick move to the heaviest and most direct types of siege combat—was followed by another, even more significant escalation. Fol-

---

18. See Gichon (1986), 287. Josephus witnessed or participated in at least five sieges prior to Jerusalem. The Jotapata narrative is rich in siege details but chaotic and untrustworthy—not a surprising fact given Josephus' role as defending commander, suicide-pact survivor, and future client of the besieging commander. Despite its interest as a source of siege incident, however, the narrative seems to be heavily doctored and does not allow for the reconstruction of a coherent siege progression.

19. Cassius Dio's brief (epitomized) account of the siege (65.4–6) treats this second stage as more or less co-extensive with the Antonia/temple stage, but his account does confirm a resetting of the progression after the first (from the Roman perspective, but previously the "third," or outer, from the Jewish perspective) wall falls, with Titus again offering good terms to the defenders.

lowing a war council (5.491–3), lines of circumvallation were belatedly constructed, an act that marked the end of any possibility of a negotiated settlement. Josephus, despite his conflicting claims that Titus wished to extend extraordinary clemency, acknowledges as much: his dramatic passages grow more hysterical, emphasizing the brutality of both sides. After the capture of the Antonia, the temple was stormed, sacked, and burnt (6.250–316), bringing the third, climactic, stage of the siege to a conclusion. Remarkably, given the scale of the slaughter and the fate of the temple, the final stage of the siege still manifested some characteristics of a "new" siege—complete with preliminary negotiations and discussions of the "laws of war" (6.346)—before the cycle of *agger*, storm, and sack was repeated for the fourth time. Among the last images is that of the smoldering fires in the ruins of the upper city extinguished by the torrents of blood coursing through the streets (6.406).

The intertwining of different tensions and escalations is difficult to unravel, especially given the tangling of the reality-based narrative with the program of exaggerations and interpolations surrounding the behavior of Titus and the fate of the temple. A close examination of the siege, however, underscores the dominant role of the moral balance between the desperate morale of the defense and the waning combat motivation of the besiegers.

The pre-contact stage of the siege of Jerusalem consisted of the arrival of a force of 600 cavalry and a swift sally that drove it away. The cavalry, with Titus in personal command, approached the walls in order to "test the mettle of the Jews, (and to discover) whether they would be cowed into surrender before it came to a fight." While Josephus is nearly as untrustworthy on the subject of Jewish infighting as he is on Titus and the temple, the point that Titus considered the internal divisions of the defenders in his hope for surrender (5.53) is a fair one, and the potent mix of rebellion, civil war, and religious dispute helps explain the many deviations from the strict "laws of war" that are to come.

In any case, the high morale of the defenders was amply demonstrated by the sally, which, we are told, cut Titus off from the majority of his men, forcing him to gallop to safety under a hail of arrows, cutting down the enemies in his path (5.54–66). While the killing and personal heroism are certainly exaggerated, there is no reason to reject the fact of Titus' presence before the walls. He was given to heroic leadership and new to the role of supreme commander; he needed to view the defenses at close range before deploying his forces; and, among cavalry, he would have been in relatively little danger. There was surely no expectation of immediate surrender: Titus' appearance was both a tactical reconnaissance and a test of morale—an early beginning of intimidation.[20]

Given the formidable defenses of the city, there was no question of any hasty assault. The intimidation process began in earnest with the arrival of the four legions, which immediately began to encamp. As it often did, the spectacle of the ordered Roman deployment and the compelling statement of intention that was conveyed by entrenchments caused dismay. But Jewish morale was high, and the legions' arrival caused a cessation of hostilities among the three warring factions in the city and a joint sally against the tenth legion (5.71–82), which provided evidence of the dominance of the defenders in close combat. Josephus reports that Titus' arrival stopped the rout and steadied the troops, after which he formed a screen composed of auxiliaries and guardsmen and ordered the tenth, out of position after chasing the returning Jewish force, to resume entrenching.[21] The defenders, confident and eager for battle, mistook withdrawal for retreat, and sallied forth again. This group of Jewish fighters—if they were organized or led Josephus does not tell us—is described as charging "with such impetuosity that their rush was comparable to that of the most savage of beasts" (5.85–97). Naturally, a stand by Titus ends the threat.

These two effective sallies preempted the rest of the intimidation stage. No desultory skirmishing was necessary, since the Jews had demonstrated not only their willingness to fight hand to hand but also their ability to take the upper hand. Preliminaries are now over, a fact clearly recognized by Titus (or his more experienced officers), who chose to move the camps

---

20. The miraculous escape from the hail of arrows fired from the wall—a difficult feat for an unarmored and recognizable prince—is more a reflection of Titus' starring role in the narrative than of tactical realities. The Jews were almost as deficient in skilled archers as they were in cavalry, and relied elsewhere in the siege on slings and thrown stones: there was no hail of arrows and he wasn't much within extreme range. Titus, who was present for at least five sieges, may not have always gotten away unscathed, however. Cass. Dio, 65.5.1, reports that he was wounded, a fact omitted by Josephus, probably because fortune's darling should not be seen to take hits at long range. For other examples of Roman supreme commanders imperiled by arrows or sallies see Suet. *Aug.* 14; pages 36, above, and 200–201, below. See also Levithan (2008).

21. 5.82–4. That Titus' picked guard/reserve responded to the rout of the tenth and checked the Jewish sally is not at all unlikely. This is also the first of several instances in which a tactical or operational error on the part of Titus can be discerned ex post facto, when Josephus reports his orders addressing an already-developed problem. To entrench in the face of a spirited enemy without a screening force was unwise, and probably a grave breach of the usual, conservative Roman practice. See, e.g., *BC* 1.41–2; *B Afr.* 51.

closer to the city and began four days of work to level the intervening ground. This marks the beginning of the "siege proper": the moment when the besieging general decides whether or not to dig lines of circumvallation and then chooses where and how to begin the assault.[22]

Josephus calls attention to the formal beginning of the siege in several ways. First, he announces forward movement and then plunges into a long description of the walls and fortifications of Jerusalem and a résumé of the defending factions (5.136–257), repeating the announcement of the siege's new stage at its conclusion. The digression is grandiose, but quite accurate in terms of both topography and Roman siegecraft.[23] Second, Josephus provides an incident to concretize Titus' decision: while the prince is reconnoitering near the wall, a member of Titus' suite is shot and wounded (5.261–2). Josephus, bound to his program of portraying Titus as merciful and the defenders as crazed extremists, presents this as a criminal act which stimulates Titus to suspend hopes for negotiation and to begin the siege in anger. This is transparent propaganda: the pause that Josephus has just emphasized was the appropriate time in the siege progression—with the first assault looming as Roman soldiers prepared the ground—to attempt negotiation, and a response in the form of a missile is hardly surprising from a garrison that has already refused terms (5.114) and twice won skirmish victories.[24] This wounding nevertheless constitutes a sort of ritual rejection of parley, and Titus orders the siege to commence (5.262–3).

While the transitions in the siege progression are easy enough to find in Josephus' account, we are faced with a more difficult problem of interpretation when it comes to the potential defection of some of the defenders. Josephus has just emphasized (5.248–57) the factional strife in the city, and, given this unusual situation, it would not be surprising to learn that Titus kept up attempts to solicit surrender after the siege progression normally demanded that they cease. This is indeed what Josephus tells us, and he was himself employed in shouting surrender offers and appeals to his

---

22. The failure to surround the city was a major mistake, later rectified. It should have been clear to the besiegers that the size of the city and the roughness of the ground around its walls allowed communication with—and probably re-supply from—the outside world for months to come. Tac. *Hist.* 5.13, notes that the strength of the site "ruled out a general assault, or any of the speedier warlike operations." That is, he tells us succinctly that the progression demanded a heavily engineered assault.

23. Josephus shows, for instance, awareness of the practice of deciding at an early stage whether to batter and smash stonework or to pry and pull it apart (5.152–55). See Price (1992), appendix 13.

24. See Levithan (2008).

countrymen. This hope that propaganda and intimidation could foment dissent and cause the desertion of one of the groups may also help explain why Titus chose not to build lines of circumvallation—he may have hoped to encourage mass defection. Yet there is no evidence that Titus ever halted the progress of the siege in order to negotiate with the defenders. Detailing Aramaic-speaking captives (or recent prisoners, at least) to declaim in the direction of the walls while the next assault was being prepared does not prove a willingness to accept terms. This was, after all, no methodical Roman war of conquest but the suppression of an extremist revolt, and the convergence of the "crazy rebels" theme with Titus' clemency makes such a passage highly untrustworthy.[25]

In any event, work now began on siege ramps against the "third," or outer wall. Since its strength was not great, it was evidently the high motivation and efficient fighting of the defenders that precluded a lightly engineered assault. The ramps were protected by archers and artillery, and a new period of skirmishing for moral advantage ensued, in the form of both sallies and artillery duels. Josephus provides colorful anecdotes of this period of low-intensity fighting, some reminiscent of modern sieges—the Jews develop lookout systems for incoming missiles, and even invent humorous slang for the instruments of bombardment (5.266–74).

As soon as the ramps were advanced far enough for battering rams, suspended from the lower story of rolling towers, to reach the wall, skirmishing ended and a period of more direct action began. Josephus again marks an important transition in the progression by digressing to one of his polemical touchstones. As the rams first approach the wall, the factions, which had been fighting, again unite (5.277). This may indicate their knowledge of a basic convention of siege warfare, namely that the touch of the ram on the wall is the traditional point of no return for the besieged.

Two running fights, or two periods of Jewish sallies upon the works, immediately follow the arrival of the rams: "The more aggressive, dashing out in bands, tore up the hurdles protecting the machines, and fell upon the gunners, and not through skill but generally through reckless courage got the better of them" (5.280). The day is duly saved by Titus, and a period of ramming follows before another mass sally with firebrands attempts to burn the ram-houses. Here too, "Jewish daring outstripped Roman discipline" and many of the front fighters were killed. A crack detachment of

---

25. On the three factions within Jerusalem see Price (1992), 135–42.

Alexandrian legionaries managed to stand, however, and the sally was driven off in time to save the works.[26]

This setback in the preparation for the heavy assault leads to an escalation of atrocity—"intimidation" ceases to suffice as a description of the psychological aspects of this sort of conflict. A Jewish fighter has been captured, and Titus orders him crucified before the walls "in the hope that the spectacle might lead the rest to surrender in dismay" (5.289).

The next section of Josephus' account is focused on the advantages of Roman technology. Three large siege towers, carrying not only rams but artillery, now approach the walls. While Josephus makes much of the panic occasioned by one tower falling over during the night, the largest of them, dubbed *nikon* (i.e., "Victor"), soon succeeds in breaching the wall. An anticlimax follows, in which the Jews fall back and the Roman troops easily secure this lightly built section of the city. Titus moves his camp within the third wall and begins the assault on the second. The first stage of the siege, from the beginning of the assault phase to victory, has taken fifteen days. Despite the preparations, it is important to note the lack of a contested assault upon the walls—fatalities will have been few.[27]

The new wall presented a different set of problems, and so a new stage of the siege began. With it the progression reset. While the pre-contact stage was of course elided, it seems that Titus did indeed adopt an early-siege methodology, hoping to carry elements of the second wall by a testing assault. Josephus, after marking the new phase of the siege with a review of morale (the Jews still hoped for "salvation"; the Romans for "speedy victory") details a series of assaults, wall fights, and sorties in small groups, made without benefit of any works or machines (5.305–7). That this is a testing assault and not a general assault is indicated by the ad hoc nature of the fighting as described by Josephus and also by the fact that the Romans never elsewhere in the siege attempt even a lightly engineered assault. When staunchly defended, the wall cannot be taken without heavy engineering: the hope here is that the initial Roman victory has altered the defenders' morale; that they will soon break and run.

The next passage is a highlighted dramatic episode, a spate of skirmishing that took place while the heavy assault was being prepared. Its relation

---

26. 5.281, 284–8. We may safely discount the tale of Titus killing twelve Jews amidst the burning siege equipment.

27. 5.290–303. See Price (1992), 132, for the topography.

to the siege progression, to borrow Josephus' own metaphor, is that of a scene played at the foot of the stage, before the curtain, during a change of scenery (5.309–16). Josephus recognizes the need for each side to solicit volunteers, and he examines the morale of each side further, noting a "rivalry (concerning) who should be foremost in the fray." Unfortunately, the presence of Titus in the passage warps Josephus' description of combat motivation at this important point, attracting an idealized vocabulary of courage that does not speak for the likely motivations of Roman fighters.[28] Josephus does not tell us what we know to be a major reason for Titus' presence: the eliciting of heroic assaults through the promise of the leader's witnessing and rewarding exceptional valor.

This skirmishing episode covers a period of less flashy activity. The legionaries have been preparing the heavily engineered assault, and the second stage of the siege leaps ahead to this phase. A battering ram is deployed against a part of the second wall, but as soon as the battering begins, Josephus reports another ruse by the wily defenders—a feigned dispute among the defenders of a tower. Titus, ingenuous and merciful, is taken in and actually stops the work of the rams, standing stupidly by while the Jews on the wall enact a farce of arguing over whether or not to surrender, thus buying time for the defense. When volunteers come to the foot of the wall to aid the Jews in their escape, they are attacked by the would-be defectors (5.317–28).

It is difficult to know how much we should credit the credulousness of Titus. Given the difficulty of the siege to come and the real possibility of factional defections, it is possible that he was willing to violate the mounting intimidation of the siege progression, which normally forbade accepting surrender after the ram had been brought into action.[29] But Josephus' handling of Titus' character and his frank acknowledgment elsewhere in the text of the "laws" concerning the ram militate against such an exception—Titus' halting of the rams is most likely a knowingly situated

---

28. A "habit of victory and inexperience of defeat" are good reasons for confidence, but impossible as "incentives to valor" for volunteer fighting—there is little connection between national military greatness and the chance of surviving an assault by escalade. The fact that he is resorting to a topos rather than properly describing the action is also indicated by the closeness of his language here to Thuc. 4.55, which Thackeray notes in the Loeb footnote to 5.310. As in a subsequent incident (see note 33), there is a strong similarity here with the debacle at Gergovia (*BG* 7.47–52). Titus incites aggression among his men but then, after a reverse, proclaims the importance of valor tempered with appropriate risk management (5.316).

29. See pages 74–77.

fabrication.[30] Josephus was well aware of the meaning of the ram's contact with the walls (see 5.277 and 6.346), and he knew that a Roman would be loath to undercut the moral force of desperation by halting the rams. Nevertheless, he invents the episode in order to emphasize the viciousness of the "zealot" defenders, as if the violation of the laws of war were theirs. Titus, the innocent hero, becomes a proxy for the reader, and through him we are made to experience the treachery of the defenders: "When Caesar saw how he had been tricked he realized that it was fatal to show pity in war."[31]

Thus the reader is prepared for the escalation of the siege. Titus orders the resumption of the battering with a vengeful rage that has been missing from the Roman attack so far.[32] By pausing dramatically in the midst of the first heavy assault, Josephus has concretized the progression of the siege, through Titus and for us.

Despite Titus' realization, Josephus immediately uses the trope of his trusting, hopeful nature to cover another blunder. The tower in question falls quickly to battering (five days after the fall of the first ["third"] wall) and the breach is assaulted and carried. But Titus fails to control his troops who, instead of widening the breach, push into the narrow alleys of the city, where a counterattack drives them back out through the breach (5.331–41). This should not be surprising: the Jews have already shown a willingness to follow a tactical retreat with a counterattack, the assault troops would have lost their tactical cohesion in the rush to the breach, and there could hardly be more favorable ground for a prepared ambush. Yet Josephus spins it, quite ridiculously, as an act of treachery, pretending that Titus' failure to widen the breach was intended as an act of city-preserving generosity.[33]

---

30. That is, the general desire to depict him as preeminent in *clementia* trumps the urge to portray him as a superb warrior. Josephus prefers to draw a merciful and dimwitted Titus (Josephus rather disloyally slips in an aside noting that he himself did not fall for the ruse) in such situations, despite the fact that when Titus' character is not in the spotlight there is ample evidence of the ruthlessness of the siege.

31. 5.329. Trans. Williamson.

32. Similarly, Josephus celebrates Titus (5.31–6) for his unwillingness to shed the blood of his men—a lovely attribute for any commander but not a realistic one in a siege such as this. He is now, by dint of his righteous indignation, excused from future consideration of such a secondary concern.

33. This incident is similar in several ways to Caesar's assault on Gergovia, on which see pages 136–37. Caesar's excuse is an excess of combat motivation in his heroic but rash centurions while Josephus blames the defenders—but in both cases the commander was responsible.

Four days of fighting elapse before the Romans retake the breached second wall. This assault, barely described by Josephus, concludes the second stage of the siege. The morale within the city was still very high, as Josephus is compelled to admit. With the heart of the city and its most formidable defenses untouched after weeks of hard fighting, there is cause for confidence against future Roman assaults. Titus chose, then, to pause and savor his initial progress and "to afford the factions an interval for reflection" (5.342–8). What they are meant to reflect upon, it seems, is the fact that their relative success is absolutely limited: behind the preferred progression of this four-part siege, as in any siege, is the fact of blockade, of finite food resources. Even if the Romans continue to "fail" by progressing slowly, starvation will loom steadily larger, and it is never more than briefly absent from Josephus' narrative from this point on.

The halt in operations lasts four days, and accomplishes several things. It is, properly, the intimidation phase of the third stage of the siege—the progression has once again been partially reset. Despite the words that Josephus will shortly put into his own mouth, it seems incredible that Titus would at this point consider leniency toward any active resisters who might decide to surrender, yet it still behooves the Roman cause to heighten the sense of desperation and to try to draw out deserters from among the defenders.[34] The pause allowed the besieging army to rest their bodies, and it also provided a period of decompression to address the truncated siege progression. The Roman troops had put in several weeks of labor and they had lost men in the assaults and the "ambush" beyond the second wall. Frustration and rage were building, but neither true victory nor the release of a sack had followed the end of the second stage of the siege, although they had at least had the chance to smash up the captured parts of the city. To make up for the missing reward of the sack, Titus shrewdly took this time to stage an elaborate pay parade, which bolstered morale by rewarding those who had distinguished themselves during the first two stages of the siege and would have presented a depressing spectacle to the hungry and trapped fighters within. Sadly, Josephus is too distracted by the gleaming Roman arms to give us details of the awards and exhortations that took place.

---

34. Josephus makes this quite clear in an unusually devious manner. He gives us a glance into the collective mind of the rebels (5.353–5), who assume correctly that the Romans will no doubt kill them by torture (an assumption based on the previous crucifixion of one of their own, 5.289). Therefore, they conclude that they may as well go out fighting. A few sentences later (5.372–3), Josephus writes into his own speech hopeful hints at a mercy he had just declared to be impossible.

Unsurprisingly, intimidation does not result in surrender and so the third stage begins (5.356). Four new siege ramps are begun, each constructed by a single legion, and resisted by sallies and fire from large numbers of artillery pieces, with which the Jews have now had much practice. Two of the ramps are directed against the Antonia fortress bordering the northern end of the Temple Mount and two face a portion of the "first wall" protecting the upper city.

Josephus again chooses to set the scene for an assault phase only to emphasize the transition with a digression—in this case, a spate of dramatic speechifying. The political situation continues to complicate the siege as Titus remains interested in the efforts to elicit surrender or defection. Josephus is clearly aware that this is not standard Roman procedure, and gives Titus the plausible but suggestively vague excuse that "the preservation or destruction of the city vitally affected himself." He also tells us that Titus continued to "blend operations with negotiations." This is unusual, but if we accept that a new stage of the siege—against new walls as yet untouched by the battering ram—has begun, it still abides by the rules (5.356–419).

As the ramps mount toward the walls of the Antonia, Josephus acknowledges the brutality of a long siege. Whatever the possibility of negotiation in the early "third stage," the punitive morality of siege warfare reflects the lateness of the overall siege. Desperate civilians, caught between the besieging army and the factions in the city, are discovered searching the ravines outside the city walls for food—they fight back against the Roman patrols only because they think it too late to surrender. These wretches, noncombatants who seem to have had combatant status forced upon them in their capture, are then tortured in view of the walls; the Roman soldiers amusing themselves by crucifying the prisoners in different postures. We are told that up to 500 people a day are killed in this manner, and when this is used by the insurgent leaders to demonstrate the preferability of resisting to the death, Titus attempts to reinforce his claim that mercy is still available by merely mutilating some prisoners and sending them back into the city, alive (5.446–59).

This strains belief. It could not have been doubted that, at this stage, the siege would end with some group of hard-core insurgents fighting to the end—a negotiated surrender was essentially impossible. Moreover, how were non-fanatic Jerusalemites to defect from under the noses of the "zealots," especially when starving foragers caught by cavalry were treated as combatants and tortured to death? "Psychological warfare" was certainly going on, but it could not really have been aimed at chipping away non-combatant support. The torture and mutilation was intended to crush the hopes of the actual fighters. Moreover, despite one of the weaker invocations of Titus' *clementia* (in the form of "commiseration" with the tortured Jews), Josephus characteristically leaves enough of the purely military logic visible: it would be risky to release so many captives, and to guard them would occupy too many troops (5.450).

Another possible reason for the crucifixions should be considered. Titus, whose last reported orders were to press on with the ramps and to patrol the ravines, is being excused by Josephus not for ordering the crucifixions but for not stopping them. Moreover, the soldiers are crucifying the Jews in any position that takes their fancy: it seems possible that Titus was actually not responsible. He may have stood idly by, allowing the soldiers their grim entertainments. The torture and killing can be read, then, as another piece of the "missing" period of violent release—a stand-in for the sack that did not take place after the first two stages of the siege. It is more than likely that Josephus has allowed an indication of Titus' slipping control over the troops to slip into his narrative. A further breakdown of discipline into sack-like behavior—the disemboweling of defectors in search of swallowed coins—is not far off.[35] Josephus, carried away into his dramatic mode of lurid tales of atrocity and fate, informs us in passing that Titus' efforts to punish the incident came to nothing.[36]

Returning to the operations of the third stage of the siege, Josephus lightens the mood with a strange, almost comic, story. Antiochus Epiphanes, crown prince of Commagene, arrives, assesses the situation, and volunteers to assault the walls with his "Macedonians"—a band of specially selected soldiers. Titus smiles as he gives his permission—it seems we are meant to chuckle at the rueful words of these non-Macedonian Macedonians who, retreating wounded from their failed assault, reflect "that even genuine Macedonians . . . must have Alexander's luck" (5.460–5). Such bravado can't be denied, and their relatively bloodless repulse allows them (no deaths are noted, though many are wounded by arrows) to live and learn.

---

35. 5.551–2. There could hardly be a more graphic representation of the connection between violent conquest and cash value.

36. 5.553–61. The conflict of rhetorical/propagandistic themes is the surest way of finding truth in Josephus: this reflects very badly on merciful Titus, but it must be so, in subordination to the greater theme of the crimes of the rebels and the passing of ultimate power, by divine will, to Rome.

The arriving prince "expressed his surprise that a Roman army should hesitate to attack the ramparts," a comment which would directly challenge the honor of Titus were it not for the stereotyped nature of siege warfare: Antiochus does not understand that the direct-assault phase is long past. He is described as being both strong and brave, and his forthright bravado—he sees a wall and wants to charge it—is not entirely wrong but merely belated.

A period of seventeen days has elapsed between the end of the Roman pay parade and the completion of the two paired earthworks. Typically, we hear nothing of the experience of the Roman troops during this long stretch of dangerous labor. That they are crucifying prisoners for amusement speaks to their psychological state, but we are left to imagine the myriad woundings and backbreaking work. The emotional investment in the seventeen days of labor becomes clear, however, when the first really serious setback of the entire siege strikes.

The two ramps facing the Antonia had been undermined. The rebels waited until the towers were being dragged to the top of the ramp and then fired the mines. "The Romans were in consternation at this sudden catastrophe and dispirited by the enemy's ingenuity; moreover, coming at the moment when they imagined victory within their grasp, the casualty damped their hopes of ultimate success" (5.472). This reference to "ultimate success" is telling: Roman morale was very low. This is further demonstrated two days later when three Jews sally and succeed in burning the towers that have begun to batter the "first wall." Then a general sally routs the troops protecting the engines and is stopped only by a desperate stand at the ramparts of the Roman camp. The excuse that these three heroic Jewish fighters were acting as crazed berserkers—they are called the "most daring" and "most terrifying" fighters of the entire war—only emphasizes the moral advantage possessed by the defenders at this stage. This is a serious crisis, a fact that Josephus emphasizes by nearly repeating himself: "The Romans, their earthworks demolished, were deeply demoralized, having lost in one hour the fruit of their long labor, and many despaired of ever carrying the town with conventional siege engines" (5.473–90).

Titus responds to the situation by calling another council of war. Josephus reminds us of the basics of the siege schema by presenting the Roman leaders as being of three minds: the aggressive are for an all-out assault on the walls, the middle group for a return to engineered assault, and the more cautious for a retreat to blockade. This party invokes the trope of the desperate defense: "there was no contending with desperate men whose prayer was to fall by the sword, and for whom, if that was denied them, a harder fate was in store" (5.491–501).[37] The debate frames Titus' next decision as the commander of the siege. The casualties inherent in a direct assault against such highly motivated defenders (it is unclear how a mass assault on such formidable fortifications would be carried out—presumably with many ladders) would be very high, but Roman prestige and the possible moral effects of conceding tactical defeat rule out relaxing into a blockade.[38]

This council may well have taken place, although the non-Latinate Judean courtier would have either been excluded or understood little, and is thus depending upon his Roman sources. It is also perfectly possible that Titus talked with his senior commanders every night (who would he dine with, if not the only other high-ranking Romans in the vicinity?) and Josephus is merely creating a formal war council when he wishes one. In either case, this recap of the facts of the siege is for the benefit of the reader. As for the three possible courses of action, the end result is that the only one that had been pursued so far—a full, heavily engineered siege—was continued, despite its recent failure and the daunting psychological and physical difficulties of reconstructing the earthworks. Titus also made the very belated decision to build lines of circumvallation. This tells us three things. First, that, as Titus is made to admit openly, the moral and prestige value of the eventual victory is depreciating with time—"rapidity was essential to renown." Second, that, despite the horrors of famine already described, significant amounts of food were being smuggled into the city and the fighters, at least, were still healthy. Finally, that the issue of the defenders' desperation was, even at this late stage, still subject to manipulation.

Titus wishes to build the wall so that "the Jews would then either in utter despair of salvation surrender the city, or, wasted by famine, fall an easy prey" (5.500). The Jews' courage and the success of their fanatical fighting style are by now well established, and there could hardly have been hope that starvation would achieve capitulation within a time frame that

---

37. See chapter 3, note 62.
38. The context makes it fairly clear that a blockade would have succeeded if it had been prosecuted from the beginning, but honor clearly demanded a continuation of operations. To resort to a blockade and hope for surrender after the work already done would be humiliating—in Josephus' milder obfuscation, total inactivity would be "undignified"; see 3.156.

would be acceptably "renowned"—especially given that the fighters, a minority of the trapped population, could continue to monopolize the available food stores. This move, then, is a forceful message aimed at a deeper level of Jewish morale. They are confident and they know that they will stay the course both because they are committed to defend their holy city and because the only likely choices are victory or a painful death. Nevertheless, even the committed rebel, if he stops short of true fanaticism, would prefer victory to death. Rome's failure to properly contain the city earlier in the siege can now at least be turned to some moral value—and the message is more forceful for being belated. Rome, too, is committed to victory.[39] Titus underscores this commitment by theatrically insisting on taking the first night watch of the renewed siege.

The wall was built in the impressively short (i.e., barely credible) span of three days, and Josephus gives an idealized (but essentially accurate) account of the roles that emulation, leadership, and competitive rivalry played in stimulating the construction work.[40] It seems possible that the wall did effect an immediate change in morale. Josephus claims that hunger amongst the fighters (a problem inconsistent with the newness of the wall and the long run of fighting still remaining) has brought a temporary end to the sallies, while the Romans were well supplied and infused with confidence, which they showed by taunting the starving Jews on the walls with displays of food. Despite the scarcity of wood, four large new earthworks were begun, all facing the Antonia fortress. Titus toured the works, exhorting his men (5.502–26).

The centrality of this episode in the narrative of the siege is signaled once again by a shift in both subject and tone. Although Josephus has failed to explain why these new works will be more effective, he has nevertheless introduced the final major engineering work of the siege: the new ramps will permit the crucial assault of the Antonia, and thus, the temple. The climactic scene is set, so Josephus launches into a long digression, devoting the rest of book five to horror stories and propaganda, leaving the actual siege operations suspended in proper cliffhanger fashion.

When book six begins, the ramps have been completed and Josephus melodramatically sketches the moral situation. The high pitch of despera-

---

39. Davies (2006), 21, accuses Josephus of drawing "a casuistic distinction between this work of containment and a 'passive' blockade," but this charge fails to take account of the moral impact of siege works.

40. See Goldsworthy (1999), 202.

tion among the remaining Jewish fighters shows the "ratcheting" effect of the siege progression: they have become death-courting fanatics—a type Josephus plays for its shocking novelty, though it has since become familiar—"upbraiding the Deity . . . for His tardiness in punishing them; for it was no hope of victory but despair of escape which now nerved them to the battle" (6.4). This desperation is matched by Roman anticipation, and there is agreement that the crucial stage of the siege has been reached.

> The completion of the earthworks proved, to the Romans no less than to the Jews, a source of apprehension. For, while the latter thought that, should they fail to burn these also, the city would be taken, the Romans feared that they would never take it, should these embankments too be destroyed. For there was a dearth of materials, and the soldiers' bodies were now sinking beneath their toils, and their minds under a succession of reverses. (6.9–11)

Josephus goes on to frankly acknowledge that the pressure on Roman morale stems from the resilience of the Jewish defense. Both the rationally considered military successes of the Jews—their victorious sallies and their superior daring—and the irrational aspects of their worldview add to their morale. The Romans are morally outflanked: "They fancied the impetuosity of these men to be irresistible and their combat motivation (*euthumia*) in distress invincible" (6.13–14).

As is often the case in Josephus, this is a setup. This is not the moment of Jewish victory but, of course, the sticking point for the Roman soldiers— the moment when Roman morale reaches their adversaries' and pulls ahead. The inevitable sally upon the new works comes, and is defeated. The Jews are uncharacteristically hesitant and "abnormally spiritless." They are unable to charge together but instead sally out in small groups that are easily turned aside: "some sped back, before coming to close quarters, dismayed by the admirable order and serried ranks of their antagonists, others only when pierced by the points of the javelins." Highly motivated fighters are becoming scarce, and those serried ranks—a Roman force that does not flinch and so, by retaining its cohesion, presents a solid front to its scattered assailants—indicates a profound shift in morale (6.15–22).

The siege now moves with greater momentum into the heavy assault phase. A combination of battering, the ill effects of continued Jewish undermining of the assault ramps, and the simpler technique of prying at wall stones by Roman soldiers working under the cover of a *testudo* formation weakened the wall of the Antonia enough to cause a partial collapse. But the defenders had had time to prepare for this problem by building a makeshift wall behind the breach, and thus we have a moral reversal: the Jews are heartened and the Romans discouraged. More significantly, the breach focuses operations too closely for a general assault to succeed. The breach must be assaulted, but the wall behind it cannot be approached by the siege towers, so any soldiers who survive the breach would have to assault the new wall without covering fire (6.23–32).

This is a potential climax of the third stage, yet "still, none ventured to mount; for manifest destruction awaited the first assailants." None ventured: leaders are needed, and none volunteer. Any unit would balk at being ordered to such a deadly task, but if a few fast, aggressive volunteers stormed the position, many would die while some, perhaps, might take the wall. Josephus understands the significance of this failure of motivation, and he immediately reports Titus' attempt to raise morale, to elicit "forgetfulness of danger . . . even contempt of death" (6.32–3).

The ensuing exhortation pointedly addresses the likelihood of death for the assault leaders. The solutions proposed in the formal speech that Josephus composes here for Titus are an excellent résumé of the array of awards that the Roman army used to elicit such operationally essential, near-suicidal behavior.[41] The idea of the gloriousness of death in battle is planted and then left in the background while Titus emphasizes a more appealing aspect of the assault: that it is a rare opportunity to achieve renown, to be recognized for personal heroism, and to restore the reputation of the army. Titus cites evidence for divine favor of the Roman cause: to show death-defying morale here is to prove the Romans unbeaten by an inferior and to be loyal to the beneficence of their "divine ally." But the exhortation, despite the fact that its stated purpose was to inspire great deeds from the attacking troops, now moves to spur the assault by dwelling on the negative side of this conclusion. Shame and disgrace are invoked instead of glory. For Romans, the natural conquerors of all, to sit idly by while "famine and fortune" do their work for them is ignominious. While Josephus is clearly getting carried away with his rhetorical invention here, the speech's dependence on organizational pride is striking. That men would choose near-certain death in accomplishing a task that hunger will do for them in

---

41. See also 1.349–51 and 2.535 for earlier assaults by "picked men" and volunteers.

a few weeks, largely in order to avenge the wounds to their honor, would indicate a very high degree of pride in Rome and, perhaps, the individual units (6.33–44).

The exhortation next passes to an irritating paralepsis in which Titus "refrains" at great length from discussing the doctrine "that souls released from the flesh by the sword on the battlefield are hospitably welcomed by that purest of elements, the ether, and placed among the stars" (6.46–7). Last but not least, Titus rather limpingly opines that the assault might not mean certain death after all, but that a spirited charge might result in a moral rout, a bloodless victory over Jewish cowardice. This would be a reasonable hope in the first charge of an open-field battle or in a testing assault against a shaky opponent, but it is not credible here, given the fortifications and the moral history of the siege. The speech finishes with a pointed promise of reward and promotion to the surviving volunteers (6.53).

Moving glibly from the speech to the ensuing high-drama episode, Josephus, perhaps aware that his pseudo-philosophical congeries is not a convincing imitation of an actual Roman combat exhortation, does not mind telling us that the harangue was basically unsuccessful: only a dozen men volunteer. Led by the heroic Sabinus, this tiny group charges, taking casualties from rocks and missiles, but managing to gain the summit of the rubble wall, routing its defenders. There Sabinus falls and is dispatched by the returning defenders. Some of his compatriots retreat with wounds, and two days elapse before the next attempt on the Antonia (6.54–67). Reading between the lines of this little episode, two facts become clear. First, the only method of assaulting these defenses that presents itself to Titus is the simple infantry charge. Second, Titus is having great trouble eliciting volunteers: a dozen men, followed by two days of inactivity, indicates an army made up of men now profoundly unwilling to give their lives for the cause.

Another volunteer assault on the second night is, however, successful.[42] This success has much to do with obtaining surprise and thus causing panic among the defenders, but also seems attributable to the fact that the main forces of the army are quick to exploit the initial success of the volunteer party. This is the positive side of Titus' imperfect control over his troops: a few highly motivated individuals seized an opportunity and acted.[43] There follows a dense, impressionistic account of a terrible and con-

---

42. The volunteer character is confirmed both by the absence of ranking officers and by the presence of members of different units in the (small) group.

43. 6.68–70. The role played in this assault by a trumpeter is a familiar stratagem; see

fused night battle: Jewish desperation staves off the Roman attack, but at the end of the night the Antonia remains in Roman hands. Josephus' notice that the Roman forces failed to take the temple because they couldn't bring up their full attacking strength emphasizes that the avenue of approach was too narrow to permit a forceful general assault. While this reminds us of the necessity of the volunteer storming tactics that opened the way over the collapsed wall of the Antonia, it is also a weak excuse, since the narrow frontage of the temple's northern border was not going to get any wider, and was in any case much broader than the breaches made in previous walls.

Josephus tacks on to a short description of the main fight a longer tale of exemplary Roman gallantry, featuring a Bithynian centurion called Julianus, and he also mentions Jews who distinguished themselves, presumably during the latter part of the engagement when the return of daylight allowed such gallantry to be distinguished. These stories conceal the significance of this assault. Though begun by a mere two dozen men, the first successful storming of a major fortification without the benefit of artillery or engines has taken place, and the Romans now occupy the high ground within a few feet of the temple walls. This volunteer, small-unit action is the best candidate we have for the single turning point in the siege.

Titus immediately orders an engineered approach from the Antonia to the temple, although inevitable skirmishing between adversaries now holding positions in close proximity and at the same level precludes the sort of pause and new beginning that characterizes a truly new phase of operations—stage three of the siege continues.[44]

---

page 70. See also Goldsworthy (1999), 208; Gilliver (2007), 154. A strikingly similar opportunistic assault during the siege of the Syrian town of Kafartab (Kfar Tab) in 1155 is described by Usama Ibn Munqidh (2008), 86: During a noon lull in the fighting, "an infantryman from our army went out all alone, armed with his sword and shield. He marched up to the wall of the tower that had fallen, whose sides had become like the steps of a stairway, and climbed up until he reached its highest point." This man is wounded, but "about ten" men, apparently without orders or officers, who chose to follow him succeeded in taking the objective.

44. Josephus feels the need to establish such a pause, however, so he regales us with his own act of dubious heroism, that speech to the rebels about the necessity of avoiding the desecration of the temple. This is followed, Josephus tell us, by desertions of upper-class Jews, the sending away and returning of the deserters, their imploring appearance before the walls, and a final appeal of Titus to the "brigands" (6.96–128). Josephus slips, though, making it clear that the fighting was more or less continuous: he describes heaps of dead in the temple court during his decrying of the rebels' decision to emplace artillery over the temple gates. If there were desertions at this stage, they must have come from the upper

The eventual assault on the temple consists of an organized reprise of the successful storming of the Antonia. Titus arranges for picked men, thirty from each century, to launch a surprise attack at night: this is a gamble, an unusual move this late in the progression.[45] Josephus describes Titus arming to join the assault only to be restrained by his generals, who insist that he save himself—and fulfill his motivational role as witness-in-chief: "Caesar yielded, telling his men that his sole reason for remaining behind was that he might judge of their gallantry, so that none of the brave might go unnoticed and unrewarded."[46] The assault fails, due to the vigilance of the Jewish guards, and degenerates into a confused scrum. Josephus describes the battle as a contest of the carrot and the stick: the Romans are motivated by Titus' approving gaze and the hope of reward and promotion, while the Jews, desperate for themselves and their temple, fear the rebel leaders. It was, writes Josephus, "like a battle on the stage, for nothing throughout the engagement escaped the eyes of Titus or of those around him" (6.142–6). Moonlit visibility notwithstanding, Josephus describes a crucial aspect of the massive front-fighting requirements of such a siege. Semi-suicidal though it may be to lead a charge, a man doing so with his commander looking on will not go unrewarded, should he succeed. Given the fact that Josephus provides notable names of Jewish heroes but mentions no Romans, we might infer that Titus' gaze was unavailing.

But Titus had hedged his bets, ordering the construction of four broad ramps to approach the temple, which are completed after seven days of labor. Josephus fills the interval with tales of desperate Jewish sallies, another single combat, and a continuing drama of skirmish and stratagem

---

city, where most of the civilians remained, and not from the immediate precincts of the temple, where the assault was focused.

45. Thirty men from every century in the army would yield far too large a force for a surprise assault on the relatively small frontage of the temple's northern end. Of course, several thousand men could have been selected to comprise both the initial assault force and troops designated to exploit any breakthrough. Thus the existence of this very large "picked" force indicates something quite different from the small numbers of heroic volunteers featured earlier in the siege: that perhaps only around half of the troops (thirty men from centuries that probably did not number more than sixty at this stage of the war) are still trusted to fight.

46. 6.132–5. This perfect little commander-as-witness vignette makes perfect sense here—alas, then, that this is a night attack under a waning moon (the date was close to the 23rd of Panemos/Tammuz), aimed at the far side of the fortifications. Perhaps there were large fires.

along the frontage of the temple portico near the Antonia (6.149–89). Then, marking the new stage of operations with a lengthy description of the mounting miseries of famine inside the walls (culminating in a famous incident of maternal cannibalism), heavy assaults resume. Two large rams are brought up two of the new ramps. Attempts to undermine the temple wall with hand-tools fail, and an assault by escalade, presumably covered by fire from the ram towers, is violently repulsed. Yet we can be sure that the next assault will succeed, for Josephus interrupts the narrative to describe (or fabricate) another council of war, solely, it seems, in order to absolve Titus of any responsibility for the destruction of the temple (6.222–43).

Again, like an architect overfond of ornament who nevertheless expresses the major load-bearing elements of his building, Josephus has indicated a major transition in the siege progression despite his high dramatic mode. Rams have only just been brought into play, and at the council Titus is urged to "enforce the laws of war" and destroy the temple (6.239). Josephus cannot be trusted anywhere near the temple, but we can rest assured that, even if the generals and Titus deliberated, the exhausted and wounded legions were fully prepared to enforce the "laws," which dictated that the city be put to the sack. This is a skillful setup by Josephus: Titus has his alibi, and when, shortly after, the temple is set alight by his soldiers, Titus can try to fight the flames. Josephus is consistent: whenever he conceals Titus' likely intention of destroying the temple, he reveals his inability to control his troops.

Afterwards, the alibi having served its purpose, Titus becomes a stickler for the laws of war. He proclaims to a few starving priests belatedly seeking to surrender that "the time for pardon had for them gone by." Yet Josephus frankly tells us that they really must be killed because their temple has been destroyed, rather than to fulfill the "laws" attending the assault upon it. Titus will remind a group of rebels, seeking terms even after the execution of the priests, that "I brought my engines against your walls; my soldiers, thirsting for your blood, I invariably restrained." But a Roman general deep into a siege would not have felt the need for the last three words—this was, truly, "in deliberate forgetfulness of the laws of war." Titus knew that the sack had been, for some time now, completely unavoidable (6.322–46).

The main temple courtyard is stormed, a firebrand is thrown into the sanctuary, and the temple begins to burn. Josephus' various ulterior motives have now briefly come together in such a way as to admit the unvarnished truth: Titus finds himself "unable to restrain the impetuosity of his frenzied soldiers." The Roman army, releasing the pent-up fury caused by months of labor, suffering, combat, and casualties, is "further stimulated by hope of plunder." They sack the temple and its precincts, alternating between killing and stripping the temple of its fittings.[47]

There was yet a fourth stage of the siege, a brutal anticlimax, which, despite the extremity of the situation, still sketched its way through some of the earlier stages of the siege progression. Tens of thousands of Jews remain in the upper city, and there is a brief intimidation-phase negotiation. But when the remaining Jewish leaders attempt to win favorable terms Titus becomes angry—they are refusing to accept the consequences of their actions in having persisted in the siege. The temple had been destroyed, and he was not inclined to offer terms to the last desperate holdouts of a long and terrible siege, even if they were, technically, in possession of an unassaulted position. Instead, he declared the final end of his clemency, announcing that "all his actions henceforth would be governed by the laws of war. He then gave his troops permission to burn and sack the (upper) city." This declaration can only be explained either as a redundancy interpolated by Josephus in a particularly awkward and ex post facto attempt to demonstrate Titus' reluctance to damage Jerusalem, or as a formality of the reset siege progression—the pre-assault phase of the fourth stage of the siege is declared to be over. The defenders have refused parley and the assault begins (6.328–53).

So, for the last time, siege ramps are raised. Wood is collected with great difficulty, and the construction consumes eighteen days of labor. We

---

47. 6.244–64. A portion of Titus' bodyguard is detailed to protect the sanctuary, "but their respect for Caesar and their fear of the officer who was endeavoring to check them were overpowered by their rage, their hatred of the Jews, and a lust for battle more unruly still." Titus' intentions regarding the temple at this stage are still much discussed; see, e.g., Barnes (2005); Rives (2005). It is an interesting question, but only an academic one. Rives, 148, is right in pointing out that the decision to storm the temple precincts "made at least its partial destruction inevitable." Josephus also reports that the legionaries set up their standards in the temple court and sacrificed to them (6.316), an act of sacrilege (or religious triumphalism) which hardly speaks to any respect for the temple. Technically, such behavior, at least in the conservative tradition of Polybius (5.9), was contrary to the laws of war, and it is possible that Titus did not intend to completely ruin the temple. But given the nature of the siege there is little need for additional speculation: it would inevitably be plundered, and any fire would be almost impossible to contain. See also chapter 8.

learn that Titus went back on his word and permitted some defectors to live—a claim not too difficult to accept, especially since Josephus seems to share his patron's exhaustion and does not bother to make much of it. Yet the more important reason for clemency is probably that the soldiers "have had their fill of killing and hoped to profit" by selling survivors as slaves. Not long after the cathartic and horrible sack of the temple, the profit urge reconquers the lust for violence in the volatile blend of the plunderer's motivation (6.383).

The engines were once again brought up the ramps, and the upper city was stormed. In the assault on the upper city the defenders' morale finally broke—most of the best fighters were dead and the rest were starving—and they abandoned their defenses. Josephus's exaggerated claim that the towers of the upper city's citadel were impregnable makes it clear that there was, at long last, a collapse in morale that speeded the last stages of the Roman assault. The remaining defenders fled, seeking to save themselves in the confusion, and the last sack began: "Pouring into the alleys, sword in hand, they massacred indiscriminately all whom they met, and burnt the houses with all who had taken refuge within" (6.374–404).

SEVEN

SIEGE WARFARE IN AMMIANUS MARCELLINUS

For three centuries after Josephus we have no informed, detailed narratives of Roman sieges. Rome made few new conquests, so fewer sieges took place—but it is the historian we lack more than the history. The early books of Ammianus Marcellinus, who knew siege warfare and wrote gripping history, do not survive, and so the second and third centuries can contribute little to our understanding.[1] But we do have the portions which cover his own turbulent time, specifically the years 353–378 CE. Much of this history involves the conflict between Rome and Persia, which hinged on the possession of a few border cities, some of which were repeatedly besieged. Ammianus describes seven sieges, three of which are examined here in some depth: the Persian siege of Roman-held Amida in 359, and the Roman sieges of Pirisabora and Maiozamalcha in 363.

Three centuries brought many changes to the Roman world, and Ammianus describes a Roman army outwardly much different from the force commanded by Titus. Yet Ammianus chose to emphasize the continuities,

---

1. The only extended narrative of a contemporary siege from this period is Herodian's tactically unavailing account of the siege of Aquileia in 238; Cassius Dio's account of Hatra (76.12) is brief and problematic. A mention in Zosimus of the siege of Cremna in 278 is used in the remarkable reconstructed archaeological narrative of Mitchell (1995). There is also the early second century siege narrative on Trajan's column and the latterly famous siege of Dura-Europos (see James, 2004) dates from the third century, but no accompanying writings survive.

referring to the army in anachronistic terms and placing the deeds and heroes of his history in the context of an unbroken Roman martial tradition stretching back over a millennium.[2] I will do the same. Despite the differences in army organization, and despite the changes in Roman society, the basic technological and tactical structures of siege warfare had hardly changed between Caesar and Ammianus, and the progression remained essentially identical.[3] Just as the difficult, four-stage siege of Jerusalem tested its flexibility, the somewhat more ritualized and more diplomatically constrained sieges described in Ammianus test the boundaries of the cruel "laws" of siege warfare, which were less often followed. Intimidation looms larger in Ammianus' accounts, yet the task of finding sufficient volunteer assault leaders remains central to success. We can also find more evidence for the idea that the cultural construction of siege warfare was understood by both sides by examining the very similar practice of the Persian Empire—regardless of who was besieger and who besieged, both sides shared the same expectations. The fourth century, then, strengthens the notion of a common Roman siege progression, while also demonstrating the diversity of practice that permitted its adaptation to a variety of physical and cultural situations.

SIEGE WARFARE IN THE FOURTH CENTURY

Technological changes between the first and fourth centuries were few.[4] The cities of Mesopotamia, though, often possessed strong lines of masonry defenses focused on stone towers, their fortifications resembling Jerusalem more than the low, battery-resistant fortifications of the Gauls.

---

2. See, for example, 17.13.25, 25.3.13, 28.3.9.

3. The weapons-system changes between the mid-fourth-century Roman army and the sixth-century army described by Procopius were much greater than those between Caesar and Ammianus. The differences in the handling of siege conventions, which are discussed later, were the product not of technological changes but rather of the particular cultural/strategic situation of Roman-Persian border warfare.

4. See Hölscher (2006), 56, on terminological consistency. Mining was more common in the East, as was the diversion of rivers in order to weaken the foundations of fortifications—but this was a Mesopotamian specialty of long standing. Marsden (1969), 198; (1971), 249ff., reflects the older assumptions about late antiquity when he remarks that Roman artillery may have actually maintained its quality. In fact, the new heavy, single-armed "onager" (technologically simpler but more effective in some situations—see Rance 2007, 362) may indicate, as Ammianus also seems to, that artillery was more important than it had been. Lander (1984), 258–59, lays out the archaeological evidence for the defensive use of onagers.

The Roman army looked very different than it had under the principate, and it used different terminology for many units and positions. More importantly, and it was divided into field armies (*comitatenses*) and less mobile border troops (*limitanei*), and a "legion" now numbered only around a thousand men.[5]

Certain elements of Roman discipline did not survive the traumatic third century: the marching camp was no longer *de rigueur*, and close reading of Ammianus suggests that field engineering had grown sloppy. The use of circumvallation as a siege tactic decreased accordingly.[6] These are not insignificant changes, but Ammianus' fourth century must be read as proudly and eternally Roman, with perfect ignorance of the coming loss of power and knowledge. His sieges were contested by the professional soldiers of the field army, fighting with the same calculations of risk and reward, death and glory as their institutional-cultural forefathers.

The sieges described by Ammianus were different from those of Caesar and Josephus—and in their strategic context generally more similar to Polybius and Livy—in that they involved neither the conquest of "uncivilized" tribes nor the suppression of revolt among strongly identified, non-Roman peoples. Northern Mesopotamia was a borderland, its cities composed of a heterogeneous mix of people and nationalities, all long accustomed to the imperial back-and-forth between Persia and Rome. Later, when Julian besieged several places in the Mesopotamian heartland,

---

5. See Nicasie (1998), 16–22, 43–74; Elton (1996), 88–101. Armies were generally smaller, which would make general assaults less likely to succeed. Yet, *pace* Lendon (2005), 308, we need not imagine that "the army of the fourth century needed to be treasured" at all times. As we will see, highly risky assaults were still launched when sieges progressed far enough to render them unavoidable.

6. Gilliver (1999), 149; Vegetius 4.28. Ammianus uses *circumvallo* four times, but only twice of the actions of a besieging force. Both instances (17.2.2; 18.6.10) describe a loose, blockade-like action, and it is unclear what works were constructed—literal circumvallation seems very doubtful. This, too, can be seen as evidence for a "decline in intensity," yet huge ramps were still constructed and massive assaults still launched, and the comparatively frequent attempts to breach by ramming (see 23.4.9) hardly lack for intensity. Besides, there is ample reason to suspect that fewer true circumvallations indicates a rational preference for less exhausting methods of blockading and intimidating the enemy. See McCotter (1995), 430ff for a somewhat convoluted discussion of the nature of late antique/Byzantine siege warfare. See also Rance (2007), 360; Davies (2006), 18, 66. Suffice it to say that the evidence is vague enough to support whatever decline/continuity narrative a historian might already be inclined to, and that generalization about late antiquity yields little actionable intelligence, while consideration of the immediate strategic and operational context of a siege often casts light on the "departures" from earlier practice. This is another good reason to examine the few good narratives on their own terms.

he could hope neither to crush resistance with one successful siege nor to separate his enemies—each operation was subordinated to the success of the larger expedition against Persia, and Persia's own version of Fabian strategy (with thirst and mounted archers supplementing the classic model) won a decisive victory. Every siege threatened a sack, but the larger context lacked the same desperation: two empires, despite persistent internal problems and intermittent incursions on their farthest frontiers, repeatedly fought for local advantage and royal bragging rights. The very fact that this endemic warfare hinged on the possession of cities meant that each siege was less the culmination of a campaign than a play for future advantage.

For these reasons, and because of the technological equilibrium of the warring parties, the intimidation and negotiation phases were more significant than hitherto. There seem to have been no major differences between Roman and Persian fortifications, and, despite the proliferation of siege engines, both sides depended primarily on two basic techniques. These were the creation of a breach—usually by ramming—and assault under cover of missile fire.[7] When it came to dismounted archery and the use of slings, artillery, and battering rams, there was no appreciable difference in the military capabilities of Rome and Sassanian Persia.[8] The combination of familiarity and equality meant that the sieges between Rome and Persia were finely calibrated: impregnable fortresses were recognized as such and bypassed, and indefensible places were abandoned before the enemy arrived (24.2.2, 24.4.1). Moving past the preliminary phases of a siege, the progression was predictable. Testing or lightly supported assaults were few. Whatever skirmishing, intimidation, or stealthy assaults took place did so in the context of the laborious buildup to a heavy assault.

AMMIANUS AS A MILITARY HISTORIAN

Ammianus Marcellinus has made great strides over the last few decades. Once scorned for his flamboyant style or simply overlooked, he is now

---

7. The Romans even used a famous old Persian ram (20.11.11). The siege engines in Ammianus have attracted a great deal of scholarly attention, in part because Ammianus makes much of them, digresses about them, and contradicts his own descriptions. His fascination is neither unusual (see page 3) nor does it detract from his portrayal of morale and motivation. For the digression on siege machines, see note 41; on the ram and, more generally, on our fascination with ancient "superweapons," see Whitehead (2010), 94.

8. This (common) assessment of Sassanian siege proficiency seems to rest almost entirely on the evidence in Ammianus and from Dura, which is clear enough—but it is less clear why, as is often assumed, this prowess should necessarily indicate a marked improvement of Sassanian over Parthian capabilities. See James (2004), 16.

widely recognized as one of the great classical historians. After a debate over his veracity and his loyalty to the genre of history, recent work on Ammianus, even as much of it tries to cope with his embroidering of the narrative, accepts the essential accuracy of his account—albeit with various caveats.[9]

Ammianus, calling himself "a onetime soldier and a Greek" (31.16.9), was a native of the Roman East, as well as an upper-class Roman who chose to write in Latin. We know that he served in the Roman army during much of the period described in the surviving books of his histories, but little else.[10]

Ammianus presents the reader with a variety of seemingly contradictory authorial identities: he can write in the fashion of a Greek universal historian, taking a long and detached view of events, yet he also echoes the Roman annalistic tradition. He enjoyed citing Homer and celebrated the Hellenism of the emperor Julian, but he also sought to demonstrate the factual basis of his work, struggling to reach the standards of the Latin historians that preceded him.[11] With regards to siege warfare, he has received high marks,[12] and he wrote cogent and instructive military narratives: "for all the selection of detail and the rhetorical colouring that have seemed to compromise his accuracy, Ammianus never leaves unexplained the specific character of a battle or the strategy of a campaign, even though he may not always be so clear as to its purpose."[13] But, given his prose style, can we rely on Ammianus' descriptions of actual combat?

Ammianus' battles are indeed impressionistic—attending to the sights and sounds of combat rather than describing tactics. He gives us the cries of the fighters, the clashing of arms and the whirring of missiles, as well as the glint of sunlit armor and the terrifying sight of elephants

---

9. For Ammianus generally, see Matthews (1989); Drijvers and Hunt (1999), 1–11; with additional bibliography in Lenski (2007), note 5; and Sabbah (1978). See also Barnes (1998), generally *contra* Matthews, and Kelly (2008).

10. Matthews (1989), 6–17.

11. Ammianus tells us that he wrote of things *visa vel lecta;* that is, he combined reading and autopsy. Naturally the history that was personally experienced by Ammianus has a very different tone from the more concise reports of far-off political events. This paragraph, and my understanding of Ammianus in general, follows Matthews, who writes, (1989), 5, that Ammianus "is in many respects the most self-revealing of ancient historians."

12. Demonstrated by Crump (1975), but see Matthews (1989), 521, n12.

13. Matthews (1989), 286. Ammianus himself (26.1.1) is intelligently defensive about the steps he has taken to streamline his narrative.

on the rampage.[14] Indeed, his writing is highly "cinematic": while the proliferation of circumstantial details and the absence of a sequence of clearly emplotted events result in a sort of panoramic view, Ammianus is also a master of the "close-up." As we will see, he tends to punctuate the narrative with accounts of the great deeds of particular combatants. This combination of techniques has frustrated many commentators, but it is a fundamentally appropriate—that is to say, accurate—way of writing about ancient warfare.[15]

In fact, Ammianus can be seen as an early practitioner of the "Face of Battle" style.[16] This is perhaps frustrating in accounts of running battles, where it can be difficult to tease out a tidy tactical sequence. But sieges are a different matter—there his readers have their understanding of the siege progression to structure the account.[17] When the assaults do come, the vivid language conveys the emotional experience of morale, representing the tactical consequences of moral and psychological events. Yet the old charge that Ammianus' flowery and allusive style obscures our understand-

---

14. E.g., 24.6.8, 25.1.18, 28.5.3, 29.5.15, 29.5.38, 31.7.2, 31.13.1.

15. The important recent book by Gavin Kelly (2008) makes a compelling case for skepticism regarding Ammianus' own emphasis on autopsy by focusing rather on his use of allusion—which is opposed (although not diametrically) to the elements of the text that assert authenticity based on the personal experience of the author. Kelly provides a detailed discussion of long-recognized Ammianian biases as well as a careful reconsideration of the effect of literary technique on historical veracity (see, e.g., 64–65, which effectively rebuts the idea that Ammianus is outside of historical convention while persisting in recognizing the unusual extent of memoir-like material in a large-scale history). Kelly's arguments do not, however, threaten the approach to siege narratives taken here. Although Ammianus is writing history—which is literature—in a rather "literary" way, his history still belongs in what is in the end a sturdily constructed (and habitually allusive) genre. Even if the combat scenes which he himself witnessed are at the same time visually impressionistic and draw heavily upon his reading about war, they can still claim to be true in a historical sense. In any event, we have no better way to parse our unsatisfactory evidence of chaotic events into a more convincing truth: reading Ammianus alongside Paul Fussell or Tim O'Brien would be a different project altogether.

16. Ammianus' resemblance to Keegan, a similarity first remarked upon by Matthews (1989), 521, n1, is treated at length by Kagan (2006), 22–39. Kagan is critical of this resemblance, remarking that Ammianus' "face of battle-style narrative technique limits the abilities of military historians to investigate" his battles. Alternatively, his exuberant literary style—which incidentally conveys truths of historical experience—may work, perhaps even intentionally, to resist invasively rigid historical analysis.

17. Kagan (2006), 38, argues that Ammianus' siege narratives "do not . . . indicate much about the conduct of the siege at the tactical level." This is true; but Ammianus provides the information necessary to reconstruct the siege progression, and the progression informs the tactical course of the siege.

ing of his combat narratives keeps cropping up. This is more than an issue of literary taste—it is about "the modern reader's expectations of learning anything" about warfare.[18] Yet to lower these expectations after rejecting information because of the style in which it is presented would seem to be a self-inflicted interpretive limitation. Ammianus' fevered descriptions of the battlefield neither obscure nor explain either tactical facts or psychological insights—yet they describe battle. When Ammianus writes of battle as being "like a theatrical performance," he is reaching for images that will help the reader understand the surreal experience of close combat. There are no historical grounds for claiming that Caesar's terse prose possesses greater "credibility" than Ammianus' overheated similes.[19]

Ammianus has also been chided for making authorial decisions "to the detriment of what he must have known as an active soldier."[20] Indeed, Ammianus' presence in his own history is, along with his portrayal of Emperor Julian, the area of scholarly concern that is most relevant to the present examination of his siege accounts. There has been a lively debate about what Ammianus' military specialty may have been,[21] but this must not obscure the important fact of his intimate knowledge of warfare.

> He had been in battles, had fought for his life, had seen people killed and had undoubtedly killed some himself, not at a distance but hand to hand ... He is better qualified than many ancient historians to convey not only the strategic and tactical shape of war and battles, but a sense of what it was actually like to take part in them.[22]

---

18. Harris (2006), 314–16. Ironically, Harris' criticism of Ammianus as a military source is far more extreme than Kagan's, yet he concludes that this is in part because Ammianus takes "very much the view from the command post."
19. 16.12.57. Recall Josephus, *BJ* 6.142
20. Harris (2006), 314.
21. Variously an artillerist, cavalryman, logistics specialist, or intelligence officer; see Kelly (2008), 125–27 for a full rundown of scholarly guesswork. Matthews (1989), 301–3, concludes that Ammianus had wide experience of warfare and was not a specialist. His membership in the *protectores domestici,* however, should not be used to hint at specialized training—to write that the *protectores* were "not line officers" (Kagan 2006, 25) or were "staff colleges" (Elton 1996, 101) lures nonspecialist military historians into indulging in anachronistic comparisons—there were no formally separate "staff officers" in the Roman world.
22. Matthews (1989), 287–88; see also Kelly (2008), especially chapters 2 and 3.

More than Caesar or Josephus, Ammianus seeks to show his readers what an active soldier knew and felt in combat.

Ammianus fought at the siege of Amida, which will be discussed here at length; he was also either with the Roman army throughout the siege-intensive Persian campaign of Julian or very well informed by his compatriots about its sieges. In the first case, his own participation complicates the narrative; in the second, it is his partiality toward the young emperor which does so. Julian enters Ammianus' narrative long before the Persian campaign, when he is suddenly elevated from scholarly obscurity to the rank of Caesar.[23] Ammianus loved Julian for his bookishness and his reactionary Hellenism and praised him for his seriousness as an administrator. But throughout Ammianus Julian's charisma is charged by, and demonstrated through, his military accomplishments. Ammianus acknowledged that his description of the young prince, whose valor and good fortune led Ammianus to see a direct divine influence upon his life, was "nearly panegyric."[24] Although Ammianus insists that it is all true (16.1.3), his portrait of Julian as a natural and exemplary leader who fights "among" the troops, "firing every man with a desire to rival him in deeds of valor," rather than as a commander and witness of deeds, will need careful attention.[25]

AMMIANUS AND THE SIEGE PROGRESSION

Pre-Contact and Contact Phases

Given the imperial balance of power, the contextual pressures of siege warfare—although present even at the beginning of the siege—played in a diminished key. As we will see, however, the progression made up ground as the fighting during the assault phases accelerated the pace of moral escalation: the late stages of the siege were just as bloody and absolute in fourth-century Persia as they had been in first-century Gaul.[26]

---

23. Among many allusions to the Roman past, Ammianus compares Julian to Titus (16.1.4) and seems to echo one of the more famous deeds of Caesar in his description of Julian physically intervening to prevent a rout (25.4.10), Suet. *Iul.* 62.

24. Ammianus' obituary of Julian (25.4) praises him inordinately and with feeling, and the attempt to balance the encomium with criticisms of Julian's excesses is forced: very serious flaws are presented almost as foibles. Ammianus was a partisan, but one who consciously strove to write history rather than, like Josephus, panegyric or propaganda.

25. 24.1.1. See also 16.12, 23.5.24–25, 25.4.4–12.

26. The following application of the progression is essentially a refinement of/expan-

Ammianus describes much negotiation, parley, and intimidation before the first assault. Negotiation seems to have been obligatory during conflicts between Rome and Persia, and nearly every siege included both pro forma invitations to surrender and real attempts to negotiate capitulation. The constant combination of "promises and threats" during the first few phases of the siege progression are in perfect accordance with the "laws" of siege warfare, but the real hope of leniency plays a larger role in Ammianus' borderlands than we have seen. The willingness of the besiegers to offer favorable terms, their greater focus on obtaining the fortifications (as opposed to eliminating the defenders), and the occasional reappearance of negotiations during the later phases of a siege show the local customization of the larger system.[27]

A good example is Julian's deal with the defenders of Thilutha—a river-rock fortress—who refused to surrender immediately but promised to do so once the Romans had consolidated the area (24.2.1). Julian bypassed the fort, saving time while the garrison saved its honor and avoided the rigors of a siege. While logical in the military context, this seems almost medieval in its detachment from the partisan passions of war (24.2.2).[28]

The image of the fleet floating by the quiet fortress after the deal was done demonstrates another important point: these negotiations were attempted before the army was in position to begin the siege, so this was a pre-contact capitulation. Ammianus is rare among Roman historians in giving a clear sense of this distinction, and rarer still in doing so with consistent attention to the moral choice of the defenders. The approach of an army to a fortified place initiates the siege progression, but only in the broadest sense of a potential siege. Thilutha became a non-siege by agreement, but every siege that progressed to the point of contact did so only because the inhabitants decided to resist. When the army of Sapor approached Singara,

> Its defenders saw the enemy a long way off and quickly closed the gates. They manned the defenses, highly confident, and prepared

---

sion upon Matthews (1989), 289: "there is a regularity, even a certain ceremonious repetition in these [siege] narratives . . . which in no way excludes the likelihood that the regularity was part of the events themselves."

27. Promises and threats: 24.2.9. See also 20.7.17–18; 20.7.1, 4–5; and 21.12.1–4. Only the Goths—who, not coincidentally, are unable to wage proper siege warfare—omit the cajoling and content themselves with threats. They were unsuccessful; see 31.15.5, also 31.6.3 and Gilliver (1996), 223.

28. See Bradbury (1992), chapter 10.

the mural artillery and ammunition. When all was ready they stood to arms, prepared to repel the enemy if they launched a testing assault.[29]

This description makes clear the shared initiative of the pre-contact stage. While the army is still far away, but contact is imminent, they close the city—their armed posture indicating refusal of open warfare and their confidence expressing a preemptive riposte to the coming intimidation of the besiegers.[30] Alternatively, a city might go so far as to meet a potential besieger on the road, bearing torches and bouquets (21.10.1).

Arriving at a closed city, the commander of the besieging force generally deployed his men and began the process of negotiation and intimidation. The usual beginning seems to have been a combined reconnoiter/intimidation similar to Titus' misadventure before the walls of Jerusalem.[31] Approaching Bezabde during the campaign of 360, Sapor hoped to take the fortress "by force . . . or by flattering promises," but nevertheless began by riding into missile range of the walls (20.7.1–2). Ammianus makes much of the tall, gleaming appearance of the King of Kings. Mural artillery fired in his general direction formally inaugurated the siege. Sapor nevertheless "sent heralds in the customary manner," even though it was quite clear that the heralds, too, would be shot at. To protect themselves and to demonstrate their previous successes and their ruthlessness, the heralds brought men captured at nearby Singara to serve as human shields. The defenders held their fire and gave no response to the surrender demands. Thus the siege moved into the assault phase (20.7.1–5).

That negotiation was part of the ritual even when the intent is to take the city by force is suggested by the terse account of Constantius' approach to Bezabde, now in Persian hands, later in the same year (20.11.6).[32] The army arrives and immediately fortifies a camp in the old style—a demonstration of serious intent. Constantius reconnoiters in person, but is not shot at from the walls, so he offers favorable terms: abandon the city and preserve your freedom. When this first offer is rejected the preparations for assault immediately begin. Similar in approach but with the opposite result is Julian's approach to the Euphrates island village of Anatha (modern

---

29. 20.6.2, trans. adapted from Hamilton. Despite their pose, the defenders listen to contact-stage overtures from the Persians before refusing and suffering assault.
30. See also 29.6.9–12.
31. See pages 149–50.
32. See also 27.12.1–12.

Ana, 24.1.6–9). After failing to surprise the garrison, Julian, mindful of the need for strategic speed, combined promises of leniency with threats. The garrison surrendered, trading their freedom for the fort, after speaking with Hormisdas, a Persian in Roman service.[33] This siege progressed to the contact stage (Ammianus describes the approach of the floating siege train before the negotiations), but was then terminated before any assault was launched. The role of Hormisdas illustrates another reason for the prominence of negotiations in Roman-Persian siege warfare: given the multitude of defectors, transmigrant locals, and multilingual soldiers and officials, overtures were easily made.[34]

Whatever negotiation took place, intimidation was ongoing. The besiegers did what they could to terrify the defenders by raising the specter of sack and massacre.[35] The commander's survey was itself intimidating, especially when it confirmed the personal presence of the opposing king—an additional motivation for the attacking troops. One form of intimidation was to simply deploy the army around the city, emphasizing the defenders' isolation and making concrete the threat of annihilation. The best example of this, at Amida (19.2.2), is discussed later in this chapter; but Julian's forces did the same at Aquileia in 361, with the explicit goal of aiding the negotiations by presenting a threat (21.12.4).[36] Intimidation, of course, was only effective when the invasion force possessed the technological skill to mount a real siege. The Gothic attempt to intimidate Adrianople (31.6.3), "threatening it with the horrors of a siege," was not credible, and they withdrew after an abortive attempt at general assault. Similarly, Julian ignored the attacks of the Alemanni who had trapped him in Sens (16.4.1–2), and they withdrew after a month of fruitless skirmishing.

Engagement and Initial Assaults

True testing assaults—in which the attacker hopes that a massive advantage in combat motivation will lead to victory even as he expects his troops to be driven back from the wall—were rare in the Roman-Persian wars.

---

33. Lib. *Or.* 18.218 reports that the inhabitants surrendered through fear (i.e., of the sack).

34. See also 24.1.10, 20.7.7–9; Den Boeft et al. (2002), 17.

35. See also 18.10.1–2 and 24.2.9.

36. Ammianus elsewhere emphasizes the intimidation factor of a wall of gleaming shields (e.g., 29.5.38) and the flashing of ornaments and standards (28.5.3, 29.5.15).

Instead, a prolonged intimidation/negotiation phase tended to determine the initial levels of commitment from each side until at least the first heavy assault.[37]

Quite common are skirmishes, like the one at Amida and the initial day of fighting at Pirisabora. "From dawn until dusk they fought with missiles" describes a skirmish and not a sincere attempt to take the walls (24.2.9). Similarly, the first Persian assault on Bezabde seems to have been intended as a general assault (we learn later that ladders were carried) but became a skirmish. "The whole Persian force fiercely attacked the rampart, screaming and cruelly threatening, but when they had almost reached the walls they began to fight with the defenders" (20.7.5).

The general assault made without benefit of siege works was rarely successful—a fact Ammianus emphasizes by describing the straight-ahead attack as typical of barbarian behavior. Goths attacking Adrianople "rushed on the city in disordered and unconcentrated fashion," or, in a later attempt, "the besiegers with their innate ferocity rushed into swift death."[38] To assault a heavily defended position requires a bestial ferocity, an unreasonable unconcern with death.[39] In each of the assaults on Adrianople a notice follows of the death of the most prominent fighters. The second, a five-hour-long slaughter, encouraged the Goths to make a far-fetched attempt at suborning treachery.[40] When the general assault is relaunched, the Goths carry ladders, and Ammianus again makes much of their moral advantages. The Gothic leaders are foremost in the charge, motivated to seize the treasures stored in Adrianople, and their men follow, drawn by the pull of heroic leadership and eager to compete in winning glory. But

---

37. The expedient of treating each of the major target sites in the Roman-Persian wars as a generically strong fortification is, unfortunately, necessary. Ammianus gives very few details of fortification or topography: the longest, at twenty-two words, is at 20.7.1, while the interesting description of Pirisabora (24.2.12) is an exception. More typical are the terse descriptions at 20.6.1, 21.7.7, 26.8.7, and 16.3.2. See Crump (1975), 97–99, who surmises that Ammianus understood military topography well enough, but omitted it—he was writing a universal history, not a *commentarius*.

38. 31.6.3, 31.15.3. Caesar's characterization of Gallic and German siege behaviors is similar; see chapter 5, note 18.

39. See also 21.12.13, where, in the assault on Aquileia, the men who try to cross the moat suffer heavier casualties. Significantly, the more reckless men are killed while the others are only wounded.

40. 31.15.7–9. This is one of only two instances of treachery or trickery stratagems in Ammianus' sieges—for the other, at Amida, see page 188.

they do not succeed in seizing the wall, and "they were no longer cohesive, but fought in scattered groups, which is a sign of extreme desperation" (31.15.13–15).

Ammianus includes in this attack narrative a vignette of the Goths' amazement at seeing the artillery of Adrianople in action (31.15.12). These are ignorant barbarians, of course, but the emphasis on the effectiveness of both stone-throwing and bolt-shooting artillery is consistent throughout. If the defenders are well provided with artillery, then suppressing fire is necessary to allow assault troops to even approach the wall, and artillery firing over their heads would also protect them from the arrows, sling stones, and makeshift projectiles that rained down as they climbed or worked at the foot of the wall—thus large Gothic armies might fail while smaller Roman and Persian forces were successful.[41]

Assault

The narrative of Sapor's siege of Singara in 360 (20.6), begins with confident pre-contact preparations by the defenders. A day after the Persian army's arrival assaults began, and lasted for several days. These included several light engineering techniques: escalade, attempts to undermine the wall at ground level, and the preparation of "machines." These certainly included artillery, and it seems probable that Sapor had ordered the construction of ram-bearing towers from the outset. The turning point of the siege is the first application of the ram to a weak point in a tower's walls. The general assault continues, but once the tower collapses, tearing open a breach, resistance ceases. The city is quickly taken as the defenders flee, and few are killed, the rest taken prisoner.[42]

At Bezabde, too, Ammianus' manner of introducing the rams "prepared for the purpose" strongly suggests that the heavy assault had been planned from the outset. Although the combat is sketched in only a few dramatic sentences, it is among the best ancient descriptions of the particular psychological challenge of laboring on siege works:

---

41. See Crump (1975), 109–10; Den Hengst (1999). See also Marsden (1969), 179–98; Julian *Or.* 1.23c-27c; and Kelso (2003).

42. The repetitive nature of warfare in this part of the world is underscored by Ammianus' notice that the breach is effected at precisely the same point where the wall was breached in the siege of 348—the repaired masonry was weak. That the ram's actual damage to the wall, rather than its imminent use, forces the decision to surrender is unusual in that it follows the medieval/early modern convention rather than the Roman tradition.

Although the narrowness of the paths made the approach to the walls more difficult and the rams prepared for the purpose could hardly be moved forward in the face of a hail of arrows and thrown rocks, the ballistae and scorpions kept firing, one shooting large bolts, the other scattering stones. At the same time, wicker baskets, smeared with pitch and bitumen and ignited, bounced down the slope one after another. As a result the machines with the rams stuck fast as if rooted to the ground, and were set alight by the incendiary materials hurled at them.

But despite all this and despite the heavy losses of both sides, the assaulting troops were all the more eager to destroy the town before winter, even though it was protected by its location and its fortifications. They believed that the king's fury could not be assuaged until this was achieved, and neither the mortal wounding of some nor all the bloodshed deterred the remaining troops from taking the same risks. In a long and destructive fight they exposed themselves to extreme danger, as the further progress of the rams which were brought up was checked by the massive weight of the stones that fell on them and by various combustibles.[43]

The first ram to reach the wall succeeded in collapsing a tower, but these defenders fought on. "An intense fight broke out in the tight space between the walls, our men and the enemy forced bodily together, fighting with drawn swords and no quarter" (20.7.14).

At the siege of Aquileia (during the civil war of 361), the nature of the ground essentially precluded the use of rams, and a general assault with the full complement of light equipment—ladders, protective sheds and screens, as well as iron tools for undermining by hand—was driven back by mural artillery and stone throwing. The defenders took heart.[44] An effort was then made by the besiegers to approach the walls with floating siege towers. This striking initiation of the heavy assault phase ended in disaster when the towers capsized, and the besiegers were forced to move back down the progression and resume their attempts at lightly engineered assault. Yet this exception enforces the rule. Although Ammianus insists on the superior motivation of the assault troops as they repeatedly storm the city, he seems to do so only to illustrate the effects of repeated failure upon

---

43. 20.7.10–12. Trans. adapted from Hamilton.
44. 21.12.6–7. Evidently, as they soon sally in force (21.12.13).

morale. The defenders are implacable, and the siege has in effect thrown a gear. Beaten back again and again, the attacking troops "began to conduct the siege with less enthusiasm" and the siege lapses into blockade.[45]

The account of an action of Gratian's in 378 against the (Alemannic) Lentienses, who had taken refuge in a natural redoubt high on a mountain, emphasizes the heroics necessary in siege-like assaults. Although there are no fortifications, Ammianus tells us that the attackers "were to be opposed by obstacles like those of city walls" (31.10.12–13). Five hundred men were selected from each legion and were treated to a special effort to elicit high combat motivation: "the emperor himself was busily engaged among the front ranks."[46] While it is possible that Gratian actually fought, Ammianus' careful choice of words make it much more likely that he is practicing close-range heroic leadership, showing himself to his men and risking himself slightly in the missile fire, rather than actually striking blows at the enemy.

Even without the tip-off of "like city walls," it is clear that Ammianus considers this uphill battle to be more like a siege assault than any sort of open combat.[47] The features he chooses to emphasize make up a useful checklist for the siege assault: the selection of the more highly motivated troops to lead the actual charge, the emphasis on the effective plunging fire of the defender's missiles, the unusually prominent role of the emperor, and the desperate resistance put up by men cornered together with their families.

As we have seen, well-fortified cities protected by mural artillery and an active defense were likely to defeat any assault by escalade. Such a defeat preserved the defenders of Aquileia and Adrianople and forced the besiegers of Bezabde and Singara to move to heavy assaults, often involving ramming.[48] At Bezabde, Singara, Pirisabora, and Maiozamalcha the decisive action of the siege came when a ram destroyed a tower. Despite the fact that the section of the siege machine digression that deals with the ram has

---

45. 21.12.8–19. The besieging army, loyal to Julian, would have been forced to raise the siege had Constantius not died, which resulted in the belated capitulation of the city.
46. 31.10.13–17.
47. Very similar in this regard is the assault on Solicinium (27.10.8–16).
48. Siege towers and the "helepolis" were also used (see note 77), although these seem to have been combinations of the two separate elements that together were decisive—artillery and the ram. Ammianus uses *agger* to refer to a man-made siege ramp only at Amida, Pirisabora, and the Persian siege of Virta (20.7.18).

not attracted much comment (it is unenlivened by technical errors or other confusions), the ram is the most effective city-taking instrument: "if used with vigor, once the walls have been cleared of defenders, even the strongest fortifications are dissolved and the city laid open."[49] Despite this fact, or perhaps because of it, the relative mercy shown to the defenders of Singara indicates that the heavy emphasis on the moment in the siege progression when the ram touched the city wall has shifted.[50] At Bezabde the ram was used and there was a massacre; the same was true of Maiozamalcha and Amida, as well as the siege of a fortified estate in Africa by the general Theodosius (29.5.25). Moreover, the surrender at Pirisabora is linked to the arrival of the "helepolis" and its ram—a possible analogue of preemptive surrenders occasioned by rams in earlier Roman history.

A curious comment on the battering ram occurs during the Roman attempt to retake Bezabde from its new Persian possessors (20.11.8–31). Constantius' army first worked through the siege progression in much the usual way. After surrender demands were rebuffed, the first day saw a general assault in which the Roman troops attempted to undermine the walls by hand. After a day's pause (no doubt to prepare the protective screens), they attacked with mantlets, but were driven away from the wall by heavy (i.e., thrown/dropped) missiles. Ammianus then elides six days, which were probably spent assembling rams and other machines and engineering their approach to the wall. On the tenth day the ram is brought into action: it is particularly large and has its own history, having been used by the Persians over a century before during their successful siege of Antioch and later abandoned to the Romans at Carrhae. Ammianus here acknowledges the conventional meaning of the first use of the ram: the sight of the ram "would have daunted the besieged, who had already almost decided to surrender, had they not taken heart again and prepared to defend themselves against this threatening machine" (20.11.11). While Ammianus is generally fond of such counterfactual conditional phrases, the reference to near-

---

49. 23.4.8–9. Despite problems with the text at this point. See Den Hengst (1999), 33–34; Matthews (1989), 293.

50. The easiest way to account for this violation of the "laws of war" is to note the context of endemic competitive imperial warfare. Specifically, Sapor took Singara early in the campaign, and could ill afford to lose control of his army in an extended sack. The possibility of another sack in the near future (which did take place, at Bezabde) could have been used in a promise of delayed gratification to the siege troops. Finally (see note 42) there is the possibility that the emphasis moved, as it was to do in medieval and early modern Europe, from the instrument of breaching to the breach itself.

surrender seems to be an acknowledgment that this moment in the siege progression—the ram approaching but not yet in action—was a logical point at which to surrender. "Taking heart" would be out of place if it did not comment on the intimidation effect of the ram and the meaning of its approach—a demonstration of an unusual access of morale on the part of the defenders.

The morale of the besieged was indeed very high. After days of fierce fighting around the rams and their embankments, they sallied twice in an attempt to destroy the rams. The first force clashed directly with the leading Roman fighters and was repulsed, but the second effort, launched under cover of a smoke screen, succeeded in burning most of the Roman siege engines.

This disaster forced Constantius' hand, and the Roman troops abandoned their machines and attempted to take the city by general assault. To support this attempt, the rams and destroyed engines were replaced on the siege mounds with extra *ballistae,* in the hope that the enemy "would not be able to put up his head" against such point-blank fire. Despite the increased artillery support, escalade and hand-undermining were so much less threatening to the defenders than the rams had been that this reversal to an earlier stage of the progression must have seemed desperate. The Persians were certainly confident, sallying again and burning down one of the siege mounds. The telltale council scene follows, and Constantius admits defeat, first by resorting to blockade and then by raising the siege (20.11.20–25, 31). It is important to note how the arc of morale follows the stalled siege progression: the Persians consider capitulating as the ram approaches, but once they stand fast at the moment of maximum moral tension they never lose that advantage. The Roman soldiers not only suffered the typical psychological stress of a siege but were also forced to continue even after the Persian moral victory reversed the siege progression. The thoroughness of that victory is clear: Constantius raises the siege because he fears mutiny.

Blockade

A passive blockade signaled either the inability to properly conduct a siege or the failure of more aggressive tactics. In the fourth century there were no huge armies that could be trapped by a blockading operation as at Alesia or Dyrrachium, and there were generally too many different forces active in the theater of operations for an army to securely blockade a border city without being harassed or engaged by the enemy. The only instance of a successful blockade is a sort of police action led by Julian against a group of Germanic raiders (17.2).[51] This is very far from the normal siege context in Ammianus, and the other notable blockades all come after the failure of siege assaults: Constantius at Bezabde (20.11.24), Julian's forces at Aquileia (21.12.17), and the Goths at Adrianople (31.6.4).

THE SIEGE OF AMIDA IN 359

Ammianus' account of the siege of Amida (Diyarbakir) is strikingly different, in several ways, from the other sieges given prominent placement in this book. First, our informant was within the city throughout the siege. Second, the Roman forces were defending rather than besieging Amida—and they were defeated. Finally, while this siege is a highlight of Ammianus' history, it was a relatively minor historical event, a classic example of the operational success that led to strategic defeat—no people was subjugated, no war concluded.[52] Yet for all this, Amida represents an almost perfect example of the siege progression in practice.

The scale of description is also different from the other sieges in Ammianus. The siege, which lasted exactly seventy-three days (19.9.9), occupies well over half of book nineteen, and is cast in epic terms.[53] Knowing the length of the siege reveals to his readers Ammianus' habitual compression. He elides long periods of preparation or skirmishing in order to focus on the actual assaults: of the seventy-three days, only twenty can be securely placed—fourteen at the beginning, and six at the end of the siege.[54]

Happily, the specificity, the elision, and the choice of notable events can all be explained: there is, again, a method to Ammianus' mercurial

---

51. With the partial exception of Gratian's pursuit of the Lentienses (31.10.13–17; page 184, above.

52. While the Persians were victorious, the length of the siege forced Sapor to abandon plans for a major invasion. See Matthews (1989), 57–66.

53. Troy is a touchstone throughout the account, as Ammianus makes four explicit references to the *Iliad* and probably alludes to it (and perhaps the *Aeneid* as well), at several other points. See Kelly (2008), 59–61; and pages 86–88 above. Certain details, such as the fight over the corpse (19.1.9) of Grumbates' son, may indeed be invented, but studding a narrative with exaggerations, allusions, and even inventions may, as in this case, detract little from its overall coherence and fidelity to historical experience. Allusion in the participant's narrative may also reflect the allusive habits of the experiencing and remembering brain, necessarily prior to any conscious literary decision-making; see note 15, above.

54. Matthews (1989), 58. See also chapter 4, note 30.

narrative. The fourteenth day was marked by a bloody general assault (19.2.12); the final attempt to take the city before heavy engineering. The final six days (19.16.13, 7.1,6, 8.1) comprise three days of preparation for the last assault and the three of its duration.[55] Ammianus supplies only two major episodes with which to fill the intervening period of some forty-five to fifty-three days—a ten-day plague that weakens and adds to the garrison's misery (19.4.2–7), and the sudden seizure of one of the city's defensive towers by an infiltration force of Persian archers (19.5.4–8). Each is a dramatic incident that allows Ammianus both to showcase his storytelling skills and to garnish the narrative with classical allusion, but both incidents represent a detour from the main axis of the siege progression, namely the escalating assaults. The pestilence represents, metonymically, the threat of hunger, thirst, and disease inside the city. The infiltration of the tower—arranged by a deserter—combines elements both of treachery and stealth, and is the only use of such tactics by Sapor's forces. While Ammianus omits the long period of siege construction and skirmishing, he takes care to demonstrate that Amida experienced the full range of dangers inherent in siege warfare.

Ammianus arrives at Amida only by hazard, after being separated from his comrades during an encounter battle on the shores of the Tigris. He spends the night crowded along a cliff path with refugees, soldiers, and corpses before reaching Amida in the morning. This harrowing experience is told in the first person, but the final two chapters of book eighteen resume the detached historical third person, describing the tactical situation at Amida (18.9) and the operational prelude (18.10). Book nineteen begins in the first-person plural, which Ammianus uses for the entirety of the siege, until his last-minute escape is marked by a conspicuous reintroduction of narration in the singular.[56]

Once an insignificant place, Amida had been heavily fortified by the young Constantius. It was also protected by the Tigris, supplied with its own spring, and geologically difficult to undermine. Its garrison, normally

---

55. See Matthews (1989), 60–61. While he indicates at least the passage of other days, some thirty are omitted entirely. See also Kagan (2006), 31.

56. 19.8.5. See Matthews (1989), 64–65. This unlikely escape may recall Josephus after his failed defense of Jotapata. Yet, while Ammianus tells some eyebrow-raising stories (see Kelly 2008, 53–58), it would be shame to lump the incident together with Josephus' defection-with-strong-suspicion-of-base-treachery. See also Kelly (2008), 42–43, 59–65, for a discussion of Ammianus' actual presence at Amida and his literary choices regarding allusion, person, and number.

one legion, had swelled to seven legions and an elite unit of archers, and it was also a regional artillery depot.[57] This was no mean fortress, to be assaulted without slowing down the campaign—Sapor had moved too slowly. So, when he rode forward to demand surrender, this was interpreted as a bluff that hoped to avoid committing the Persians to a siege (the army was visible but not yet deployed). Yet Sapor expected to be able to successfully intimidate the defenders into surrender (19.1.4). Ammianus invokes the heavenly powers to explain this irrational overconfidence; a literary touch, but the hope that a well-fortified, well-defended city would yield to intimidation without the direct threat of a siege does seem farfetched. The army did not actually surround the city until days later (19.2.3), after Sapor's intimidation attempt had ended in disaster.

Coming too close to the city, Sapor is recognized, fired upon, and barely escapes, his cloak torn by a missile.[58] Sapor's generals only succeed in restraining him from ordering an assault by reminding him that this might cause a fatal delay to his larger enterprise (19.1.6). Sapor then details Grumbates, king of the Chionitae, to make a second surrender demand on the following day. It was never delivered: an alert artilleryman fired on the approaching party and killed the son of Grumbates, riding beside his father. This forces Sapor's hand, "for it was resolved to propitiate the spirit of the slain youth by burning and destroying the city; for Grumbates would not allow them to go farther while the shade of his only son was unavenged" (19.2.1).

Seven days having been given to the funeral and two to foraging, the siege formally commenced with the traditional Persian intimidation en masse.

> Then the city was enclosed by a line of shields five deep, and on the third day the gleaming cavalry squadrons entirely filled the human range of vision, and the ranks of infantry quietly marched to the places assigned to them by lot. (19.2.2)

Ammianus testifies eloquently to the effect of this massive display of force, claiming that the defenders then and there despaired of survival. The entire army stood in place—utterly soundless—throughout the day, then camped and returned to the identical positions in the early morning, emphasizing

---

57. 18.9.1–4. See Marsden (1969), 197.

58. 19.1.5. Such a display of the imperial person was standard practice: see Lightfoot (1989); and note 76.

their insurmountable control of the situation. The first engagement was initiated after Grumbates himself hurled a blood-dipped spear at the walls (19.2.5–6).

The fighting begins, and Ammianus is at his cinematic best: clouds of arrows, masses of flying stone, wails of grief, death and mangling, while trumpets blare and the soldiers of both sides shout in praise of their leaders, or call for aid in pulling arrows out of their bodies (19.2.6–11). But there is also tactical specificity here, if we use the progression to read between the lines. This is no true assault—where is the clanging of weapons and armor? The focus on arrow wounds, as well as those caused by catapulted rocks, makes clear what is omitted: no Persian forces actually tried to mount the defenses of Amida. The first stage is a skirmish that enacts the segue from pure intimidation to attrition. A second assault (19.2.12–15) heightens the drama, yet there are still no references to hand weapons, ladders, or wall contact, and all wounds are caused by arrows. This may have been a more serious attempt—a testing assault that did not reach the walls due to the volume of fire from the defenders—since the upshot is Sapor's decision to abandon such attempts and begin heavy engineering.

Ammianus marks this transition first by cutting away from Amida to discuss plans for its relief and then by focusing on the pestilence in the city (19.3–4). He then brings us up to date.

> Meanwhile, the busy Persian had surrounded the city with sheds and mantlets, and siege mounds and towers began to rise—these towers were tall and fronted with sheet metal, and each was topped with a ballista, to drive the defenders from the ramparts; yet not for a moment did the skirmishing by the slingers and archers slacken. (19.5.1)

This sentence alone defeats any criticism of Ammianus as a narrator of sieges. Here we have all relevant tactical details, including a clear description of the towers' salient features; an explanation for the omission of any lightly engineered assault in the preparations for the decisive heavy assault; and, not least, a concise description of skirmishing that illustrates the psychological drain of siege warfare.

This description sets up the frustration of the Gallic legions, "composed of brave, agile men" who are useless in siege warfare and had been sallying against the Persian forces until barred from doing so by officers worried about pointless attrition (19.5.2). They chafe under this pressured inactivity, and will soon demand to launch a desperate sally in force.

Next, though, Ammianus places the second major episode of the long period between the initial assaults and the heavily engineered assault. Seventy elite bowmen infiltrate the city, through water tunnels, by night.[59] Taking possession of an abandoned tower (evidently overlooking the Tigris—a direction from which Amida had not yet been attacked), the archers wait for daybreak and then signal the Persian army: their sudden, effective fire down into the city is coordinated with an assault on the walls.

The progression is again instructive: this coup de main takes place after testing assaults have concluded but before the heavy assault has been launched—the mounds, and thus the rams, have not yet reached the walls. The Persian onslaught is a serious but lightly engineered assault: they attack in close array and with greater fury, and they bring scaling ladders (19.5.5–6). There had been no expectation of such an assault, as Ammianus indicates by means of the narrative break and the "meanwhile . . ." description of siege construction: both sides, while skirmishing, were essentially waiting for the completion of the siege works. But this is no rapid narrative shift at the expense of operational clarity—the lack of expectation is precisely the tactical point. Sapor had not intended to attempt a general assault—Amida's mural artillery, as we have seen, clearly precluded that—and both sides expected the lightly engineered section of the siege progression to be tacitly omitted. But the deserter's information evidently presented the Persians with the possibility of a successful stealth assault, and Ammianus lets us experience the event as the defenders did—with surprise.

Ammianus uses his own presence at the siege to underline the essential unpredictability of this category of assault, and the extent to which it relies upon morale to succeed: "We were uncertain and perplexed as to which force we ought to counter first (19.5.6)." A surprise attack is always a gamble, since surprise gives a temporary edge in morale which must be converted into tactical advantage before the defenders recover and fundamental tactical advantages reassert themselves. Here the defenders reacted well, soon deciding to shift five ballistae to bring them to bear against the archers in the tower. When the ballistae defeat the archers the pendulum of moral advantage swings further back toward the defenders: "this being so

---

59. That these men are volunteers seems overwhelmingly likely: they are "outstanding in confidence/bravery and skill" even among the king's own troop.

quickly accomplished, and the engines restored to their usual places, with a little greater confidence we all ran together to defend the walls" (19.5.7). The Romans are angry, and the exterior assault is decisively repulsed: "the enemy scattered in bitter defeat, lamenting the death of many, retiring in fear of wounds" (19.5.8). With great skill, with only the merest mention of his own role—his presence among the "we" that resighted the five ballistae—Ammianus has concisely communicated the salient moral and tactical details of this assault, from the operational setup to the action's beginning, decisive turn, and conclusion. So passed the only lightly engineered assault of the entire siege—a small Roman tactical victory.[60]

The briefly augmented confidence of the defenders falls again when the garrisons of other Roman fortifications are pointedly paraded by Amida on their march into captivity (19.6.1–2). Not long after this, the decision is made to let the Gallic troops attempt a sally upon the Persian camp (19.6.3–5). Ammianus has repeatedly emphasized the beast-like ferocity of these fighters, but their motives are now explained as a combination of frustration and the concern that they will die deedless. They have long been nearly mutinous, but the collapse of morale now reinforces their determination to sally before the city is taken. Ammianus again gives us his participant's insight into the tactical decisions being made within the city: "we, out of options" agreed to let the Gauls go. He uses this second notice of the coming Gallic sally to stitch together two significant events: the low ebb of morale and the approach of the twin siege mounds, which the defenders are hoping to counteract with interior mounds designed to bolster the wall and provide fighting platforms of similar height. Despite the fevered language lavished on the Gauls, they are still clearly under some control, since their sally is released at the best possible moment, when the Persian mounds are about to reach the walls. This is when a setback would have the greatest effect on their morale.[61]

The account of the sally places due emphasis on Gallic courage (19.6.7–12): they rush in with axes and swords where their enemies prefer to use

---

60. Kagan (2006), 44, remarks on the sudden increase in tactical precision in this episode, and attributes it to "Ammianus' presence and the potential decisiveness." This is certainly correct, but the same logic can be extended to the generic and cinematic depictions of the early assaults. Ammianus had no clear view of or decision making role in these indecisive skirmishes—which were likely to have been tactically amorphous in any event—hence he felt no need to be artificially precise.

61. 19.6.3. See page 159 for a strong parallel.

arrows. But despite killing many Persians and winning the glory they had sought, they are defeated, losing 400 men and failing to damage the works or to kill Sapor. The Romans, too, have gambled and lost.

The death of several prominent Persians occasions another ritual pause, of three days (for the funeral rites), before the final assault commences.[62] The Persian decision to move to the heavily engineered assault is introduced with a statement of extremely high combat motivation.

> The Persians, since open force was having little effect, now decided to settle the matter with siege works; and all of them, motivated by great eagerness for combat, rushed to meet a glorious death or to propitiate the spirits of the slain with the sack of the city.[63]

Then the Persian forces approach, arrayed for battle, and we are treated to an eyewitness description of a siege assault from the defenders' point of view—a scene as rare in ancient history as are twentieth-century photographs of attacking troops taken from their front.[64]

> With eagerness the preparations were completed, and as the morning star was rising various forms of siege engine and ironclad towers were moved forward to the walls. On the top stories of the towers were ballistae, which scattered the defenders below. When it was getting light, mail-coated soldiers appeared, in numbers that filled the entire view, and the serried ranks came on, not in skirmishing order as previously, but at a slow pace controlled by trumpet calls. No one broke ranks and ran ahead, they advanced under cover of their mantlets, holding wicker shields in front of them. When they came within range the Persian infantry had difficulty in protecting themselves against the missiles of the mural artillery, and opened up their formation. Hardly a missile failed to find its mark; even the

---

62. 19.6.13. De Jonge (1982), 132, gives *indutiae* its classical sense of formal "armistice," but in this context, as at Bezabde (20.7.5), it must mean something like "informal truce." It is unlikely that Ammianus would omit reference to formal negotiations at such a point in a siege.

63. 19.7.1. De Jonge (1982), 133: "By *vis* is meant the storming tactics used so far, the massive attacks, which as it were, overwhelm the defenders. Now they pass on to *opera*... which here has to mean the construction and especially *the use of technical siege tools,* thus also of *machinae*" (emphasis in original).

64. Keegan (1976), plate 8.

cataphracts wavered and gave ground, which raised our morale. But their ballistae on the ironclad towers were effective against our defenders below—their superior height brought success and they caused much bloodshed.[65]

This gripping passage concisely communicates the difference between the heavy assault and those that have gone before: there are no rushes, no screaming charges, no reckless movements until the towers are in position.

The advance of the towers and the missile duel lasts the entire day. The second day's effort includes elephants (presumably deployed both to terrify the Roman defenders and to provide elevated firing platforms), but Roman mural artillery smashes the two towers and the elephants are driven off by the use of incendiaries. The Persians persist in the assault from their ramps and, reading closely, it seems that this is the first time (other than the abortive escalade in coordination with the archer infiltration) that Persian infantry have actually tried to reach the walls. Not surprisingly, this attempt is coupled with a new motivational effort: Sapor himself appears in the combat zone, galloping about to inspire his assault troops—an action "unheard of" on the part of a Persian emperor. Ammianus is generously hyperbolic, declaring that the Roman archenemy "rushed into the fight like a common soldier."[66] Sapor may have become the target of long-range missiles, but the common soldiers of relevance here were fighting atop the siege works, where his mounted suite would surely fear to tread.

The final assault began the following day. Ammianus vividly describes the ferocity of the fight at the wall and the sudden collapse of the buttressing interior mound. He has again structured the narrative so that we are drawn into the vivid but "generic" action and surprised—just as the defenders were—by this disastrous and decisive development.

Ammianus' consummate skill as a writer of action scenes does not necessarily involve any omission of historical detail. The collapse of the mound brings part of the wall with it: a breach has finally been opened. "Then by

---

65. 19.7.2–5. Trans. adapted from Hamilton. I construe *non inordinatem* as "not in open order (but in close order)" and not as "not disordered (but under better control)." Incidentally, the mention of *cataphracti* here is generally taken to mean that these men are actually on horseback (Rolfe, Hamilton, Sabbah, Seyfarth), but De Jonge (1982), 139 is surely correct in insisting that they are fighting dismounted. See also Speidel (1994), 123–24.

66. 19.7.6–8. Julian's imagined description of Sapor at the siege of Nisibis in 350 (*Or.* 2.63) sitting on a platform "like Xerxes" confirms Ammianus' view—or demonstrates Julianic snark. Julian's highly rhetorical account draws both on literature and lived history—see Lightfoot (1988). See also note 76.

the king's command all the warriors were summoned, and there was a close combat with drawn swords, blood streamed from both sides amidst the carnage."[67] This is the first mass hand-to-hand assault of the siege, and although the nature of a fight in a narrow breach hardly needs elaboration, Ammianus confirms its intensity by noting the drawing of swords before going on to vividly describe the gory scrum. The end is near and, typically, Ammianus wastes no time. The plural narrator is replaced by the first person singular as Ammianus makes good his own escape in the chaos of an assault becoming a sack (19.8.5).

One of the distinguishing characteristics of Ammianus' narrative of the siege of Amida is the clarity with which he marks the progression of the siege from phase to phase. The major shifts in his narrative style correspond to the natural and predictable progression of Persian tactics. Read in isolation, the text might seem to rely on "the literary device of steadily intensifying tension" and lack any identifiable "causal chain."[68] But the ratcheting advance of tension is historical (i.e., in the positive sense—it is also "literary" in the sense of being a device of historical narrative) and the causal chain is evident if we read with the siege progression in mind. Ammianus marks the links in the ("historical") chain when he expresses (by "literary" means) the transitions between the progression's phases. He writes the moral and psychological pressure of the siege progression so smoothly that it does read like a literary imposition—but it is real history, and better history than a muted, tactical, blow-by-blow account.[69] Thus, the brilliant, brief combat scenes carry the emotional weight of the ten weeks of combat. Ammianus has chaotic battles and minutely controlled artillery actions because both happened, but also because they embody the two aspects of the siege experience: the steady accumulation of pressure and the sudden shift of tactical phases; the relentless turning of the wheel and the sudden slipping of gears.

---

67. 19.8.4: there is some disagreement on whether to accept the manuscripts' *praedatoribus*—plunderers—or emend the text to read *proeliatoribus*—fighters—or perhaps even *propugnatoribus*—assault troops. In any case, it is worth noting that Ammianus' word choice seems to emphasize that these are shock troops of some sort, and not the technicians, laborers, and skirmishers who have hitherto dominated the Persian attacks.

68. Kagan (2006), 49. Examples include the placement of 19.3 and 19.4 after the general assault phase and the prior notice of the Gallic sally, so that the delay before the actual event underlines the imminent heavy assault.

69. See Matthews (1989), 295.

JULIAN'S PERSIAN CAMPAIGN OF 363

The emperor Julian, a scholarly type and unexpected emperor, was no less keen for the glory of military conquest than his more soldierly predecessors. Despite his victory at Strasbourg in 357, he felt the need to prove himself as a strong-armed descendant of Constantine, and it seems clear that planning for an invasion of Persia began shortly after the death of Constantius in 361. Ammianus confesses Julian's twofold desire for war: to the reputation-making aspirations of the insecure new ruler were added a more personal lust for battle. Julian "dreamed of trumpets and combat." Yet the assumptions of his critics are telling—new emperors always seek to establish themselves by starting unnecessary wars (22.12.2–3).

After meticulous military and religious preparations, Julian ordered his forces across the Euphrates frontier, starting from Antioch in early March 363 to join them (22.12; 23.2).[70] His plan was to feint toward northern Mesopotamia (the usual battleground in recent conflicts) and leave a smaller army there to threaten an advance down the Tigris and distract Sapor's main force, while advancing instead down the Euphrates, hoping to catch the Persians unawares. Although Ammianus belabors the journey through the frontier zone, Julian's progress was fairly rapid. He crossed the river Abora (Khabur) into Mesopotamia proper in early April and moved down the Euphrates, trailed by a floating siege and supply train of over a thousand boats and marching in battle array because of the fear of ambush (23.3.9). This simple military detail is more eloquent of the unwisdom of the invasion than Ammianus' many portents of disaster. Julian's great force advances along the river at will: since they are supplied by boat, only fortifications on the Euphrates pose a direct threat to their lines of supply. Yet stray but a little from its banks, and harassing cavalry become a threat to operations and logistics. Rome will be dominant in open battle—which the Persians generally refuse—but inferior in the skirmishing that delays their march. Thus the only locus of tactical victory is in the sieges of those river towns too valuable to abandon, and the only chance of strategic victory lies in winning those sieges quickly and efficiently.

As we have seen, the first defended fortified places on the Euphrates were dealt with quickly, either being intimidated into surrender (24.1.6–9),

---

70. See Matthews (1989), 130–79 for a many-faceted study of the invasion. For chronology see especially Den Boeft et al. (2002), xiii–xxiii.

taken by a speed assault (24.1.12), or bypassed after negotiating a truce (24.2.1). After winning a skirmish with Persian cataphracts (24.2.5–6) and crossing the canal known as the Naarmalcha, the army reached Pirisabora, "apart from Ctesiphon the most important town on the invaders' route," some three weeks into the invasion.[71]

The siege of Pirisabora begins exactly as we would expect it to. "The emperor, after riding around and inspecting the walls and the topography, began the siege with due deliberation, hoping to intimidate the townspeople and thus deplete their motivation for defense" (24.2.9). Intimidation shades into unsuccessful negotiation, and the troops are deployed around the city, in a cordon three ranks deep. This formation, identical but for its depth with the daylong intimidation at Amida, is held only briefly: time is of the essence, so missile skirmishing soon begins (24.2.9). The defenders interrupt the fighting several times to demand further negotiations with Hormisdas, but then insult him, behavior which was soon recognized as a delaying stratagem. When night fell Julian began to prepare the engineered assault. The Romans filled in the ditch and advanced a ram to the wall, and by first light they had already breached a tower.[72] The defenders then abandoned their two circuit walls and took up position in the citadel.

How are we to account for the success of this assault? The answer seems to lie both in its speed and in the strength of the citadel. When Julian moves immediately to the heavily engineered assault he makes an effective demonstration of his will to take the place. Speed is a strategic imperative, and since extensive heavy engineering on the outer walls was evidently not necessary, the Persian defenders chose to defend the citadel in full strength and not suffer casualties at the outer walls. The elevated citadel, on a "high mountain shaped like an Argolic shield" and backing on cliffs over the Euphrates, possessed high walls "of bitumen and baked brick, than which nothing is more secure."[73] This is, for Ammianus, an elaborate description

---

71. Den Boeft et al. (2002), 29.

72. Davies (2006), 99, who praises the "dual purpose" Caesarian ramp at Avaricum (see chapter 5, note 30), argues that the ramp at Pirisabora "demonstrates a reversion to the earliest uses of these structures as simple bridging tools." The sparsity of evidence for *longue durée* trends aside, this seems like an overinterpretation from form in the face of contextual information on function: the simple bridge enabled the taking of a strong—but evidently not very actively defended—place in a single night.

73. 24.2.12: Libanius (*Or.* 18.228) reports that the inhabitants considered the citadel more defensible. On bitumen and brick, see Cassius Dio 68.27.1.

of fortifications, and we are clearly meant to envision a site of great strength. Forcing the Roman troops to move through the town and operate in a confined space also made the withdrawal tactically attractive.

Yet the withdrawal is also guided by another, unspoken assumption. Once again, we see that the use of the battering ram is closely accompanied by a decision among the defenders. This is the second instance in Ammianus (see note 42 above) that hints that the cultural consensus governing the meaning of the use of the battering ram may have shifted from the earlier Roman standard. Caesar and Cicero refer to the ram's first use, the ritual recognition of its first touch on a city's walls, as the defining point, but here it is its effect that seems to demand action. As at Singara (20.6.7), where the collapse of a tower by a ram immediately caused the defense to abandon resistance and thus escape slaughter, it seems probable that the moral implications of stubbornly defending a breach contributed to the decision to withdraw to the citadel.[74] Avoiding the defense of the breach—and thus becoming involved in bitter close combat—preserved the possibility of surrender without widespread killing.

A day of skirmishing in the streets and before the walls of the citadel follows. The next morning Julian launched a vigorous general assault, presumably under cover of artillery. "Many fell on both sides, but neither side had the upper hand" (24.2.14). Ammianus leaves unstated the real meaning of such "equal" combat during an assault—that the besiegers have failed to gain the walls.

The next incident is one of the most striking in all of Ammianus: Julian himself leads an assault on the citadel's gate (24.2.14–15). That a Roman royal would risk himself in such a way is surprising, and our instinct to disbelief has been honed by reading Josephus' exaggerated claims for the prowess of Titus. Yet Ammianus has carefully prepared his readers for this exploit. Julian is not a typical later Roman emperor; he is both brave and attracted to combat; he believes himself to be protected by fortune; and he competes constantly with historical predecessors. This last becomes very clear when Ammianus informs us that Julian blushes with shame for not having matched a similar feat of siege assault heroics accomplished by Scipio Aemelianus—the bookish soldier is emulating his reading.[75]

The action is also not as reckless as it may seem. Julian "leads" the assault party, but as a witness and an exhorter, not a fighter. Ammianus

---

74. See chapter 3, note 62, on Machiavellian comeuppance.
75. As is Ammianus: see Den Boeft et al. (2002), 60, for the echoes here of Ovid and Vergil. See also Lendon (2005), 292–94.

makes it subtly clear in the comparison to Scipio that Julian was not at/ under the walls, but nearby; while his men batter the gates he "cheers them on," protected by several shields. Moreover, no one was killed in this assault, and only a few were slightly wounded: Julian was perhaps reckless, but not rash. Given the tighter physical space and decreased visibility (within a city as opposed to beyond its walls) his action is very similar to that of Sapor at Amida (19.7.6–8), in which the emperor exposes himself to enemy missiles in an effort to rouse his troops to greater deeds. The difference is one of cultural expectation: unusual but admirable for a Roman, but "unheard of" for a Persian. Even if his strategic foolishness stemmed from a misguided emulation of Alexander, Julian's actual leadership in combat is much closer to that of Trajan, who was almost shot at the siege of Hatra (the soldier hit at his side was probably protecting the emperor with his own shield), than of Alexander, who was once alone within an enemy fortification, having led the escalade in person.[76] The primary meaning of his action is to demonstrate the urgency of the assault by placing himself in some danger, thus giving physical expression to the need for a hasty conclusion to the siege. Sapor's northern army is coming, and Ctesiphon is still far away.

Ammianus makes reference to the "pressing" operational matters in relating Julian's next decision, which is to eschew all other types of engineering activity in favor of building a huge machine, called here a helepolis.

> To this huge mass, which would overtop the battlements of the highest towers, the defenders turned an attentive eye, at the same time considering the resolution of the besiegers—then they suddenly turned to prayer, and standing exposed on the turrets and battlements they begged the Romans with outstretched arms for protection, for mercy and their lives.[77]

This gamble pays off. It may yet have taken some time to assault the citadel: the archers and artillery on the helepolis (which may also have mounted a drawbridge enabling wall-top assaults) would not have been immediately

---

76. Alexander: Arr. *Anab.* 6.9–10. Trajan: Cass. Dio 68.31.3. Thus the "apologetic handling of the episode" detected by Den Boeft et al. (2002), 59, may be literal apology rather than excuse making: Ammianus is careful to show that Julian is not (yet) acting irresponsibly. See also Levithan (2008); and pages 35–36, above.

77. 24.2.18–19. For the odd fact that this helepolis, while generally familiar, does not resemble the helepolis of the siege digression, see Matthews (1989), 293.

decisive against the mail-clad defenders and their fearsome bows. Nor would its ram have quickly opened a breach in the unusually strong walls. If the defenders had resisted it seems quite likely that Julian would have had to invest time in belatedly assembling equipment to support a more general assault (24.2.18).

But the defenders surrendered, due in large part to psychological acuity on Julian's part, subtly communicated by Ammianus: he recognized the defenders' unwillingness to defend the no-quarter-given assault that follows a breach, and he saw that their confidence was based largely on the advantage of altitude. Simultaneously confronted with a tall tower and imminent battering, they called for a truce, and, after being guaranteed their lives, surrendered. This was a victory of intimidation: had the defenders been perfectly confident, they could have waited out the initial battering of the helepolis, surrendering only when a breach began to form—but their resolve collapsed too quickly (24.2.20–22).

At Pirisabora Julian read the morale of his opponents quite well, but he was less attuned to the moral state of his own troops. He had already pushed them far, and with too little recompense. Although Pirisabora had been short and relatively bloodless, it was preceded by a long march and ended without the satisfaction of plunder—not only was the garrison released, but most of the population, and hence the city's portable valuables, had been evacuated. When Julian announced a reward to his assembled troops they were angered by its small size, and he forestalled mutiny largely by emphasizing the riches of Persia, still to be won—a risky mortgage to finance their loyalty (24.3.3–9).

Difficulties immediately ensued, as the Romans had to march through low-lying land intentionally flooded by the Persians. The passage of the marshes is further complicated by demoralizing cavalry attacks, and after ten days the army reached a place called Maiozamalcha, "a great city surrounded by strong walls." Julian adopted precisely the same procedure here as at Pirisabora: camping at some distance away, he went to the city to reconnoiter and perhaps intimidate.[78] As the emperor's party observed the

---

78. 24.4.2. The account, including the unprecedented detail that he went on foot (probably due to the marshy nature of the ground around the fortress), favors a simple reconnoiter, yet Julian was "conspicuous," so this was no stealthy intelligence-gathering mission. The camping and special notice of fortification are due to the necessity of guarding against sudden attacks by Persian cavalry. That is, Julian ordered his army to camp where the day's march left them, somewhere near Maiozamalcha, thus allowing him to intimidate in the pre-contact phase and preserve the faint hope of a quick capitulation or favorable

city, they were attacked by a group of ten Persians, who sallied from a postern gate. Julian was suddenly in mortal peril, and fought with sword and shield against the assailants, killing one himself.[79]

The incident becomes another opportunity for Ammianus to compare Julian to heroic Roman predecessors, but its greater significance is the resolution of the pre-contact phase. Not only will Maiozamalcha not capitulate, but morale is running so high that the defenders are willing to sally and take the fight to the Romans. Julian responds decisively. The camp is quickly moved to a site more suitable for the siege, which begins with the intimidating encirclement by three rows of shields and a sober assessment of the physical and moral challenges facing the Roman army: a lofty site, walls and high towers, and a hand-picked defense force resolved to fight or die. Unsurprisingly, the usual negotiations are rejected and a testing assault or skirmish is ordered (24.4.6–11). This is quickly called off despite a widespread, nearly mutinous insistence on attacking. Instead, work begins simultaneously on filling the ditches, building siege mounds, reassembling the artillery pieces, and mining.[80] While the heavy works are being built (command of the mining is delegated to two professionals but Julian himself takes command of the artillery) Julian takes an aggressive action not seen at Amida or Pirisabora, ordering a large-scale, lightly engineered assault.

Although the grim operational situation has just been sketched, Ammianus seems to make an effort to elevate his style as he describes what will be the last successful major action of the campaign. The assault is preceded by a report from a scouting party that the road to Ctesiphon is open, and the soldiers, "wild with joy," are eager to begin what they hope to be the final battle.[81] This is described in a flurry of dramatic language and fantas-

---

truce. That the camp must be moved to begin the siege indicates that the fortification of the first camp was not due to the coming siege—the nearby notice of "at Maiozamalcha" setting up Julian's reconnoiter—but rather to the threat of cavalry attack.

79. 24.4.3–4. Ammianus is probably guilty of exaggerating the martial heroism of Julian, since Zosimus and Libanius record the incident but not Julian's personal "kill."

80. Other than the notice of the high natural position, which demands mounds to approach the walls but would stand to make tunneling slightly easier, there is no clear indication why mining is first mentioned as a tactic only at Maiozamalcha. It is possible, of course, that Ammianus omits mention of mining at sieges where it was abandoned or unsuccessful; here the mine tunnels will prove decisive.

81. 24.4.14. Den Boeft et al. (2002), 119–20: "one senses some reservation on the part of the author." They also point out that *efferatus* is not a word used to describe disciplined but motivated Roman soldiers. Yet I think that Ammianus describes not an undesirable frenzy

tic images: the mailed Persians are like ironclad birds; the roaring assault troops wield their interlocking shields (24.4.15). But this description mentions only missile weapons, as does a sentence on the screaming artillery and the stones and incendiaries thrown from the fortress—it is impossible to determine if the first day's fighting constitutes a stalled assault or a fierce skirmish that covers the advance of the heavy machinery.

The next day sees the siege continue "with combats of various kinds," and Julian again appears among his men, although not so spectacularly as at Pirisabora. Ammianus reminds his readers (for the third time) of the time pressure. "In the face of every danger the emperor stayed very close to his troops, urging the destruction of the city lest by wasting too much time around its walls he might have to abandon his more important objectives." Toward the end of the second day, a tower, higher than the rest and only newly addressed by a ram, collapses, pulling down the adjacent wall and opening a great breach. "This at once transformed the situation," and a fight around the breach ensued between the desperate defenders and the Roman troops "who were in a fury of rage and resentment" (24.4.18–20). Ammianus moves on quickly to the climax of the siege, and the assault itself is described in cinematic terms without any specific mention of close combat—but this is a major event. The new situation, with the defenders' obstinacy now fully matched by the rage of the assault troops, marks the full engagement of the unforgiving "rules" of siege warfare.

This fight is still undecided at nightfall, and an assault of the breach is forestalled because a tunnel has succeeded in getting under and beyond the walls, providing the opportunity to launch a surprise assault from within the fortifications. Julian accordingly opens an attack on two areas of the wall in order to cover the noise of the completion and opening of the mine. At the appropriate time, Roman troops leapt out of the tunnel, led by a soldier, a *notarius,* and a military tribune. These volunteer assault leaders are named by both Ammianus and Zosimus, so we may assume that they were "mentioned in dispatches" as a reward for their heroism.[82] Ammianus awkwardly digresses into a comparison with an ancient deed of daring and then leaps ahead in the narrative to show Julian rewarding the

---

on the part of the troops but instead the effects of mounting desperation: their motivation is colored by their strategic plight.

82. 24.4.22–23; Zosimus 3.22.4. See Den Boeft et al. (2002), 130–32, on the names. Lendon (2005), 302, uses this to bolster his contention that heroic leadership by higher officers was more common in the fourth century than previously; yet one *miles,* one civilian notary, and one tribune seem to average out to approximately the status of a centurion.

most deserving storm troops.[83] Strangely, he avoids describing the action itself. It is possible that the eliding of the assault is intended to convey the speed with which organized resistance ceases when infiltration is combined with attacks on many breaches (24.4.25). Nevertheless, it is a curious aspect of Ammianus' narrative that he avoids giving any extended description of the final assault at either Amida or Maiozamalcha.

As we would expect, given the pointed notice of the soldiers' extreme anger and the continuing defense after the initial breach, Maiozamalcha is brutally sacked and its inhabitants "killed without distinction of age or sex."[84] The moral imperatives of siege warfare are very much in operation. In addition to the punitive sack, the commander of the garrison, one Nabdates, is burned alive because he had promised to betray the city but then defended it (24.5.4). This action is explained with reference to Julian's increasingly erratic behavior, but the death, if not necessarily its manner, is justified by the "laws of war."[85] After all, the defenders of Pirisabora also stalled by pretending a willingness to surrender, but they were spared. Nabdates' guile only earned death when he fought on after the walls were breached.

"Thus a great and populous city, destroyed by Roman strength and valour, was reduced to dust and ruins" (24.4.30). Under great operational pressure Julian had managed to take a strong fortification in only four days. This was no mean feat, but each day lost on the siege was a step toward the disastrous defeat of the larger project. Julian's army pushed on for another month, taking a smaller fortress in a two-day siege, suffering from constant skirmishing attacks and even winning an engagement with an arriving Persian army. But the main Persian force still lurked on the horizon, preventing any siege of Ctesiphon, which was too formidable to be taken quickly by general assault. Julian's strategy had been predicated on moving swiftly into the Persian heartland and seizing the capital, but he

---

83. 24.4.24. Julian was well-read and astute in restoring the practice of pointedly decorating the most conspicuously brave. His antiquarianism (or Ammianus') is imperfect, however: he awards "siege crowns"—proper only to the general who raises a siege—instead of mural crowns. Den Boeft et al. (2002), 135–37, defend Ammianus by questioning the canonicity of the much earlier statements of classical authors, citing Maxfield (1981), 64. This is a good point, but the award still carries considerable weight and is in any case not terribly appropriate for soldiers who emerge from a tunnel.

84. 24.4.25. The commander and eighty soldiers, who hid or held out in an interior fortification during the early part of the sack, as well as some women and children, were spared.

85. Den Boeft et al. (2002), 155.

had been too slow—and he had not defeated the Persian army. The inescapable conclusion is that the lack of an obtainable objective had long since doomed the expedition to bog down in southern Mesopotamia, lacking any viable exit strategy. Roman technology and the fierce motivation of its best assault troops had resulted in a string of impressive siege victories, but without defeating Sapor's army Julian could not resolve the war, nor could he supply his army indefinitely in hostile territory. By the middle of June 363, Julian had no choice but to turn toward home. Not long after, he was mortally wounded while riding to rally his troops (25.3), and his successor, Jovian, concluded a humiliating peace with Persia.

Ammianus is an invaluable source for Roman siege warfare, and he gives due attention to its aftermath. His accounts of the sacking of Amida and Maiozamalcha demonstrate how the psychological pressure of siege warfare is sustained by the promised release into pillage and murder. The rape, killing, and destruction of the sack are the last and heaviest weight on the moral scales of siege warfare, rounding out the culture of ancient siege warfare in a spasm of superabundant violence. The following chapter attempts to describe, and to go some distance toward explaining, the sack.

EPILOGUE
The Sack

At the end of the siege came the sack. As an event, a trope, and a narrative object it needs separate treatment. Here we will consider the sack as the closing act of the siege narrative, a necessary part of the siege story yet not a part of the siege event. The sack is an epilogue, but one long anticipated—the complementary unspooling of the siege progression.

The primary activity of the sack was the thorough plundering of the captured place. While pillaging, both for operational advantage and as a source of post-combat profit, went hand in hand with most military activity, a sack was rare and different, coming only after the siege's long containment of potential violence, under pressure. The release of pent-up force into the contained, civilian-inhabited space of the city was an apotheosis of violence: pillage was now as much about destruction as gain. Greed or lust drove the attackers, and they made the bodies of the townspeople into chattel or the objects of sexual violence, but the worst sacks resulted in the wholesale slaughter of the population and a destruction of both people and place that went far beyond any such motives. The sack was outside the normal boundaries of Roman culture and, despite its immediate context, it was an essentially nonmilitary event: command, control, coordination, and discipline did not exist.

It is a curious hazard of military history that—whether reading of ancient, medieval, or early modern sieges—the latter stages of the narrative are likely to feature a statement (usually generalized and unsourced) that the sack was well known and understood to be the inalienable right of assaulting troops, and that this has always been the case.[1] This seems to be quite true, as a matter of fact. But as a matter of historiography it still amounts to tacit complicity, with a long line of historians choosing each to throw up his hands in dismay and avert the gaze of history from a particular horror.

In the Roman historical sources the assumption that any sudden capture of a city results in a sack seems pervasive. Polybius (who, as we will see, tries to cover up a Roman sack) tells us that the citizens of Tarentum assumed that the strange noises they heard at daybreak came from the Roman garrison since the lack of looting or open violence meant that the city could not possibly have fallen.[2] Appian finds several different ways to use the expectation of sack for dramatic purposes.[3] The Latin historians, too, tend to indicate a similar assumption by making minimal acknowledgments of each such event.

Other genres found the sack to be more useful, and the sure knowledge

---

1. Ironically, sacks began to be suppressed or prevented in the nineteenth and twentieth centuries, just as modern warfare had progressed to the point of regularly targeting civilian-inhabited urban areas during ongoing campaigns. But in the early nineteenth century the ancient traditions were still going strong. See, e.g., Myatt (1987), 6–7, 15, on the Peninsular War: "When [the] preliminaries had reached a certain stage however, brute force then took over . . . this in its turn being frequently succeeded by conduct so hideous on the part of the assaulting troops as to defy description. It is perhaps one of the strange paradoxes of human nature that orderly, well-disciplined soldiers would behave with supreme gallantry until success had been achieved, when, in a flash, they abandoned all pretext of discipline, decency, or human feelings." Myatt's subsequent dodge of the issues such a description raises also applies, and with equal dissatisfaction, to the present book: "This said, it may be as well to add that this book is mainly a study of military affairs, and is only incidentally concerned with human depravity." For additional examples of the common assumption of the right to sack, see also Fletcher (1999), 29, 81; Bradford (2005), 130, on the sixteenth-century siege of Malta; France (2008), 163; or Strickland (1996), 222, on "the right of storm" in the Middle Ages. Such a firm convention is handy for historical fiction, as well—see, e.g., Cornwell (1999), 360.

Watson (1993b), 143, notes of sieges generally that "if the siege lasts long enough, if the fighting is both frequent and bloody, self-generated parameters of behavior will emerge that eschew traditional norms of military conduct." This is bloodless language for bloody deeds, and strangely located amid Watson's analysis of the spatial containment of a sack—surely an important explanation, but hardly the only one. Yet few other writers have attempted any sort of explanation.

2. Polyb. 8.30–2. In fact, the city had been taken by stealth during the night—this, then is an exception that proves a rule that Polybius would rather not acknowledge.

3. App. *Embassies* 4.2, *Pun.* 131, *B Civ.* 5.122.

of what will come when a city falls is worked into our most fundamental texts, whether Mediterranean or Near Eastern. Rahab knew what would happen to Jericho.[4] Priam describes for Hector what defeat will mean for Troy—women raped, babies slaughtered, dogs tearing at the genitals of his own pitiful unburied old man's corpse. The epic cycle dwelt on these horrors, and Vergil puts them to use in the *Aeneid*, not only by having Aeneas describe the destruction of Troy with similar details, but also by invoking the paramount fear of an enemy break-in at the moment of Dido's suicide.[5]

To make sense of the Roman siege, in any event, there must be some discussion of the sack. Conversely, if something so awful had become an expected event, endorsed by "law" and "custom," then we need to think about how exactly the siege worked to contextualize (or normalize) large-scale atrocity. But we are immediately stymied: the ancient writers evince as much discomfort as do their modern counterparts. Some choose terse and oblique descriptions; others run in the other direction, shifting abruptly into a tragic or melodramatic mode. Yet the sack is not about narrative closure, or not only: it was, to a large degree, the promise of the sack that made the prosecution of difficult and drawn out sieges possible. The desire for valuable booty and the need for an explosive release of psychological tension were inseparable from the continued participation of the soldiers in the siege. The same soldiers that are praised elsewhere for discipline and courage commit rape and murder in the wake of their victory.

This was not how it had to be, of course: a siege only came about because the defenders refused to fight in the open. Swift resolution, rather than a bloody sack, was the usual strategic goal of the Roman general. Ideally, this would come in the form of a glorious battlefield victory followed by a quick capitulation, the terms of which would personally enrich him.

---

4. Joshua 2:6. See also the laws of Deuteronomy (chapter 1, note 40; this chapter, note 32) and Morris (1995), for visual and literary evidence from the ancient Near East.

5. *Il.* 22.59–76; *Aen.* 2.506ff, 4.669–71 (see also Luc. 3.99); Vergil moves the corpse of Priam from a doorway to a beach, perhaps to evoke the death of Pompey. Ovid, too (*Met.* 12.225), uses the capture of a city as a reference/comparison for chaotic acts of sexual violence—see also note 28.

Much later, the *philosophes* were still making use—both serious and satirical—of the paradigmatic horribleness of sieges. One of the hyperbolic claims for the state of nature as Rousseau envisioned it in the second part of the *Discourse on the Origin of Inequality* was that "there were more horrors in the storming of a single city" than in centuries of pre-civilized life. Voltaire includes dark jokes about slavery, rape, and the usual "laws" of siege warfare in chapter 12 of *Candide,* adding an episode of pygiphagia for good measure.

But if the defense was prolonged, the "laws of war" treated continuation as escalation, and as the siege progression reached each new stage it presented a harsh "double or nothing" choice to the defenders. This dynamic could, by encouraging surrender, have the effect of limiting overall violence, but it also justified the exaction of maximal punishment for continued intransigence.

Once a siege had progressed to the point of heavy investment in engineering, the sack was very difficult to avoid, for two reasons. First, because the refusal to fight in the open required punitive damages. Second, because the horror of the sack would serve as a deterrent to the next city unwilling to capitulate to the Roman army.

This was the broad military and cultural mechanism that linked the sack to the siege progression, our metaphorical ratchet: unidirectional, locking into place at a higher level of tension with each turn.[6] The gear can be seen as storing the mounting tension in the besieging army: not only does the growing pressure risk damage to the machinery, but when it releases there will be a burst of speed. With no braking mechanism to slow it down, the wheel spins on, slowing to a stop only when environmental friction saps all its speed.

CONTROLLING THE SACK

The missing brake would be discipline, conceived as either a cultural force or the commander's ability to rein in his men, and its absence goes a long way to explaining the reticence of Roman historians. Polybius and Livy, as Adam Ziolkowski has demonstrated, almost never describe the process of sacking a city. Livy most often simply notes that a sack occurred, usually with a form of the verb *diripio*.[7] Ziolkowski then takes on Polybius' unusually full account of the sack of New Carthage, arguing that this disciplined and highly organized "model sack" is not so much idealized as impossible. We will examine the evidence for the emotional state of the inrushing troops later, but it bears mentioning here that the sources do not convincingly adduce any means of controlling the sack, once the troops have passed out of the commander's sight and into the city. Control depends upon communication, and the one example of attempted communication at the moment when an assault becomes a sack—the "plundering signal" (*signum praedae*)—is better understood as a signal of the

---

6. See pages 48–49.

7. Ziolkowski (1993). See also Shatzman (1972); Harris (1979), 51–53; and Gilliver (1999), 154–59. Paul (1982) and Urban (1966) discuss the sack as a literary trope.

relinquishing of control, a concession to the looting that began as soon as resistance broke. So, when such a *signum* was given (sounded, presumably, on trumpets) it communicated the general's judgment that killing no longer served a military purpose, and could cease. This killing, then, was the slaughter of combatants, or at least *puberes*—men of military age—that took place in the immediate aftermath of virtually every successful storming.[8] But the killing might continue: all the commander was really acknowledging was the end of the military phase, and in the worst sacks many died after the besiegers had finished "mopping up" or securing the city. If some sacks included massacres of women and children, then some post-*signum* plundering included continued killing of adult males. This signal is sometimes linked with the express command to take prisoners (instead of killing), as in the archetypical siege narrative of Veii. This action is implied in any case: people, too, qualified as *praeda*, booty. Nevertheless, it seems to have been usual for many or most of the men of the city to be killed.[9]

TELLING THE STORY

The commander lost control of his troops as they disappeared over a wall or through a breach. So too did the ancient historian, who so often shared the same vantage point, both literal and figural.[10] And if the chaos of battle is difficult for participants to explain, surely the maddened assault troops

---

8. See Tac. *Ann.* 12.17; Ov. *Ars Am.* 1.114. See also Livy 10.45.11, 37.32, 42.63.10–12, and the story of the controlled sack at 5.21.13–14.

9. Ziolkowski (1993), 77–83. Veii: see pages 86–88. Most men: (e.g., Livy 10.45.10, 42.63.10–11). Elsewhere the *signum praedae* makes more sense within a military context, as at Livy 25.25.9, which describes not a sack from a running assault but the result of a partial capitulation by the defenders.

10. This is an inalienable condition of the basic physical circumstances of the siege. The commander positioned himself to best observe what took place at the wall during the assault; he could not observe what took place beyond the wall. Even such a paragon of military command as Wellington (see Keegan 1987) was unable either to direct the final assault (which, it should be noted, took place at night) or to prevent the sack of Badajoz. Although his written orders for the assault ran to sixteen paragraphs, he was still reduced to asking a wounded private, dragging himself past the general's suite toward the camp, whether any of his troops had entered the fortifications. They eventually did, and sacked the city for three days. Myatt (1987), 105, 114: "for although Wellington was furious he seems also to have been powerless, a very strange condition indeed for him. It is impossible to believe that he condoned the sack, although being a realist he may have regarded it as inevitable. . . . The line between discipline and anarchy was, and in many ways still is, a very narrow one, and once it has been crossed chaos can soon result."

were not offering careful accounts for posterity. The historical sack, then, has another good excuse for being dangerously literary, perilously rhetorical. The historians may be silent or terse because they can't see what is going on, but they may also avoid describing the sack because it cannot reflect well on the army perpetrating it, however expected its behavior might be. These are decent explanations for silence, but the historiography of the sack is not only meager but deformed: the trajectory of the siege narrative is warped out of shape by the proximity of the historian-satellite to the great gravity of the commander.

The sack of the city is not a convenient place to demonstrate the martial virtues of the great man—but the resourceful writer can still make a silk purse from a sow's ear by taking the opportunity to comment on other forms of virtuous behavior. Heroic leadership, in this context, consists largely of declining silk purses, or the opportunity to acquire them. Plutarch, who made Themistocles the epitome of this trope, also has Coriolanus not only skip the plundering of Corioli in order to fight on but also turn down the booty offered to him and free a prisoner.[11] Turning down the sexual opportunities of the sack was an even better demonstration of virtuous self-control, and, predictably, it is Scipio who becomes the Roman exemplar (see note 39). Not for nothing does Agamemnon—the classical antitype of the prudent general—insist on taking Cassandra before the process of alotting the other captive women of Troy among the victors is begun.[12] Even when conspicuous nonconsumption of booty is not plausible, the general may still show certain virtues—and set himself off from the rampaging of his men—by expressing a philosophical sadness, as Marcellus and Scipio Aemilianus are said to have done as they witnessed the destruction of Syracuse and Carthage.[13]

But these are diversions from the insoluble problem of the commander and the sack narrative itself. Just as the linear and segmented nature of the ancient siege narratives is determined both by the events themselves and by the strong bias in favor of the commander's perceptions (and overempowered self-perception) so too the brevity and chaos of the narrative are shaped by the commander's distance from, and inability to control, events.[14]

---

11. Plut. *Them.* 18.2. Pointing to the gold-adorned bodies of fallen "barbarians" he tells a companion "Help thyself, thou art not Themistocles." *Cor.* 9–10.

12. Eur. *Tro.* 294–7.

13. Scipio: App. *Pun.* 132. For Marcellus see immediately below.

14. Tacitus may hint at the basic absurdity of attributing ordinary historical causality in

In addition, the ancient historians were dealing with a particularly well-established tragic and rhetorical trope.[15] Here, Quintilian describes a rhetorical sack:

> So, too, we may move our hearers to tears by the picture of a captured town. For the mere statement that the town was stormed, while no doubt it embraces all that such a calamity involves, has all the curtness of a dispatch, and fails to penetrate to the emotions of the hearer. But if we expand all that the one word "stormed" [*expugnatam esse*] includes, we shall see the flames pouring from house and temple, and hear the crash of falling roofs and one confused clamour blent of many cries: we shall behold some in doubt whither to fly, others clinging to their nearest and dearest in one last embrace, while the wailing of women and children and the laments of old men that the cruelty of fate should have spared them to see that day will strike upon our ears. Then will come the pillage of treasure sacred and profane, the hurrying to and fro of the plunderers as they carry off their booty or return to seek for more, the prisoners driven each before his own inhuman captor, the mother struggling to keep her child, and the victors fighting over the richest of the spoil. For though, as I have already said, the sack of a city includes all these things, it is less effective to tell the whole news at once than to recount it detail by detail.[16]

This is the sort of thing that gets an avowed plain-truth-teller like Polybius up in arms.[17] Polybius takes a moment to attack the dramatizing style of the historian Phylarchus, who

> being eager to stir the hearts of his readers to pity, and to enlist their sympathies by his story . . . talks of women embracing, tearing their hair, and exposing their breasts; and again of the tears and lamenta-

---

a sack narrative by making the sack of Cremona the result of a misunderstood joke in a bath; see note 44.

15. See Pritchett (1991), 152–57 on the Greek historians, who also avoid describing sacks, leaving out details "which the ancients apparently took for granted."

16. Quint. *Inst.* 8.3.67–69. For the sense of *expugno* as encompassing "storm and sack" (i.e., as closer to *diripio* than to *oppugno*), see Briscoe (1973), 197–98 (on Livy 32.17.9).

17. Gibbon (1788), chapter LXVII, is despairingly happy to acknowledge Quintilian's victory here: "In the fall and the sack of great cities, an historian is condemned to repeat the tale of uniform calamity ; the same effects must be produced by the same passions . . ."

tions of men and women, led off into captivity along with their children and aged parents.

The problem is not exaggeration, however, but context: "Phylarchus, in most of the catastrophes which he relates, omits to suggest the causes which gave rise to them, or the course of events which led up to them: and without knowing these, it is impossible to feel the due indignation or pity at anything which occurs."[18] Would that Polybius went on to spell out the siege progression and its implication that defenders deserve this treatment. But the idea is there: the context of the siege explains—even if it does not forgive in any sense that takes justice and freedom into consideration—the treatment meted out in the sack, "the relationship," in other words, "between the sack's occurrence and the circumstances of the city's seizure by the Romans."[19]

It is important to note that while Polybius might not enjoy "arousing pity," he does not condemn it—or dramatic history generally—if it is linked to a causal explanation of events. Context matters, and Polybius certainly accepts colorful language as a useful tool: it keeps the reader interested, and if it is true it may well explain why what happened happened.[20] The sack of Syracuse is a good example: a long, hard-fought siege that lapsed into blockade before ending with a series of sharp assaults. A jewel of the Hellenistic world was destroyed and a famous old man was needlessly killed, yet Rome had gained a crucial victory in its most desperate war. How to tell this story? Alas, Polybius' account does not survive. We do have Plutarch and Livy, however.

Livy begins his tragic plotting early, prefiguring the destruction by telling us that Marcellus wept as his standards advanced (the crucial breakthrough of the walls of Epipolae had just taken place, but most of the large city was as yet untouched), and tried to give the defenders one last chance—unusual mercy—to come to terms. This is prevented by Roman deserters among the defenders, the quintessential desperate men, and so the siege goes on. The physical complexity of the city and the political complexity of the conflict seems to have allowed for unusual accommodation: when the city finally did fall there were efforts to preserve the lives of ordinary Syracusans, to protect the property of those who had fought for

---

18. 2.56, trans. Shuckburgh.
19. Ziolkowski (1993), 70.
20. See D'Huys (1987).

Rome, and to seize the treasury. But that is all that was even attempted: the city was still given over to the soldiers to sack, which Livy will not describe. He writes only that "many shameful examples of anger and many of greed" took place. The slaughter of Archimedes stands for the rest of the chaos and waste: "in the midst of plundering soldiers dashing about" he is killed while tracing geometric figures in the dust.[21]

Plutarch, as we might expect, makes more of this. Marcellus' weeping becomes the tragedy of a general's inability—his hand, too, forced by the inexorability of the siege mechanism—to prevent destruction: he "is said to have wept much in commiseration of its impending fate, bearing in mind how greatly its form and appearance would change in a little while, after his army had sacked it. For among his officers there was not a man who had the courage to oppose the soldiers' demand for a harvest of plunder."[22] Plutarch cannot resist, either, giving three different stories of the murder of Archimedes: in one, a soldier has been sent to bring him safely to Marcellus but, upon being made to wait as Archimedes works out a problem, flies into a rage and slays him; in another, he is simply cut down by a soldier bent on murder; in the third, he is killed for the presumed value of the scientific instruments he carries.[23] So: undisciplined rage, simple bloodlust, and greed.

Later, Plutarch has a chance to contextualize this unusual sack by reporting accusations that Marcellus did not respect the surrender of some of the Syracusans. His response is simply that "in return for many injuries which they had done to the Romans, they had suffered nothing except what men whose city has been taken by storm in war cannot possibly be prevented from suffering; and that their city had been so taken was their own fault, because they had refused to listen to his many exhortations and persuasions."[24] This is a Greek author demonstrating the commitment to

---

21. Livy 25.24.11; 25.31.7–11. Marcellus' specific instructions to his troops to plunder but not harm any free citizens are clearly meant to be read, with the slaughter of Archimedes, in a tragic mode, illustrating his inability to control the events of the sack.

22. Plut. *Marc.* 19.1–2. Nevertheless, Plutarch converts the reported events of the sack in Livy into Marcellus' strict orders, as if he had prescribed the extent of the violence that was to take place. The point of this is to show that Marcellus, by letting most Syracusans live (and become important allies), should be considered magnanimous—which is reasonable, considering the length of the siege and the lack of massacre or total destruction.

23. Plut. *Marc.* 19.4–6.

24. Plut. *Marc.* 23.4. Elsewhere (*Sull.* 14.4), Plutarch is happy to measure the effects of a sack in terms of the area covered by spreading blood.

justice that tempered Roman ruthlessness: a tragedy, but a fair one. Still, we have very little in the way of actual narrative of a sack so famous that Cicero can rely on his audience's familiarity with the details.[25]

Livy is fairly consistent in avoiding giving convincingly original details of a Roman sack, preferring a thoroughly rhetorical treatment, but he does occasionally elaborate when unusual circumstances present themselves. He is drawn to the drama of a mass suicide that forestalls a sack (see pages 225–27), and he will occasionally describe a generic sack to emphasize what did not take place, or to dwell on the guilt or unusual inhumanity of Roman enemies.[26] One historian who makes the most of an opportunity to describe a sack is Tacitus, since the sack of Cremona embraces two of his favorite themes: the foulness both of soldiers generally (not an opinion usually held by an ancient historian) and of civil war in particular. His account is melodramatic, but it provides a context not only for the siege but for the particular motivations for the assault troops' hatred of the people of Cremona—and it does go into the specific components of the sack.[27]

THE LAWS OF WAR AND THE DESTRUCTION OF CITIES

The sack has four essential components: slaughter, pillage, rape, and destruction.[28] The mass killing of the defenders—that is, of any men of military age—is the normal segue from combat, and often continued even after resistance had collapsed.[29] Generally, this phase, which a commander may seek to stop once the target has been secured, runs out of momentum after a relatively short time, and the inrushing army turns to pillage and rape. A particularly brutal sack is often marked by a notice that the soldiers chose to continue killing well after the collapse of resistance. Unusual rage

---

25. See Jaeger (2008), 88.
26. Not take place: (e.g., 1.29.2, 6.3.10). See also 21.57.14, with Pomeroy (1989), 168. Ogilvie (1978), 320, writes that "almost all of Livy's accounts of captured cities are variations on the *Ilioupersis* theme."
27. Tac. *Hist.* 3.32–4.
28. Here epic faithfully imitated—and influenced—life. See, for example, *Il.* 9.590–4, 22.59–76; Paul (1982). As Van Wees (2004), 124 points out, post-Homeric epic dwells on the experience of siege and sack, especially the most disturbing and grisly aspects of pillage and massacre. Ovid's concise sack of Troy, at *Met.* 13.408–17, nevertheless includes each crucial element of the historical/literary catalogue (see also note 5). In histories, the basic elements of the sack were so well established that writers could allow their readers to infer what went on. See, for example, App. *Hann.* 58.
29. Ziolkowski (1993), 276, sees slaughter as "the last phase of the assault."

or a determination on revenge meant that large numbers of old men, women, and children would also be killed before the turn to pillaging—frequently, here, the fact that bloodlust temporarily trumps greed for booty is remarked upon.[30] When, after some hours or days, the massacre ended, the survivors were taken prisoner and assessed for their value as hostages or slaves.[31]

Such a massacre was explicitly permitted by the customs governing siege warfare.[32] These "laws," as several ancient authors refer to them, were well known: the Massiliots understand that "the fortunes of war" rendered their lives forfeit after a certain level of resistance; Tacitus, too, makes broad reference to "the law of war" during a siege; Josephus repeatedly cites violations of "the laws of war."[33] Nevertheless, a thorough slaughter of noncombatants was unusual enough that the sources generally feel compelled to offer an explanation, and these usually led straight back to the question of motivation. Rage was an essential motivator for the assault troops, but it was an excess of rage that might turn a sack into a massacre.

The determinative power of the soldiers' will can also be seen in the customs of plundering. Although all booty technically belonged to the general possessing *imperium,* and the property of a surrendering city could be calmly given over to the conquering general, anything taken during the

---

30. See, e.g., Caesar, *BG* 7.28; Ammianus 24.4.25; Procop. *Pers.* 2.8.34; App. *Hisp.* 32; Livy 9.14.11–14, 10.45.13–4, 28.20.6–7. See also Tac. *Hist* 3.32; *Ann.* 12.17; App. *Mith.* 28; Josephus *BJ* 3.133, 304–5, 336–9.

31. At Jerusalem, those too old to be valuable as slaves were killed, children were sold and the proceeds given to the troops, and prisoners over seventeen years of age were sent either to imperial plantations or to die in the arena. Josephus, *BJ* 6.415–20.

32. The standard "laws" of siege warfare reflected in the Roman sources were already old when they were first invoked by Rome: of many instances in Livy, see especially 26.31.2, 8, 30.31, and 33.13.6–14. See also Deuteronomy 20:13–14: "And when the LORD thy God hath delivered it into thine hands, thou shalt smite every male thereof with the edge of the sword: But the women, and the little ones, and the cattle, and all that is in the city, even all the spoil thereof, shalt thou take unto thyself; and thou shalt eat the spoil of thine enemies, which the LORD thy God hath given thee." This applies to far-off cities; those of intimate enemies "thou shalt utterly destroy."

33. Massilia: Caesar *BC* 2.6. Tacitus: *Ann.* 6.12; Josephus: *BJ* 6.346, 353, 383–6. See generally Watson (1993), 49–71. The crucial point was the engagement of the battering ram with the city wall—after this, the defender lacked any rights and could be massacred. See pages 74–77, above. See also Xen. *Cyr.* 7.5.73 and Polyb. 2.58, who differentiates between the laws (νομοί) of war, which demand the enslavement of the defeated, and more lenient customs built on the "practice" (ἦθος) of war which may recommend leniency to a trapped garrison. There seems to have been a similar gap between law and custom in the Medieval period as well. Keen (1965), 119–20.

sack was understood to be the property of the army.[34] Livy makes explicit the significance of the unification of personal violence and profit: "there would in every instance be more satisfaction and pleasure in what a man took with his own hand from the enemy and brought home, than if he received many times its value at the discretion of another."[35]

After the pillaging of the most obvious targets, prisoners were rounded up. Every person in the stormed city became a prisoner without rights and could be kept or sold as a slave. Although the sources are rarely as explicit as Tacitus was about the sexual aspect of the sack of Cremona, it seems clear that any sack included rape.

> Without any respect for age or for status they added rape to murder and murder to rape. Aged men and decrepit old women, who were worthless as booty, were dragged off to make sport for them. If some grown girl or a handsome boy fell into their clutches, they would be torn to pieces in the struggle for possession, while the plunderers were left to cut each other's throats.[36]

The association was so strong that rape in other contexts, especially the rape of children, could be described as a sack-like behavior, suggesting both that child rape was a frequent occurence and, again, that the sack was a suitable byword for brutality.[37] Ancient historians generally gloss over the

---

34. Shatzman (1972) defines the general's authority over booty. But Shatzman, like Harris (1979), accepts the cold statements of law and literary whitewashings without due allowance for the violence and chaos of the sack. Ziolkowski's conclusion that "once a thing got lost under a legionary's cloak, there was no power on earth which could snatch it away" is surely right. *Contra* Roth (1999), 148–50, who ratifies Shatzman.

35. Livy 5.20.8. See also Plut. *Cam.* 5.3–4; Livy 4.59.6–10.

36. Tac. *Hist.* 3.33. Ziolkowski (1993), 73–76, argues this position strenuously, describing rape as "of all the aspects of *direptio* the one most strongly emphasized in the Latin sources." In doing so he leans heavily on the idea that rape must be a personal undertaking—part of the chaos of the siege and not something ordered by a general. But we know that mass rape is a commonly occurring horror of war, and that gang rape has been encouraged as a terror tactic.

37. The archetype of sexual misconduct in Livy is the rape/abduction of the freeborn maiden Verginia by Appius Claudius (3.57.1–3): he took her *velut bello captam* (i.e., in a sack, for women were rarely present on the battlefield). Similarly, the depravities of Tiberius are exemplified by the fact that the boys he desires for sexual purposes are sometimes taken by force (Tac. *Ann.* 6.1). See also Diod. Sic. 13.58; Livy 8.25.6–13; and Cic. *Phil.* 3.31, which lists the infamous deeds of M. Antonius. There being no especially cruel sack to make a

fact of mass rape when they are describing the simple sack of an enemy city by Romans, yet the contours of the hidden practice are easily discernible. Appian, in an exceptional incident, has Sertorius put many of his own soldiers to death for raping after a sack.[38] Onasander advises that prisoners be preserved and then makes references to feasts and implicitly sexual "celebrations" of the victorious soldiers. Or we can see the absent sexual violence in the narrative dalliance on the virtuous commander's continence. When Ammianus praises the restraint of Julian—he passes up the beautiful Persian women offered to him after the sack of Maiozamalcha, accepting instead a boy, dumb and skilled in sign language—he is placing him in the tradition of commanders too noble to rape along with their men.[39] (The near-silence is not always preserved in nonhistorical literature: Ovid adapts the *signum praedae* to a context in which it can only mean the seizure of women, and he calls the Sabine women "nuptial booty" and praises Romulus for his ability to reward his soldiers with women.)[40]

The fourth essential element of the sack was a senseless, superabundant rage directed against physical objects, as if the walls and buildings themselves could be punished for the hardships of the siege. The invaders smashed whatever was too bulky to be borne off and burned whatever couldn't be smashed. As with the case of the overkilling of potential slaves, the destruction of potentially saleable booty signified a particularly frenzied sack.[41] Interestingly, Roman siege warfare was generally innocent of the sort of religiously motivated hatred that characterized the most vicious sacks of the medieval and early modern periods, since no sieges in our period were primarily driven—on both sides—by monotheistic disagreement. Since Roman policy usually sought to preserve, if at all possible, any

---

rhetorical meal of, Cicero accuses him of sacking villas and raping mothers, girls, and boys.

38. App. *B Civ* 1.109. The harshness of the penalty is due to Sertorius' brutality, the fact that rape is in this instance treated as a crime to the fact that this was a Roman woman, raped during a civil war.

39. Onasander 35.4–5. Ammianus 24.4.26–7. Scipio (see Polyb. 10.19.3, Val. Max. 4.3.1) and Alexander (Curt. 3.12.21, 4.10.24) are mentioned by Ammianus, to which, as Rolfe (vol. II, 447) notes, we might add Cyrus the Great. See also Procop. *Pers.* 2.8.34, 2.9.9.

40. *Ars am.* 1.114–32.

41. Josephus (*BJ* 6.404–6) is the master of such imagery, elevating the baroque Plutarch (e.g., *Sull* 14, see note 67) and Tacitus (*Hist.* 3.33–4) into a rococo extravaganza of piled corpses, dripping blades, screaming victims, and rivers of blood flowing with sufficient force to extinguish the flames of burning buildings. This is embroidery, but not fabrication. *BJ* 6.271, 284.

temples or shrines, the destruction of these buildings was either a problem to be explained, or an indication, again, of unusual rage.[42]

Last, some mention should be made of other extreme acts of violence that share aspects of several of these categories. Atrocities such as the creative killing of babies and deliberate acts of torture and mutilation have a long history in literature, and the fall of Troy was remembered as much for the hurling of the infant Astyanax from the battlements as for the butchering of Priam, the pillaging of its temples, the rape and enslavement of the Trojan women, or the burning of the city.[43] Knowing this tradition, and Quintilian's instructions, and having read of Josephus' account of atrocities during the siege of Jerusalem, it is impossible to feel confidence in any general judgment about the frequency or meaning of such acts in Roman siege warfare. That they happened shouldn't be doubted: a recent find of thirteen skeletons dating from the Roman sack of Valencia in 75 BCE included several that were bound and deliberately dismembered and one that was impaled, through the rectum, on a spear.[44]

MOTIVATION

The direct connection between combat motivation and the sack needs more emphasis than it has received. Rage and the lust for booty were commonly adduced as explanations for soldiers' desire to sack, while, sepa-

---

42. See chapter 6 for Jerusalem; See, variously, Livy 1.29.6, 29.16–21, 31.30.2, and 38.43, with much emphasis on the temple ornaments in this debatable sack. See also Plut. *Fab. Max.* 22.4; Tac. *Hist.* 3.32; Memnon 35.5–7; and App. *Pun.* 127–33, where those who desecrated shrines at Carthage are punished. Diod. Sic. 13.57 plays on this trope, highlighting the criminal depravity of the Carthaginian captors of Selinus by describing their sparing of the women taking shelter in temples as being motivated only by the fear that entering will provoke them to burn down the temples around them and thus ruin much potential booty. Generally, it seems that, as at Jerusalem, Roman culture allowed for great flexibility in the interpretation of the proper fate of the shrines within the city—in general, burning was to be avoided, but clearly the cult statues and ornaments were often plundered. Polybius' ruling out of any such sacrilege (5.9–11) is probably a hopeful piety, a position more conservative than that of Roman armies, then and, especially, later. The thorough destruction of temples—down to the door-hinges—as an exemplification of defeat and suffering goes back at least to around 2000 BCE, and the Sumerian *Lamentation over the Destruction of Sumer and Ur.*

43. Psalm 137, beginning with the waters of Babylon, proceeds to remember the sack and destruction of Jerusalem, and concludes with wishing "a blessing on him who seizes your babies/ and dashes them against the rocks" (trans. JPS).

44. Ribera i Lacomba (2006), 80; James (2011), 100.

rately, the stimulation of these emotions is often cited as the key to combat motivation. But the siege, "toilsome and dangerous,"[45] does not merely link the two together. A long siege causes the commander to overdraft his soldiers' obedience, with the penalties to be paid out at the time of the sack. An imperfect analogy, but when they went through the excessive toil and danger, the feeling was that he was in their debt. The sources rarely admit that the sack was inevitable, but when they reliably list the labors of the soldiers as an explanation for the violence of the sack, they are drawing a straight line between the submission of the troops to authority during the siege and the fugue state of the sack.[46]

That "it was certainly good for morale to give soldiers the opportunity to pillage captured towns" is certainly true.[47] But it was more than merely good—it was a military necessity. The diverse array of incentives and threats that kept the Roman soldier to his duty sufficed for most tasks, including open-field warfare, but it could not long hold an army to a difficult siege, which was willingly prosecuted only with the promise—implicit or explicit—of plunder to come.[48] Roman soldiers were accustomed to heavy labor and they were conditioned to the danger of fighting, but the combination is more onerous than the sum of its parts. Legionaries hated to work under harassing missile fire, and yet the anxiety of imminent battle persisted in any situation where the defenders might suddenly sally. And the labor of the siege was of an entirely different order than the ordinary hardships of marching and camp building—no legionary would do it for simple hatred and 225 *denarii* a year.[49] Nor was there much opportunity for periodic psychological compensations, such as the glory that even a skirmish might provide or the casual booty of the open campaign.

If a commander forestalled a sack by allowing terms to be struck late in a siege, mutiny was likely to result. The fact that the legate Trebonius commanded at Massilia in his stead allows Caesar to admit that his troops were

---

45. Livy 39.1.6.
46. See, e.g., Caesar, *BC* 2.13, *BG* 7.28; Tac. *Hist.* 3.60.
47. Gilliver (1999), 129.
48. There are innumerable references in the sources to the soldiers' desire to sack a city or town solely for its loot. Some instances dwell on the soldiers' greed and assertion of their "right" to plunder places they have taken, while others focus on the commander's inability to avoid sacking places that he wishes to preserve either for his own benefit or for reasons of strategy or mercy. Another trope is the commander's generous gift of cities to be sacked to his loyal troops. See, e.g., Caesar *BC* 3.31; Plut. *Cam.* 11.1, *Luc.* 14.2; App. *B Civ.* 4.3, 5.49, 5.122; Livy 10.44.1, 36.24.7, 43.1.3, or 43.10.25.
49. See pages 49–50.

"with difficulty" restrained from sacking the city after the first truce had been struck. Constantius' failure to take Bezabde required the raising of the siege because the prospect of a blockade (and thus an eventual surrender on terms rather than a sack) left him fearing mutiny. Similarly, the very late surrender of the defenders of Pirisabora left Julian's army feeling cheated and close to mutinous: even though they had plundered the surrendered town, burned it, and been given a cash donative, they had been denied rape and slaughter. Cassius Dio describes an actual mutiny that ended the siege of the Syrian town of Hatra. The emperor Severus failed to exploit a breach because he hoped that its existence would force surrender, thus allowing the city's treasure to come into his hands. When this delay only allowed the defenders time to repair the breach, his order to recommence the assault was met with stark refusal by his best troops, and the siege was raised soon after.[50]

INDISCIPLINE

> What rein can hold licentious wickedness
> When down the hill he holds his fierce career?
> We may as bootless spend our vain command
> Upon the enraged soldiers in their spoil
> As send precepts to the leviathan
> To come ashore. Therefore, you men of Harfleur,
> Take pity of your town and of your people,
> Whiles yet my soldiers are in my command . . .
>
> —*HENRY V*, ACT 3, SCENE 3

The conduct of the soldiers, too, within the last hour, had undergone a complete change; before, it was all order and regularity, now it was nothing but licentiousness and confusion—subordination was at an end, plunder and blood was the order of the day, and many an officer on this night was compelled to show that he carried a sabre.[51]

---

50. Massilia: Caesar: *BC* 2.13; see also Frontin. *Str.* 3.16.5. Bezabde: Ammianus 20.11. Pirisabora: Ammianus 24.3.3. Hatra: Cass. Dio 76.12; see also note 64.

51. Grattan (1847), I, 204–5, describing the sack of Ciudad Rodrigo on January 19, 1812.

Indiscipline—total chaos, the sudden snapping of psychological bonds—defined the sack both as a release and as a threat. The looming possibility of a sack played the dominant role in the psychological warfare of intimidation and refusal, as Henry's threat makes clear, and, once begun, it was beyond any willing back of the commander or his officers.

Caesar lost control of his men during the assault on Gergovia just when the storm seemed about to become a sack. Early in the civil wars, too, when intimidation and the morale of his soldiers was less important than preserving the towns he brought under his control, the problem of being unable to prevent his men from sacking hung over his negotiations. This fear left him open to the treachery of the Massiliots, and it drove the elaborate precautions that delayed the handing over of Corfinium.[52] Another way to dramatize the rage of the troops—and rage, being linked to motivation but beyond the control of even a good commander, was a good excuse when actions needed excusing—was to declare their unconcern for profit. At Avaricum, none of Caesar's troops "had any thought for plunder. Thus, being angered by the massacre [of a few Romans, months before] at Cenabum and the fatigue of the siege, they spared neither the elderly, women, or children."[53]

Josephus emphasizes the complete lack of discipline during the late stages of the Jerusalem siege, admitting that even Titus could not control his men, who pretended not to hear his orders to desist from burning the temple.[54] Livy's account of the sack of Phocea in 190 BCE is telling: despite the fact that the praetor has accepted the surrender of the town, the angry and greedy soldiers rush in "as if he had given the signal to sack the town."[55] Appian's description of the sack of Locha during the second Punic War is similar: the townspeople sue for peace just as an assault by escalade is getting underway, and Scipio sounds the retreat, "but the soldiers, angry at what they had suffered in the siege, refused to obey. They scaled the walls and killed both women and children indiscriminately."[56]

Discipline is not easily reasserted, either—sacks only end when the sol-

---

52. Gergovia: *BG* 7.47. Massilia: *BC* 2.12–3. Civil war (Corfinium): *BC* 1.21. See also Suet. *Iul.* 65.

53. *BG* 7.28, trans. adapted from Edwards. The point, of course, is in the generic plausibility of Caesar's claim, even if the incident at Cenabum hardly seems sufficient provocation to rage for thousands of legionaries.

54. *BJ* 6.252–60.

55. Livy 37.32.11. See also 6.4.11, 9.25.8–9, 24.19.6–10.

56. App. *Pun.* 15, trans. White.

diers are sated with slaughter and plunder.[57] Other authors preserve some fiction of control by pretending that excesses occurred simply because the commander was absent.[58] These obfuscations have led some modern scholars to take a rather hopeful view of the ability of such commanders to prevent unwanted sacks.[59] Nevertheless, the evidence from our period—with Caesar's frank admission standing out from the rest—ratifies Ziolkowski's conclusion: "First and foremost, the essence of *direptio*... was the suspension of any form of control from above. An 'orderly' sacking is a misunderstanding."[60]

GREED AND ANGER

There were several ways to get rich from the storming of a city. Valuable decorations could be obtained, and Roman commanders often offered awards of extra booty or cash prizes to those who would lead the way during a dangerous assault.[61] But the haul of booty that resulted was also a broad motivational tool—every soldier would profit, once the campaign and the siege were done.[62] Horace makes light of this incentive, while even Josephus steps aside from his praise of Titus' motivational efforts to note that the troops storming the temple, having heard of its gold furniture and fittings, "were further stimulated by hope of plunder."[63]

This appeal was made explicit in the exhortations of Roman commanders to their troops. Corbulo urged his men to the assault of Volandum for the sake of *gloria et praeda,* glory and plunder. Livy's Gaius Marcius strikes a bargain with his troops: "I now give to you the camp and city of the enemy for plunder, if you promise me that you will exert yourselves bravely in the field, and that you are not better prepared for plunder than for fighting." Onasander is enough of a psychologist to advise the same habit: "It is not only necessary in victory to distribute rewards to individual men but also to make recompense to the army as a whole for its dangers. The sol-

---

57. Josephus, *BJ* 6. 406–14. Other historians describe sacks of several days' duration. See also Pompey's reaction to indiscipline at Plut. *Pomp.* 11.3–4.

58. Tacitus (*Hist.* 3.32–4) puts the responsibility for the internecine outrage of Cremona squarely on the shoulders of the commander, Antonius Primus, who left the scene to take a bath. See also Cic. *Leg. Man.* 13.

59. Kern (1999), 335; Harris (1979), 59.

60. Ziolkowski (1993), 90. See also Gilliver (1996), 153.

61. See, e.g., Livy 2.20.12; Onasander 42.16; Caesar *BG* 7.27; Josephus *BJ* 6.33–54.

62. See Shatzman (1975); Harris (1979).

63. Hor. *Epist.* 2.2.26–40; Josephus *BJ* 6.264.

diers should be allowed to plunder the possessions of the enemy if they should capture a camp or baggage train or fortress, or sometimes even a city, unless the general intends to put it to more profitable use."[64]

But the most powerful appeal a general could make was to both greed and anger. Proper motivation focused on the two inseparable qualities of the sack—violence and acquisition. Metellus successfully whips up his troops to storm a Numidian town by calling for revenge and promising booty. Ammianus balances his description of the massacre at Bezabde by noting both motivations, although he describes the Persian troops' lust for booty as overtopping even their bloodlust.[65] Nor could generals overcome this combination to enforce restraint: at Phocea, *ira* and *avaritia*, rage and greed, lead to the sack of a surrendered city, and the sack of Cremona was brought about not only by booty-lust but by a complex hatred of its inhabitants.[66]

THE LAWS OF WAR AND THE REFUSAL TO FIGHT

The inhabitants of a city that closed its gates and pursued an active defense knew that defeat meant the forfeiture of their property and their freedom. The destructive rage that moved the assault troops might be fueled by ethnic or political hatreds, but it stemmed in large part from outrage over the fact that the defenders of the city had hidden for so long, avoiding proper open combat, fighting unfairly. The desire to use terror as a strategic tool—to make an example of a city—might encourage the commander to drive his troops toward massacre. But even if there might be some political or strategic reason to hope for clemency, the dominant consideration in the calculations of the refusing garrison was the knowledge that, whatever

---

64. Corbulo: Tac. *Ann.* 13.39; Gaius Marcius: Livy 7.16.4. Onasander 34.4; Less organized armies, such as the massive Gothic force that destroyed the eastern Roman army in 378, launched foolhardy assaults, "intending to destroy the city (Adrianople) even at the cost of the utmost dangers," because they knew that the imperial treasures were stored within; Ammianus 31.15.3. See also Livy 36.24.7. Even when no siege loomed, the chance to sack towns—with or without the excuse of refusal and siege—could be dangled before an army to ensure its enthusiastic performance. See Caesar, *BC* 3.31. See also Plut. *Luc.* 14, 24.8; Caesar *BC* 3.80. Luc. 5.305–9 gives his monstrous Caesar the thought that he would never deny his (mutinously peaceful) soldiers their right to sack, and would even allow them to plunder the temples and rape the women of Rome itself!

65. Metellus: Sall. *Iug.* 68–9. Bezabde: Ammianus 20.7.15.

66. Phocea: Livy 37.32.13; Cremona: Tac. *Hist.* 3.32. It also happened to be the time of a fair, so the town was stuffed with wealth and merchandise.

the wishes of the commander, the troops might not be kept from massacre.[67] Just as even the most technical aspects of siege warfare depended entirely on the motivation of the troops, the execution of the "laws" that sketched out the punishments for the refusal of battle were in the hands not of emperors and generals but of the soldiers who had been driven into the rigors of siege warfare by that refusal. This is the counterweight of the progression, the basic threat that made sieges both rare and terrible.

> If I begin the battery once again . . .
> The gates of mercy shall be all shut up,
> And the flesh'd soldier, rough and hard of heart,
> In liberty of bloody hand shall range
> With conscience wide as hell, mowing like grass
> Your fresh fair virgins and your flow'ring infants . . .
> What is't to me, when you yourselves are cause,
> If your pure maidens fall into the hand
> Of hot and forcing violation?[68]

Roman commanders, too, were able to terrorize defenders who might persist in defending a wall that had already been attacked with engines. Not only could they with some cause announce that "you yourselves are cause" of the sack, but they could point to the coming "liberty of bloody hand" among long-suffering assault troops.[69]

---

67. Ziolkowski (1993), 83, counts eight such massacres under the republic and demonstrates "the soldiers' freedom to kill regardless of the general's signal or the stage which the sacking had reached." The question is why they would do so. Kern (1999), 334, concludes that the massacre at Ilurgia, during the Second Punic War, was ordered by Scipio in order to terrorize nearby communities, despite App. *Hisp.* 32, which blames the massacre on the rage of the soldiers. The accounts in Appian (*Mith.* 38) and Plutarch (*Sull.* 14) of Sulla's sack of Athens make it clear that the extensive slaughter had little to do with Sulla's goals and everything to do with the bloodlust of his troops. This was also the case at Jerusalem, as we have seen, and in at least two cases where massacre followed a belated surrender: Capsa (Sall. *Iug.* 91), where the women are apparently killed with the men and the children sold, and Locha (App. *Pun.* 15), where Scipio's men, "angry at what they had suffered in the siege," refused an order to retreat (and honor the surrender) but instead sacked the town of Locha and killed the women and children.

68. *Henry V*, act 3, scene 3. A similar conversation is likely in progress on Trajan's column, scene 118, (Cichorius 89).

69. This perverse tangle of justifications was still in effect in 1812. Myatt (1987), 8, 115, ascribes the British sack of Badajoz both to an understandable rage—"They had worked hard under appalling conditions for weeks and had watched their comrades killed around

It wasn't that this was fair. War being war, heated, irreconcilable, hateful differences of opinion might lead both sides to be certain that god and justice were on their side. But more often, justice—specifically, political liberty—was a mere bystander, visible but unacknowledged. Small peoples caught in the crossfire of one of Rome's inter-imperial wars, or a town caught in the crosshairs of some senator's ambition were quite possibly innocent, and Rome technically in violation of its own law against wars of aggression. Yet those about to be besieged had only three choices: submission and loss of liberty; resistance leading to an improbable victory; and loss of liberty combined with great loss of life. Having chosen to close their gates and resist until a siege had moved deep into the progression, a few communities chose a fourth way—mass suicide.[70] This was usually carried out by having the fighting men slaughter the noncombatants, often killing their own families, and then each other; otherwise it might be accomplished by burning down the town around its inhabitants.

It is difficult to place such an act in any sort of context, to assign any historical meaning to this category of events. The reminder that a sack was not, properly, a military act may not do much to allay the discomfort felt

---

them, and now they apparently felt that the moment for revenge had come. Most were clearly looking beyond the assault to the time when the successful survivors could break loose from all the bonds of discipline and restraint . . ."—and a possible breaking of the "laws" of consent and refusal "imprecise though they were" by the defending commander Phillipon. In theory, Phillipon could have surrendered with his honor intact once his walls had been breached. Yet it was not clear—especially given the carnage of the repeated, failed assaults (the city was taken by escalade at a different point)—that these breaches were really "practicable," and Badajoz was too strategically important to cede without a fight. Nevertheless, here is the idea that Phillipon's refusal to surrender his tactically very defensible position meant that the high British casualties, and the resulting vengefulness of the sack, were his fault.

70. The most famous of these incidents is undoubtedly Josephus's account of the mass suicide at Masada, *BJ* 7.389–97, although Josephus also made much use of the idea that certain knowledge of massacre could stimulate effectively desperate resistance (e.g., BJ 3.260–1). Also noteworthy is the one extended siege narrative on Trajan's column (scenes 112–24, Cichorius 83–94). We know nothing about the conduct of this siege, but it seems to involve both light and heavy assaults and there is at least one, and probably two, scenes of negotiation. It is not surprising, then, given such extreme refusal/resistance, that when the city does fall, its inhabitants fire its buildings and swallow poison—this last depicted in an especially dramatic scene (121, "The Dacian *pietà*") of barbarian high-mindedness. Interestingly, the famously Trajan-centric monument follows the conventions of commander-centered texts by eliding any chaotic scenes of a sack, providing instead scenes of Trajan sparing survivors (123) and of a suspiciously orderly collection of booty (124)—the column does not elsewhere avoid graphic scenes of capture or killing. See also pages 73–74.

here in closing a long discussion of military affairs with a brief discussion of such horrors. But the act is still linked to the basic rules of the siege, its inevitable context in the source narratives.

Livy's description of the scene at Astapa witnessed by legionaries who ran into the burning city to discover that the inhabitants have thrown themselves, along with their valuables, into the fire, indulges in hyperbole, anticipating Josephus' description of the flames of the sack of Jerusalem extinguished by the blood of the slain. But he also reminds us, with an unlikely or exaggerated detail, of the manic greed of storm troops (and thus the overarching context of the siege): some of the Romans are burned, too, when they are pushed into the flames by those coming up behind or when they try to snatch precious metals from the conflagration.[71] The people of Saguntum, besieged by Hannibal and starving, chose a desperate sally, and, when the fighters were annihilated, the women killed their children and themselves by jumping from rooftops, hanging themselves, or by fire—but only after melting their precious metals together with base metals.[72] Plutarch too loves the suicide trope, and garnishes his theme of the kindheartedness of Brutus by detailing his efforts to save the citizens of Xanthus (whom he is subjecting to siege) from their insane urge to burn themselves alive, outdoing the historians in describing particularly horrible deaths.[73] Polybius, whose account of Phillip's siege of Abydos was examined in chapter 4, is at his most strange in describing the communal suicide there. The type scenes and the means of suicide are very similar to the other accounts, but Polybius seems to be telling the story not merely for its shock value but as the capstone to his praise of the Abydenes for their complete commitment to their decision to resist.

> On becoming master of Abydos, Philip found all the property of the citizens collected by themselves ready to his hand. But when he saw the numbers and fury of those who were stabbing, burning, hanging, throwing into wells, or precipitating themselves from housetops, and their children and wives, he was overpowered with surprise; and resenting these proceedings he published a proclamation,

---

71. Livy 28.23.4.
72. Livy 21.14.4; App. *Hisp.* 12.
73. Plut. *Brut.* 31–2. In fact, Plutarch uses Brutus' handling of the "laws" of siege warfare as a sort of measuring stick by which his character can be assessed. His greatest misdeed (*Brut.* 46) is the giving over of two unresisting cities to be sacked by his troops. See also Plut. *Cim.* 7.2.

announcing, that "he gave three days' grace to those who wished to hang or stab themselves." The Abydenians, already bent on executing their original decree, and looking upon themselves as traitors to those who had fought and died for their country, could not endure remaining alive on any terms; and, accordingly, with the exception of those who had previously been put in chains or some similar restraint, they all without delay hastened to their death, each family by itself.[74]

It is not really possible, in the end, to wrest meaning out of stories of such horrors. The survivors were traumatized and enslaved, and if any of them later left their testimony it has vanished—no one listens to Cassandra. The historians are faithful to their rhetoric or to the hard of logic of siege warfare, but they are still uncomfortable. And surely nearly all of the soldiers were uneasy, too, in the days after the sack, about what they had done—but we have none of their testimony either.

If nothing else, the massacres and mass suicides should stand at the end of an account of Roman siege warfare as a final reminder of just how different the siege really was. Instead of the sprawl of war, claustrophobic violence; instead of the two-dimensional freedom of the tactical map, the flowchart of the siege progression; instead of the positive morale of the many, bitter endurance and the super-motivation of a few. The story might still have heroes, but these were up against long odds, pinched and trapped between the slow work of engineering and the quick madness of slaughter.

---

74. 16.34, trans. Shuckburgh.

BIBLIOGRAPHY

Astin, A. E. 1967. *Scipio Aemilianus.* Oxford: Clarendon Press.
Barnes, Timothy D. 1998. *Ammianus Marcellinus and the Representation of Historical Reality.* Ithaca, NY: Cornell University Press.
Barnes, Timothy D. 2005. "The Sack of the Temple in Josephus and Tacitus." In *Flavius Josephus and Flavian Rome,* edited by Edmondson et al., 129–44. Oxford: Oxford University Press.
Baynes, John. 1967. *Morale: A Study of Men and Courage: The Second Scottish Rifles at the Battle of Neuve Chapelle, 1915.* London: Cassell.
Birley, Anthony Richard. 2002. *Garrison Life at Vindolanda: A Band of Brothers.* Stroud: Tempus.
Birley, Eric. 1941. The Origins of Legionary Centurions. *Laureae Aquincenses II,* 47–62.
Bishop, M. C. 1990. On Parade: Status, Display, and Morale in the Roman Army. In *Akten des 14. Internationanalen Limeskongresses 1986 in Carnuntum,* edited by H. Vetters and M. Kandler, 21–30. Vienna: Verlag der Österreichischen Akademie Der Wissenschaften.
Blake, Joseph A. 1976. "The Medal of Honor, Combat Orientations and Latent Role Structure in the United States Military." *Sociological Quarterly* 17: 561–67.
Bleibtreu, Erika. 1990. "Five Ways to Conquer a City." *Biblical Archaeology Review* 16: 37–44.
Blunden, Edmund. 1928. *Undertones of War.* London: R. Cobden-Sanderson.
Le Bohec, Yann. 2006. *L'Armée Romaine sous le Bas-Empire.* Paris: Picard.
Le Bohec, Yann. 2009. *L'Armée Romaine dans la Tourmente.* Monaco: Éditions du Rocher.
Bradbury, Jim. 1992. *The Medieval Siege.* Woodbridge, Suffolk, UK: Boydell Press.

Bradford, Ernle. 2005. *Francisco Balbi di Correggio: The Siege of Malta, 1565*. Woodbridge: Boydell.
Briscoe, J. 1973. *A Commentary on Livy Books 31–33*. Oxford: Oxford University Press.
Briscoe, J. 2008. *A Commentary on Livy Books 38–40*. Oxford: Oxford University Press.
Burton, Robert. 2001. *The Anatomy of Melancholy*. New York: New York Review of Books.
Campbell, Duncan. 2003. *Greek and Roman Siege Machinery*. Oxford: Osprey.
Campbell, Duncan. 2005. *Siege Warfare in the Roman World*. Oxford: Osprey.
Campbell, Duncan. 2006. *Besieged: Siege Warfare in the Ancient World*. Oxford: Osprey.
Campbell, J. B. 1984. *The Emperor and the Roman Army, 31 BC–AD 235*. Oxford: Clarendon.
Campbell, J. B. 1987. "Teach Yourself How to Be a General." *JRS* 77: 13–29.
Coarelli, Filippo. 2000. *The Column of Trajan*. Translated by Rockwell. Rome: Colombo.
Coarelli, Filippo. 2008. *The Column of Marcus Aurelius*. Translated by Patterson. Rome: Colombo.
Cornwell, Bernard. 1999. *Sharpe's Fortress*. London: HarperCollins.
Crump, Gary A. 1975. *Ammianus Marcellinus as a Military Historian*. Wiesbaden: Steiner.
Cuomo, Serafina. 2007. *Technology and Culture in Greek and Roman Antiquity*. Cambridge: Cambridge University Press.
D'Huys, Viktor. 1987. "How to Describe Violence in Historical Narrative." *Ancient Society* 18: 209–50
Davidson, James. 1991. "The Gaze in Polybius' Histories." *JRS* 81: 10–24.
Davies, Gwyn. 2001. "Siege Works, Psychology and Symbolism." In *Proceedings of the Tenth Annual Theoretical Roman Archaeology Conference, London 2000*, edited by Davies et al. Oxford: Oxbow.
Davies, Gwyn. 2006. *Roman Siege Works*. Stroud: Tempus.
De Jonge, P. 1982. *Philological and Historical Commentary on Ammianus Marcellinus XIX*. Groningen: Bouma.
Den Boeft, J., J. W. Drijvers, D. Den Hengst, and H. C. Teitler. 2002. *Philological and Historical Commentary on Ammianus Marcellinus XXIV*. Leiden: Brill.
Den Hengst, Daan. 1999. "Preparing the Reader for War: Ammianus' Digression on Siege Engines." In *The Late Roman World and its Historian: Interpreting Ammianus Marcellinus*, edited by Drijvers and Hunt, 29–39. London: Routledge.
Dobson, Michael J. 2008. *The Army of the Roman Republic: the Second Century BC, Polybius and the Camps at Numantia*. Oxford: Oxbow.
Dodington, Peter. 1980. "The Function of the References to Engineering in Caesar's Commentaries." Unpublished dissertation. Ann Arbor, MI: UMI.

Drijvers, Jan Willem and David Hunt, ed. 1999. *The Late Roman World and its Historian: Interpreting Ammianus Marcellinus.* London: Routledge.
Duby, Georges. 1984. *Guillaume le Maréchal.* Paris: Fayard.
Eckstein, Arthur M. 1995. *Moral Vision in the Histories of Polybius.* Berkeley and Los Angeles: University of California Press.
Egbert, Robert L., et al. 1957. *Fighter I: An Analysis of Combat Fighters and Non-Fighters.* Human Resources Research Office, Technical Report 44. Washington, D.C.: Department of the Army.
Eisenhut, Werner. 1973. *Virtus Romana. Studia et Testimonia Antiqua 13.* Munich: Wilhem Fink.
Elton, H. 1996. *Warfare in Roman Europe, AD 350–425.* Oxford: Clarendon Press.
Empson, William. 1930. *Seven Types of Ambiguity.* London: Chatto and Windus.
Eph'al, Israel. 2009. *The City Besieged.* Leiden: Brill.
Fletcher, Ian. 1999. *Badajoz 1812.* Oxford: Osprey.
France, John. 2008. "Siege Conventions in Western Europe and the Latin East." In *War and Peace in Ancient and Medieval History,* edited by de Souza and France. Cambridge: Cambridge University Press.
Fuller, J. F. C. 1969. *Julius Caesar: Man, Soldier, and Tyrant.* New York: Funk and Wagnalls.
Gal, Reuven. 1987. "Combat Stress as an Opportunity: The Case of Heroism." In *Contemporary Studies in Combat Psychiatry,* edited by G. Belenky, 31–45. New York: Greenwood Press.
Gichon, Mordechai. 1986. "Aspects of a Roman Army in War According to the *Bellum Judaicum* of Josephus." In *The Defence of the Roman and Byzantine East,* edited by Philip Freeman and David Kennedy, 287–310. Oxford: B.A.R. International Series.
Gilliver, C. M. 1996. "The Roman Army and Morality in War." In *Battle in Antiquity,* edited by Alan Lloyd, 219–38. London: Duckworth.
Gilliver, C. M. 1999. *The Roman Art of War.* Stroud: Tempus.
Gilliver, C. M. 2007. "Battle." In *The Cambridge History of Greek and Roman Warfare,* edited by Philip Sabin, Hans van Wees, and Michael Whitby. Cambridge: Cambridge University Press.
Goldsworthy, Adrian. 1996. *The Roman Army at War 100 BC-AD 200.* Oxford: Clarendon Press.
Goldsworthy, Adrian. 1998. "'Instinctive Genius': The depiction of Caesar as General." In *Julius Caesar as Artful Reporter,* edited by Kathryn Welch and Anton Powell, 193–219. London: Duckworth.
Goldsworthy, Adrian. 1999. "Community Under Pressure: The Roman Army at the Siege of Jerusalem." In *The Roman Army as a Community,* edited by Adrian Goldsworthy and Ian Haynes, 197–209. Portsmouth, RI: Journal of Roman Archaeology.
Goldsworthy, Adrian. 2000. *The Punic Wars.* London: Cassell.

Goldsworthy, Adrian. 2003. *The Complete Roman Army.* London: Thames and Hudson.
Grattan, William. 1847. *Adventures of the Connaught Rangers.* London: Henry Colburn.
Gray, J. Glenn. 1959. *The Warriors: Reflections on Men in Battle.* New York: Harcourt.
Griffin, Miriam, ed. 2009. *A Companion to Julius Caesar.* Malden, MA: Wiley-Blackwell.
Grinker, Roy R., and John P. Spiegel. 1945. *Men Under Stress.* Philadelphia: Blakiston.
Hamblin, William. 2006. *Warfare in the Ancient Near East to 1600 BC.* London: Routledge.
Handford, S. A., trans. 1963. "Introduction." In *Sallust*, 7–33. London: Penguin.
Hanson, Victor Davis. 1989. *The Western Way of War: Infantry Battle in Classical Greece.* New York: Knopf.
Harris, William V. 1979. *War and Imperialism in Republican Rome.* Oxford: Clarendon.
Harris, William V. 2006. "Readings in the Narrative Literature of Roman Courage." In *Representations of War in Ancient Rome,* edited by Sheila Dillon and Katherine E. Welch, 300–20. Cambridge: Cambridge University Press.
Holmes, Richard. 1985. *Firing Line.* London: Jonathan Cape.
Holmes, T. Rice. 1899. *Caesar's Conquest of Gaul.* London: Macmillan.
Hölscher, Tonio. 2006. "The Transformation of Victory into Power: From Event to Structure." In *Representations of War in Ancient Rome,* edited by Sheila Dillon and Katherine E. Welch, 27–48. Cambridge: Cambridge University Press.
Hoyos, B. D. 1992. "Sluice-gates or Neptune at New Carthage?" *Historia* 41: 124–28.
Jaeger, Mary. 2008. *Archimedes and the Roman Imagination.* Ann Arbor: University of Michigan Press.
James, Simon. 2004. *Excavations at Dura Europos: Final Report VII: The Arms and Armour and Other Military Equipment.* London: British Museum Press.
James, Simon. 2011a. *Rome and the Sword.* New York: Thames & Hudson.
James, Simon. 2011b. "Dark Secrets of the Archive: Evidence for 'Chemical Warfare' and Martial Convergences in the Siege-Mines of Dura-Europos." In *Dura-Europos: Crossroads of Antiquity,* edited by Lisa R. Brody and Gail L. Hoffman. Chestnut Hill, MA: McMullen Museum of Art.
Jünger, Ernst. 1929. *The Storm of Steel.* Translated by Creighton. London: Fertig.
Kagan, Kimberly. 2006. *The Eye of Command.* Ann Arbor: University of Michigan Press.
Keegan, John. 1976. *The Face of Battle.* New York: Viking.
Keegan, John. 1987. *The Mask of Command.* New York: Penguin.
Keegan, John. 1993. *A History of Warfare.* New York: Vintage.

Keen, Maurice. 1965. *The Laws of War in the Late Middle Ages.* London: Routledge and Kegan Paul.

Kellett, Anthony. 1982. *Combat Motivation: The Behavior of Soldiers in Battle.* Boston: Kluwer-Nijhoff.

Kelly, Gavin. 2008. *Ammianus Marcellinus: The Allusive Historian.* Cambridge: Cambridge University Press.

Kelso, Ian. 2003. "Artillery as a Classicizing Digression." *Historia* 52: 122–25.

Kennedy, David. 1983. "C. Velius Rufus." *Britannia* 14: 183–96.

Keppie, Lawrence. 1984. *The Making of the Roman Army, from Republic to Empire.* London: B. T. Batsford.

Kermode, Frank. 1979. *The Genesis of Secrecy: On the Interpretation of Narrative.* Cambridge: Harvard University Press.

Kern, Paul Bentley. 1999. *Ancient Siege Warfare.* Bloomington: Indiana University Press.

Kraus, Christina S. 1994. "'No Second Troy': Topoi and Refoundation in Livy, Book V." *TAPA* 124: 267–89.

Kraus, Christina S. 2005. "Hair, Hegemony, and Historiography: Caesar's Style and its Earliest Critics." In *Aspects of the Language of Latin Prose,* edited by Reinhardt, Lapidge, and Adams, 97–115. Oxford: Oxford University Press.

Kraus, Christina S. 2007. "Caesar's Account of the Battle of Massilia (*BC* 1.34–2.22): Some Historiographical and Narratological Approaches." In *A Companion to Greek and Roman Historiography,* edited by John Marincola, 371–78. Malden, MA: Wiley-Blackwell.

Kraus, Christina S. 2009. "*Bellum Gallicum.*" In *A Companion to Julius Caesar,* edited by Miriam Griffin, 159–74. Malden, MA: Wiley-Blackwell.

Kraus, C.S. and A. J. Woodman. 1997. *Latin Historians.* Oxford: Oxford University Press.

Lander, James. 1984. *Roman Stone Fortifications.* Oxford: B.A.R.

Lee, A. D. 1996. "Morale and the Roman Experience of Battle." In *Battle in Antiquity,* edited by Alan B. Lloyd, 199–217. London: Duckworth.

Lendon, J. E. 1997. *Empire of Honour: the Art of Government in the Roman World.* Oxford: Clarendon.

Lendon, J. E. 1999. "The Rhetoric of Combat: Greek Military Theory and Roman Culture in Julius Caesar's Battle Descriptions." *Classical Antiquity* 18: 273–329.

Lendon, J. E. 2005. *Soldiers and Ghosts.* New Haven, CT: Yale University Press.

Lenski, Noel. 2007. "Two Sieges of Amida (AD 359 and 502–503)." In *The Late Roman Army in the Near East from Diocletian to the Arab Conquest,* edited by Lewin et al. Oxford: Archaeopress.

Levene, D. S. 2010. *Livy on the Hannibalic War.* Oxford: Oxford University Press.

Levick, Barbara. 1998. "The Veneti Revisited: C.E. Stevens and the Tradition on Caesar the Propagandist." In *Julius Caesar as Artful Reporter,* edited by Kathryn Welch and Anton Powell, 111–37. London: Duckworth.

Levithan, Josh. 2008. "Emperors, Sieges and Intentional Exposure." In *Beyond the Battlefields: New Perspectives on Warfare and Society in the Graeco-Roman World*, edited by et al., 25–45. Cambridge: Cambridge Scholars Publishing.

Lillo et al. 1988. "On Polybius X 10,12: The Capture of New Carthage." *Historia* 37: 477–80.

Liddell Hart, B. H. 1930. *A Greater than Napoleon: Scipio Africanus*. London: Blackwood.

Liebenam, W. 1909. "Festungskrieg (2)." *Paulys Realencyclopädie* 6.2: 2236–55.

Lightfoot, C. S. 1988. "Facts and Fiction—The Third Siege of Nisibis (AD 350)." *Historia* 33: 105–25.

Lightfoot, C. S. 1989. "Sapor Before the Walls of Amida." In *The Eastern Frontier of the Roman Empire*, edited by D. H. French and C. S. Lightfoot, 285–94. Oxford: B.A.R.

Lowe, Benedict J. 2000. "Polybius 10.10.12 and the Existence of Salt-Flats at Carthago Nova." *Phoenix* 54: 39–52.

Lynn, John. 2008. *Women, Armies, and Warfare in Early Modern Europe*. Cambridge: Cambridge University Press.

MacMullen, Ramsay. 1984. "The Legion as a Society." *Historia* 33: 440–56.

Marsden, Eric William. 1969. *Greek and Roman Artillery: Historical Development*. Oxford: Clarendon.

Marsden, Eric William. 1971. *Greek and Roman Artillery: Technical Treatises*. Oxford: Clarendon.

Marsden, Eric William. 1974. "Polybius as a Military Historian." In *Polybe*, 209–65. Geneva: *Entretiens de la Fondation Hardt*.

Marshall, S. L. A. 1947. *Men Against Fire: the Problem of Battle Command in Future War*. Washington, D.C.: The Infantry Journal.

Matthews, John. 1989. *The Roman Empire of Ammianus*. London: Duckworth.

Maxfield, Valerie A. 1981. *The Military Decorations of the Roman Army*. Berkeley and Los Angeles: University of California Press.

McCotter, Stephen. 1995. "The Strategy and Tactics of Siege Warfare in the Early Byzantine Period." PhD diss., Queen's University Belfast.

McCullough, Helen. 1959. *The Taiheiki*. New York: Columbia University Press.

McDonald, A. H. 1957. "The Style of Livy." *JRS* 47: 155–72.

McDonnell, M. 2006. *Roman Manliness: Virtus and the Roman Republic*. Cambridge: Cambridge University Press.

McGing, Brian. 2010. *Polybius' Histories*. Oxford: Oxford University Press.

McNeill, William H. 1995. *Keeping Together in Time: Dance and Drill in Human History*. Cambridge: Harvard University Press.

Millar, Fergus. 2005. "Last Year in Jerusalem: Monuments of the Jewish War in Rome." In *Flavius Josephus and Flavian Rome*, edited by Edmondson et al., 101–28. Oxford: Oxford University Press.

Mitchell, Stephen. 1995. *Cremna in Pisidia*. London: Duckworth.

Morillo, Stephen. 2006. *What is Military History?* Cambridge: Polity.

Morris, Sarah P. 1995. "The Sacrifice of Astyanax: Near Eastern Contributions to the Siege of Troy." In *The Ages of Homer,* edited by Jane Carter and Sarah P. Morris. Austin: University of Texas Press.

Ibn Munqidh, Usama. 2008. *The Book of Contemplation.* Translated by Cobb. New York: Penguin.

Murakami, Haruki. 2011. *1Q84.* Translated by Rubin and Gabriel. New York: Knopf.

Myatt, Frederick. 1987. *British Sieges of the Peninsular War.* New York: Hippocrene Books.

Needham, et al. 1994. *Science and Civilisation in China: Vol. 5 Pt. 6. Military Technology: Missiles and Sieges.* Cambridge: Cambridge University Press.

Neill, Donald. 1998. "Ancestral Voices: The Influence of the Ancients on the Military Thought of the Seventeenth and Eighteenth Centuries." *Journal of Military History* 62: 487–520.

Nicasie, M. J. 1998. *Twilight of Empire: The Roman Army from the Reign of Diocletian until the Battle of Adrianople.* Amsterdam: Gieben.

Oakley, S. P. 1997–2005. *A Commentary on Livy, Books VI-X.* Oxford: Clarendon Press; New York: Oxford University Press.

Ogilvie, R. M. 1978. *A Commentary on Livy, Books 1–5.* Oxford: Clarendon Press.

Parente, Fausto. 2005. "The Impotence of Titus, or Flavius Josephus's *Bellum Judaicum* as an Example of 'Pathetic' Historiography." In *Josephus and Jewish History in Flavian Rome and Beyond,* edited by Joseph Sievers and Gaia Lembi, 45–69. Leiden: Brill.

Paul, G. M. 1982. "*Urbs Capta:* Sketch of an Ancient Literary Motif." *Phoenix* 36: 144–55.

Pennington, L. A., Romeyn B. Hough Jr., and H. W. Case. 1943. *Psychology of Military Leadership.* New York: Prentice-Hall.

Pepper, Simon. 2000. "Siege Law, Siege Ritual, and the Symbolism of City Walls in Renaissance Europe." In *City Walls: the Urban Enceinte in Global Perspective,* edited by James D. Tracy, 573–604. New York: Cambridge University Press.

Phang, Sara Elise. 2001. *The Marriage of Roman Soldiers.* Leiden: Brill.

Phang, Sara Elise. 2008. *Roman Army Service.* Cambridge: Cambridge University Press.

Pomeroy, Arthur J. 1989. "Hannibal at Nuceria." *Historia* 38: 162–76.

Powell, Anton. 1998. "Julius Caesar and the Presentation of Massacre." In *Julius Caesar as Artful Reporter,* edited by Kathryn Welch and Anton Powell, 111–37. London: Duckworth.

Price, Jonathan J. 1992. *Jerusalem Under Siege.* Leiden: Brill.

Pritchett, W. Kendrick. 1969. *Studies in Ancient Greek Topography, Part II.* Berkeley and Los Angeles: University of California Press.

Pritchett, W. Kendrick. 1991. *The Greek State at War, Part V.* Berkeley and Los Angeles: University of California Press.

Raaflaub, Kurt, ed. Forthcoming. *The Landmark Caesar.*
Rajak, Tessa. 2002. *Josephus,* 2nd ed. London: Duckworth.
Rance, Philip. 2007. "Battle." In *The Cambridge History of Greek and Roman Warfare,* edited by Philip Sabin, Hans van Wees, and Michael Whitby. Cambridge: Cambridge University Press.
Reddé, Michel. 2001. *Fouilles et Recherches Franco-Allemandes sur les Travaux Militaires Romains autour du Mont Auxois (1991–1997).* Paris: Mémoire de l'académie des inscriptions.
Reddé, Michel. 2003. *Alésia.* Paris: Errance.
Reddé, Michel. 2008. "Alésia du Texte de César aux Vestiges Archéologiques." In *Alésia et la Bataille du Teutoburg,* edited by M. Reddé and S. von Schnurbein. Ostfildern: Thorbecke.
Ribera, i Lacomba. 2006. "The Roman Foundation of Valencia." In *Early Roman Towns in* Hispania Tarraconensis, edited by Casal et al. Portsmouth, RI: Journal of Roman Archaeology.
Richmond, Ian. 1982. "Trajan's Army on Trajan's Column." London: British School at Rome.
Riggsby, Andrew M. 2006. *Caesar in Gaul and Rome: War in Words.* Austin: University of Texas Press.
Rives, James. 2005. "Flavian Religious Policy and the Destruction of the Jerusalem Temple." In *Flavius Josephus and Flavian Rome,* edited by Edmondson et al., 145–66. Oxford: Oxford University Press.
Rodger, N. A. M. 1987. *Wooden World: An Anatomy of the Georgian Navy.* London: Collins.
Rosenstein, Nathan. 1990. Imperatores Victi: *Military Defeat and Aristocratic Competition in the Middle and Late Republic.* Berkeley and Los Angeles: University of California Press.
Rosenstein, Nathan. 2009. "General and Imperialist." In *A Companion to Julius Caesar,* edited by Miriam Griffin, 85–99. Malden, MA: Wiley-Blackwell.
Rossi, Lino. 1971. *Trajan's Column and the Dacian Wars.* Translated by Toynbee. Ithaca, NY: Cornell University Press.
Roth, Jonathan. 1999. *The Logistics of the Roman Army at War.* Leiden: Brill.
Roth, Jonathan. 2006. "Siege Warfare in Livy: Representations and Reality." In *Representations of War in Ancient Rome,* edited by Sheila Dillon and Katherine E. Welch, chapter 3. Cambridge: Cambridge University Press.
Roth, Jonathan. 2009. *Roman Warfare.* New York: Cambridge University Press.
Sabbah, Guy. 1978. *La Méthode d'Ammien Marcellin.* Paris: Les Belles Lettres.
Sabin, Philip. 2000. "The Face of Roman Battle." *JRS* 90: 1–17.
Sacks, Kenneth. 1981. *Polybius on the Writing of History.* Berkeley and Los Angeles: University of California Press.
Scullard, H. H. 1970. *Scipio Africanus: Soldier and Politician.* Ithaca, NY: Cornell University Press.

Shatzman, Israel. 1972. "The Roman General's Authority over Booty." *Historia* 21: 177–205.
Shatzman, Israel. 1975. *Senatorial Wealth and Roman Politics.* Brussels: Latomus.
Southern, Pat and Karen Dixon. 1996. *The Late Roman Army.* New Haven, CT: Yale University Press.
Speidel, M. P. 1994. *Riding for Caesar: The Roman Emperors' Horse Guard.* London: B. T. Batsford.
Sterne, Laurence. 1759–67. *The Life and Opinions of Tristram Shandy, Gentleman.* London.
Strickland, Matthew. 1996. *War and Chivalry.* New York: Cambridge University Press.
Urban, Friedrich. 1966. "Belagerungsschilderungen: Untersuchen zu einem Topos der Antiken Geschichtsschreibung." PhD diss., Göttingen.
Van Wees, Hans. 1992. *Status Warriors: War, Violence, and Society in Homer and History.* Amsterdam: J. C. Gieben.
Van Wees, Hans. 1996. "Heroes, Knights, and Nutters: Warrior Mentality in Homer." In *Battle in Antiquity,* edited by Alan B. Lloyd, 1–86. London: Duckworth.
Van Wees, Hans. 2004. *Greek Warfare: Myths and Realities.* London: Duckworth.
Viollet-Le-Duc, Eugène Emmanuel. 2000. Translated by Bucknall. *Annals of a Fortress.* London: Greenhill Books.
Walbank, F. W. 1957, 1967, 1979. *A Historical Commentary on Polybius.* 3 volumes. Oxford: Clarendon Press.
Walbank, F. W. 1972. *Polybius.* Berkeley and Los Angeles: University of California Press.
Walbank, F. W. 2002. "Polybius as Military Expert." In *Polybius to Vegetius,* edited by Hall, 19–30. Great Britian: Hadrianic Society.
Walsh, P. G. 1958. "The Negligent Historian: 'Howlers' In Livy." *Greece & Rome* 5: 83–88.
Walsh, P. G. 1961. *Livy: His Historical Aims and Methods.* Cambridge: Cambridge University Press.
Watson, Alan. 1993a. *International Law in Archaic Rome.* Baltimore: Johns Hopkins University Press.
Watson, Bruce. 1993b. *Sieges: a Comparative Study.* Westport, CT: Praeger, 1993b
Watson, G.B. 1969. *The Roman Soldier.* Ithaca, NY: Cornell University Press.
Webster, Graham. 1998. *The Roman Imperial Army of the First and Second Centuries A.D.*, 3rd ed. Norman: University of Oklahoma Press.
Wheeler, Everett L. 2001. "Firepower: Missile Weapons and the 'Face of Battle.'" *Electrum* 5: 169–84.
Whitby, Michael. 2007. "Reconstructing Ancient Warfare." In *The Cambridge History of Greek and Roman Warfare,* edited by Philip Sabin, Hans van Wees, and Michael Whitby. Cambridge: Cambridge University Press.

White, Hayden. 1973. *Metahistory.* Baltimore: Johns Hopkins University Press.
Whitehead, David. 2008. "Fact and Fantasy In Greek Military Writers." *Acta Antiqua* 48: 139–55.
Whitehead, David. 2010. *Apollodorus Mechanicus: Siege-Matters.* Stuttgart: Franz Steiner Verlag.
Williamson, G. A. 1959. *The Jewish War.* New York: Penguin.
Yadin, Yigael. 1963. *The Art of Warfare in Biblical Lands,* vol. 1. New York: McGraw-Hill.
Yavetz, Z. 1975. "Reflections on Titus and Josephus." *GRBS* 16: 411–32.
Ziolkowski, Adam. 1993. "*Urbs direpta,* or How the Romans Sacked Cities." In *War and Society in the Roman World,* edited by John Rich and Graham Shipley, 69–91. London: Routledge.

INDEX

2 Samuel, 43n74

Abimelech, 16n32
Abydos: siege of, 88–89, 91–96; suicide at, 88–89, 91, 226–27
Achilles, armor and/or shield of, 17, 58n37
Adrianople, assaults on, 180–82, 184, 187, 223n64
Aeschylus, 57
Agamemnon, 210
agger. *See* siege ramp
Alesia, battle or siege of, 4n7, 51n11, 68, 78, 86n21, 114n103, 122–23, 126, 129n36, 130n37, 136–41; excavation of, 10n20
Alexander the Great, 35, 69n87, 158, 199, 217n39
altruism, reciprocal, 40–41, 45
Ambracia, siege and sack of, 95–99
Amida, Ammianus at, 177, 180, 188, 191–95; excavation of, 10n20; intimidation at, 58; siege of, 33n40, 170, 184n48, 185, 187–95; skirmishing at, 181
Ammianus Marcellinus, vii–viii, 170–204; and ballista sighting, 191–92; on emotion or morale, 14, 33–35, 69, 76, 177–204, 223; and *The Face of Battle*, 175; as a historian, soldier, and writer, 173–77; and his imperfect antiquarianism, 35n42, 198–99; impressed by Persian display, 58; on Julian, 174, 176–77, 196–204, 217; on/at the siege of Amida, 177, 180, 187–95; as a source, 12–14, 79, 81; and technical digression, 4n6; his use of the siege progression, 177–87
Anatha, surrender of, 180
andreia, 24. *See also virtus*
Antonius, M. (Mark Antony), 216n37
Antonius Primus, M. (Flavian general), 62, 222n58
Appian, 3n5, 5n7, 6n8, 14, 17n33, 23n5, 42n72, 46, 50n7, 52n13, 56n27, 59, 61n49, 64n61, 65, 68, 75n111, 77n118, 81n3, 89n30, 112–17, 206, 210, 216–17, 218n42, 221, 224n67, 226
aquila (eagle), 27–29. *See also signum*
Aquileia, siege of, 56n28, 170n1, 180, 181n39, 183–84, 187
Archimedes, 72, 107–9, 213

239

Aristotle, 16n30
Arrian, 33n39, 38n60, 69n87, 199
artillery: anachronistic, 84n13; concerning torsion power, 3, 13–14, 134; as covering fire, 72–73, 84, 112n98, 129, 153, 165, 198–99; as digression, distraction or historiographic problem, 4n6, 15n29, 90n32, 171n4; moral effect of, 3–4, 182, 202; mural (defensive), 17, 72, 92, 94n48, 107–9, 157, 179–86, 189, 191, 193–95; operated or powered by women, 16n32, 17n33; Sassanian, 173; in skirmishing, 60, 66–68, 152, 181. *See also* siege tower
assault, 3–6, 8–9, 16–17, 21, 24–46, 49–53, 55–62, 65–77, 79, 84–88, 92–118, 120n5, 122–41, 143–47, 150–69, 171–73, 175, 177–204, 206, 208–9, 212, 214–15, 220–25. *See also* assault, *ex itinere*; assault, general; assault, heavy; assault, light; assault, testing
assault, *ex itinere* or immediate, 56–57, 79, 84, 122–24, 126n24, 127
assault, general, 4n5, 43, 46, 53, 62, 63n57, 66, 68–73, 77, 79, 82, 87–88, 92, 94, 102, 104, 106, 112n98, 122, 127, 140, 151n22, 153, 163, 165, 172n5, 180–86, 188, 191, 195n68, 198, 200, 203
assault, heavily engineered. *See* assault, heavy
assault, heavy, 9n18, 60, 66, 71–79, 87, 97, 99n63, 111–14, 118, 123n16, 126–29, 132–35, 137n50, 143, 148, 151n22, 153–56, 162–67, 173, 181–86, 190–95, 197, 201–2, 225n70
assault, light, 53, 74n106, 84, 100, 108, 118, 127–28, 139–40, 152–53, 173, 182–83, 190–92, 201, 225n70
assault, lightly engineered. *See* assault, light
assault, testing, 61–62, 64n63, 88, 92,
102n72, 104, 108, 112n98, 125–27, 153, 164, 173, 179–80, 190–91, 201
Astapa, suicide at, 226
Astyanax, 218
Athens: sack of, 224n67; siege of, 117
Atuatuci, 59, 75
Avaricum, siege of, 30, 71, 123, 126, 129n30, 129n36, 130–36, 137n50, 197n72, 221

Badajoz, sack of, 209n10, 224n69
battering ram, 53, 66, 71–76, 95, 97, 112n99, 129, 151–55, 157, 167, 172n6, 173, 182–86, 191, 197–200, 202; as "point of no return," 74–76, 78n127, 92, 99n63, 152–55, 157, 167, 182n42, 185–86, 191, 197–98, 202, 215n33
battle, open field, 1–2, 6–9, 12n23, 14, 16n31, 18–20, 22–24, 28, 41–47, 49, 57, 63n57, 71, 78, 83n8, 84n12, 114, 119, 120n5, 122–23, 125n23, 131, 136–41, 147, 164, 174–76, 196, 207, 219, 224
Bezabde, sieges of, 69, 72, 76, 179, 181–85, 187, 193n62, 220, 223
blockade, 6, 51–53, 65, 77–79, 82, 84–87, 95n50, 98, 107n87, 109–15, 118, 123n16, 126n23, 127, 130, 137–39, 141, 143n2, 156, 159–61, 172n6, 184, 186–87, 212, 220
Blunden, Edmund, 23n4
Bray, John, 31n32
breach, creating and/or fighting in, 27, 29–30, 32, 40n66, 42–45, 49, 51n9, 52–53, 56n27, 60, 71–72, 74–75, 89, 91–98, 117–18, 122, 129n30, 132n41, 153, 155–56, 163, 165, 172n6, 173, 182, 185n50, 194–95, 197–98, 200, 202–3, 209, 220, 225n69

Caesar, G. Iulius, as essential source, viii, 12; on the significance of the

battering ram, 75–76; his commentaries as sources for siege warfare, 10, 13n26, 14, 17n33, 27, 29n23, 30, 32–33, 34n41, 37n52, 39, 42, 49n4, 51n11, 56–66, 69–72, 78–86, 99n63, 112, 114n103, 115, 118, 119–41, 147, 155n33, 171–72, 176–77, 198, 215n30, 215n33, 219–23; politically-motivated distortions, 14, 42, 78, 119–23; writing technology, 4n6, 59, 122, 125, 132, 134–36
Camillus, M. Furius, 83n9, 84, 87
cannibalism, 78, 115, 139, 167
Capsa: sack of, 51n9, 224n67; seizure of, 116
Cartagena. *See* Carthago Nova
Cartagena Lagoon, 41, 100–102, 104, 106
Carthage, siege of, 46, 64, 68, 91n34, 112, 114n104
Carthago Nova, siege of, 36, 99–107, 208
Cassandra, 210, 227
Cassius Dio, 14, 35, 60, 81n3, 143n6, 148n19, 150n20, 170n1, 197n73, 199, 220
catapult. *See* artillery
centurion, 26–33, 39, 103n76, 111, 120, 137, 155n33, 165, 202n82
chance. *See* fortune
chivalry, 4n5
Cicero, M. Tullius, 40n65, 57n33, 75–76, 198, 214, 216n37, 222n58
Cincinnatus, L. Quinctius, 18
circumvallation. *See* lines of circumvallation
Civil Wars, The. See under Caesar
Civilis, revolt of, 58
clementia. See mercy
Cohen, Brian, 28n19
combat motivation. *See under* morale
commentarius (commentary), 33n37, 68n80, 82, 112, 119–21, 124–25,
132n40, 146n13, 181n37
Constantius, 179, 184n45, 185–88, 196, 220
contravallation. *See* lines of contravallation
contubernia, 40
Corbulo, Gn. Domitius, 42, 55, 59, 68–69, 222–23
Coriolanus. *See* Marcius, G.
corona muralis, 30, 42, 102, 104n77
courage, 18–25, 31, 37–42, 62, 103, 115, 122, 145–48, 154, 160, 192, 207; desperate, 18n36, 23n5, 83n8, 93–4, 103n75. See also *virtus*, motivation
Crassus, P. Licinius, 124
Cremona, battle of, 32, 62
Cremona, sack of, 214, 216, 222n58, 223
Critognatus, nefarious speech of, 139
customs of war. *See* laws of war

de Rebus Bellicis, 3
death rays, super–hot. *See* Archimedes
deditio, 55n23, 78, 85n14, 93n42, 99n63. *See also* surrender, terms of
Delium, siege of, 3
despair. *See* desperation
desperation, 17–19, 23n5, 38, 51n9, 64–65, 90n33, 93–96, 114–15, 147n15, 149, 155–65, 173, 182, 184, 189, 202, 212, 225n70
Deuteronomy, 19n40, 207n4, 215n32
Diodorus Siculus, 17n33, 216n37, 218n42
disciplina. See discipline
discipline, 25–29, 37–40, 43–46, 49, 58, 63, 87, 103, 106, 111, 135–36, 147, 150, 152, 158, 162, 172, 193, 194n65, 201n81, 205–9, 221, 225n69. *See also* sack
Diyarbakir. *See* Amida, siege of
Donatus, 58n37
Dura-Europos, 10n19, 73, 170n1, 173n8

242 • Index

Dyrrachium, field fortifications at, 126–27, 133, 139n57, 186

eagle. See *aquila*
embankment, siege. See siege ramp
engagement. See under siege progression
escalade, 13, 30, 43–45, 52, 61–69, 72, 74, 84, 88, 99n63, 102–6, 110, 112n98, 117, 127–29, 154n28, 160, 167, 181–84, 186, 191, 194, 199, 221, 225n69
Euripides, 210n12
Euryalus. See Nisus and Euryalus
ex itinere. See assault, *ex itinere*
expugnatio, 52n11, 78, 85n14, 88, 98n62, 124n19, 137, 211. See also sack

Face of Battle, The, 7–8, 175–76, 193n64
Ferentinum, assault on, 67
Florus, 17n33
forlorn hope, 93–94
fortification: as conceptual boundary, 15–21; as distraction from issues of motivation, vii, 2, 10, 12n23, 18, 20; field, 18, 63, 122, 125–29, 137–41 (*see also* lines of circumvallation, lines of contravallation); Gallic, 75n109, 132n40, 171–72; natural strength and thus counterintuitive weakness of, 101n67; Near Eastern, 16n31, 75n109, 171–73; as subject for historical novel, 61n51; as unmanly advantage, 15–16, 18n37, 141. See also wall
fortune, 6, 29–35, 37, 39–41, 44n80, 49, 53n18, 100, 120, 127, 150n20, 158, 163, 177, 198, 215
Frontinus, 8n13, 14, 28, 59n40, 60n46, 220n50
Fulvius Nobilior, M., 95–99

gadget or gadgetary turn, 3–5, 13, 70, 90n32, 95n49, 116

Gallic Wars, The. See under Caesar
Gamala, siege of, 72, 75n109
gates, closing of, 2, 6–7, 18–19, 50–51, 55–56, 59, 71, 85, 125, 223–25
Gergovia, assault on, 30, 33, 126, 136, 155n33, 221
Gibbon, Edward, 211n17
Goldberg, Rube, 5n7
Gomphi: sack of, 56n28, 125; taking of, 128
Gratian, 184, 187n51

Hadrian, 34n41
Hatra, siege of, 60n47, 170n1, 199, 220
helepolis, 73, 76, 184n48, 185, 199–200. See also siege tower
Henry V, 27, 220–21, 224
Hercules, 35
heroism, 5, 18, 27–35, 37–38, 41, 43n74, 44n81, 45, 61, 83n9, 103, 111–13, 134–36, 144, 149, 154, 155n33, 159, 163–66, 181, 184, 198, 201–2, 210
Herodian, 30n27, 56n28, 143n2, 170n1
Herodotus, 30n27, 101n67
Heron of Byzantium, 17n33
Historia Augusta, 14
Homer, 16, 36n47, 40, 46, 174
Horace, 31–32, 222
Horatius (Horatius Cocles), 35

Ibn Munqidh, Usama, 39n62, 165n43
Iliad, 3, 6n8, 17n34, 38, 40n66, 58n37, 187n53, 207n5, 214n28
Intercatia, assault on, 46
intimidation. See under siege progression

Jericho, siege of, 101, 207
Jerusalem: excavation of, 10n20, sack of, 34, 142, 148–49, 156, 158, 167–69, 215, 218, 221, 224n67, 226; siege of, 14, 30, 35, 38, 46, 58, 70, 73, 76, 142–69, 171, 179; temple in, 60, 68–

69, 142–45, 148–49, 161, 165–68
Josephus: actions at Jotapata, 68n83, 77n121, 188n56; on desperation, 23n5, 64n62, 149, 155–62, 165–68; as essential source, viii, 6n8, 12, 14, 79, 145–48; as historian, generally, 33–34, 38, 57–62, 66n70, 68–72, 74, 76–79, 142–69, 215–17, 222, 225; as liar and propagandist, 14, 143–45, 151–52, 161; writing horror or melodrama, 4n7, 161, 167–69, 217n41; writing Titus, 30, 36, 38, 76, 100n65, 144–45, 147–69, 221
Joshua, 207n4
Jotapata, siege of, 23n5, 68n83, 75n109, 77n121, 147–48
Julian, 18, 30, 34, 36–38, 58–60, 172–82, 187, 194n66, 196–204, 217, 220
Jünger, Ernst, 45–46

Keegan, John. See *Face of Battle*

ladders: breaking during assault, 103–5; determining height of, 106n84, 110. See also escalade
"laws" or customs of war, 19n40, 50, 54–56, 75–78, 97–99, 111n97, 126, 131n38, 140, 149, 152–57, 167–68, 171, 178–79, 182n42, 185, 202–3, 206n1, 207n4, 208, 214–18, 223–27
Libanius, 180n33, 197n73, 201n79
lines of circumvallation, 52n12, 59n39, 63–65, 71, 78, 85n14, 95n50, 102n69, 114–15, 122, 125–28, 137–41, 143n2, 149, 151–52, 160–61, 172. See also under siege progression
lines of contravallation, 33n39, 63n58, 102n69, 137n49, 138–41
Livy, committing "howlers," 96–97; on desperation, 23n5, 93–94, 96; as essential source, vii–viii, 12–13, 79; as fabulist, 86–89; as historian more generally/*Ab Urbe Condita*, 6n8, 13, 14n34, 17–18, 29n23, 30, 37, 43n77, 51, 55–57, 60, 64–68, 72n99, 74n108, 77–89, 91–97, 101n67, 105–13, 172, 208; and historical factuality, 80–83, 86, 89n30, 92, 105, 208; interest in morale, 82–85, 98–99, 101–3, 107, 117; on the sack, 208–16, 218–19, 221–23, 226; writing drama or melodrama, 86–88, 91, 93–94, 120, 226
Locha, sack of, 221, 224n67
Lucan, 4n5, 18n35, 18n38, 42n72, 51n11, 66n72, 76n115, 207n5, 223n64
Lucian, 4n6, 107n86
luck. See fortune

Machiavelli, 18n37, 53n16, 64n62, 100n65,
Maiozamalcha, siege of, 34, 170, 184–85, 200–4, 217
manliness. See *virtus*
Marcellus, M. Claudius, 108–11, 210, 212–13
Marcius, G. (Coriolanus), 83n9, 210, 222, 223n64
Marcus Aurelius, column of, 36n51
Marius, G., 46, 116
Marshall, William, 6n9
Masada: siege ramp at, 59n39, 72; suicide at, 225n70
Massilia (Marseille), siege of, 66n72, 72, 129, 132n41, 215, 219, 221
Memnon, 77n121, 218n42
mercy, 56, 74–76, 90n33, 145, 151–58, 185, 212, 219, 224
military revolution, Hellenistic, 3n3
mine, mining, undermining: 10n19, 15n29, 71–72, 87–89, 92–93, 95–98, 117, 133, 167, 171n4, 182–83, 185–86, 189, 201–2; defensive undermining, 129, 133, 159; as transition in siege progression, 75n111; to infiltrate a city, 87–89, 202–3; tunneling vs. undermining, 53, 71–72, 97–98

Montfort, Simon de, 16n32
morale: and combat motivation, vii, 5, 22–24, 28–36, 42, 46, 53, 67, 102, 111, 122, 130, 162, 180, 184, 193, 218–19; definition of, 19, 22, 23n4, 24, 25n11; endurance, 25; gauging through combat, 57n32, 61, 87n24, 124–26, 128, 137, 149–52, 181, 201; general importance to siege warfare, 1, 7, 17–24, 48–53, 57, 61–62, 64, 66, 69, 83, 87, 90n33, 92, 95, 102, 104–5, 116–17, 122, 130–36, 153–54, 161–63, 169, 173n7, 186, 191–92, 194, 201, 219, 227; leadership and 35–37, 130, 135n46; unit cohesion and, 25–29, 39, 116. See also desperation, *virtus*

Napoléon I, 22, 46n88, 99
Napoléon III, 10n20, 119n5, 137n49
narrative: characteristics of siege narratives, 3–5, 12–14, 47–48, 53–54, 82–85, 87–90, 95, 99–100, 103–13, 117, 120–22, 125, 130, 132, 134–36, 141, 146, 174–77, 187n53, 188, 191, 194–95, 207, 210; centrality to history of, 10–12, 70n88, 80–81, 144, 205; of sieges more possible than of battles, 1–2, 8–11; theory of historical, 9n16, 11, 54, 80n1, 82n6, 172n6, 175n15; visual, 73–74
Nero, 55
New Carthage. See Carthago Nova
Nisus and Euryalus, 32, 60n46
Noviodunum, assault on, 59, 124, 129n30
Numantia, siege of, 46, 113–16

obsidio, 52n11, 84n14, 126n23, 127, 130n37
Onasander, 14, 30, 40, 44, 57n29, 63n59, 64n62, 65n69, 70, 78n127, 101n67, 217, 222, 223n64
opera, viii, 63n58. See also lines of circumvallation; lines of contravallation; mining; siege ramp; siege tower
oppugnatio, 52n11, 84n14, 125–27, 138. See also assault
Orlando Furioso, 6n8, 66n69
Orongis, siege of, 88
Ovid, 32, 198n75, 208n5, 209n8, 214n28, 217

Paradise Lost, 24n5, 52n14,
Parthian empire, siege capabilities of, 19n39, 21n41, 173n8
Pericles, 16n31
Persia, 16n31, 18, 21n41, 34, 55n22, 58–59, 69, 72–73, 76, 170–204, 217, 223
Perusinae glandes, 10n19
Petilius Cerialis, Q., 69
Phaedrus, 37n55
Phocea, sack of, 221, 223
Phylarchus, 211–12
Pirisabora, siege of, 58–60, 76, 170, 181, 184–85, 197–98, 200–203, 220
Plataea, siege of 3n4, 33n9
Plato, 15
Plutarch: on gadgets, 4n5; *Lives*, 4n5, 16–18, 29–30, 33, 35, 38, 42, 46, 51, 60, 64, 66, 70, 71, 99, 101, 107, 116, 210, 216–19, 222–26; on the sack of Syracuse, 212–14; as siege warfare source, 14, 81
Polybius: as essential source, viii, 12–14, 79; *Histories*/as historian of siege warfare, 6n8, 19n40, 26n13, 43–45, 51, 59n42, 60–61, 74n108, 77n121, 81–85, 88–98, 102–5, 107n85, 108–14, 118, 215n33; on morale, 23n5, 35–36, 92, 95, 102–3; opinions on rhetoric and historiography, 12, 211–12; relationship with Scipiones, 14, 99–108, 112, 217, 218n42; on the sack, 51, 93, 106, 206, 208, 211–12, 217, 226
Pompey (Gn. Pompeius Magnus),

37n55, 78, 122n12, 125–26, 139n57, 207n5, 222n57
pre–contact stage. *See* siege progression
Priam, 207, 218
Procopius, 171n3
Psalms, 43n74
Pseudo–Zachariah the Stylite, 110n94

Quintilian, 211, 218

ram. *See* battering ram
ramp, siege. *See* siege ramp.
Reeds, Sea of, 101
refusal (of battle or open combat), 15–20, 82, 93–94, 111n97, 114, 122, 123n14, 136, 138–41, 147; and the siege progression, 20, 63n57, 65, 78, 82, 93–94, 118, 179, 196; and the sack, 17–19, 47, 168–69, 207–8, 221, 223–27. *See also* gates, closing of
Rhodes, siege of, 116
Rigodulum, assault on, 69
Robinson, Heath, 5n7
Romulea, assault on, 67

sack, 51n9, 56n28, 59, 67, 76–78, 84, 86, 93, 97–99, 106–7, 111–12, 131, 135–36, 148–49, 156–58, 180, 193, 195, 203, 205–27; avoided by historiography, 12, 89n29, 209–14; components of, 214–18; indiscipline in, 20, 78, 106–7, 145, 167–69, 185n50, 208–9, 220–22; intimately connected with siege progression, viii, 7, 19, 47–51, 76–78, 94, 97, 204–8, 218–20. *See also* "laws" of war, refusal
sacramentum, 26
Saguntum, suicide at, 88, 93n44, 226
sallies, by the besieged, 17, 18, 25, 49, 53n18, 57, 63–64, 72, 74, 82, 84, 87, 95–96, 102, 104–5, 117, 126, 129, 134–36, 139–40, 147–53, 157–59, 161–62, 166, 183n44, 186, 190–92, 201, 219, 226
Sallust, 14, 16, 39, 43–44, 51n9, 70, 101n67, 115–16, 223–24
sambuca, 105n79, 108–9, 116
Sapor (Shapur II), 178–79, 182, 185n50, 187–96, 199, 204
Sarmizegethusa, siege of, 73–74
Sarpedon, 40
Satricum, assault on, 84
Scaeva, M. Cassius, 33, 42
Scipio, L. Cornelius (Asiaticus), 88
Scipio Aemilianus, P. Cornelius, 6n8, 36, 46, 89, 112–16, 198–99, 210
Scipio Africanus, P. Cornelius, 99–108, 111, 210, 217n39, 221, 224n67
scorpio, 134, 136, 183. *See also* artillery
Sertorius, 217
Servius Tullius, 28, 40
Severus, Arch of, 73n104
Severus, Septimius, 36, 60, 142n2, 220
Sforza, Catalina, 64n62
Shandy, Tristram, 17n32
siege engines. *See* assault, heavy; artillery; siege tower
siege lines. *See* lines of circumvallation, lines of contravallation
siege progression: 2, 15, 20, 47–54, 85, 89n30, 92–93, 95–96, 107, 108n88, 109, 112n98, 115, 117–18, 121, 123, 127–29, 132n41, 138, 143, 145, 148, 151–56, 162, 166–8, 171–73, 175, 177–78, 185, 187–91, 195, 205–8, 227; assault phase of, 65–77 (*see also* assault; assault, *ex itinere*; assault, general; assault, heavy; assault, light; assault, testing); circumvallation as stage in, 63–65 (*see also* lines of circumvallation); initial engagement phase of, 60–62, 125, 180–82 (*see also* assault; assault, *ex itinere*; assault, general; assault, heavy; assault, light; assault, testing); intimidation phase

of, 55n24, 56–62, 77, 79, 102, 104, 106, 108, 116, 125, 150–57, 168, 171, 173, 178–81, 189–90, 197, 221; lapsed into blockade, 77–79, 186–87 (*see also* blockade); pre-contact stage of, 54–56, 77, 88, 116, 123, 149, 153, 177–79, 182, 200n78, 201; ratchet as metaphor of or analogy for, 48–49, 71, 94, 162, 195, 208,

siege ramp (also referred to as *agger*, embankment, or mound), 38, 53, 59, 66, 68, 71–74, 79, 97n59, 98n63, 112n98, 117–18, 122–23, 127, 129–30, 132n39, 133–36, 149, 152, 157–62, 166–69, 172n6, 184n48, 186, 190–94, 197n72, 201

siege tower, 3, 4n5, 5n7, 43, 49, 53, 59, 66, 68, 71–76, 82, 99n63, 112n98, 117–18, 123, 128–30, 132, 134–36, 152–54, 159, 163, 167, 182–84, 190, 193–94, 199–200. See also *helepolis*

siege works. *See* lines of circumvallation; lines of contravallation; mining; siege ramp; siege tower

signum, 28–30, 34, 68, 168n47, 208–9, 217

Singara, siege of, 33, 178–79, 182, 184–85, 198

skirmishing, 57n32, 60–62, 87n24, 125–27, 131, 133, 137, 149–54, 165–66, 173, 181, 190–93, 196–98, 201–3, 219

standard. See *signum*

storm. *See* siege assault

stratagem, 4n5, 5n7, 19n39, 28, 29n23, 51–52, 66, 70, 71, 79, 82, 87, 122, 124n18, 141, 164n43, 166, 181, 197

Suetonius, 14, 28n22, 33n36, 42n72, 78n124, 121n10, 143n6, 150n20, 177n23, 221n52

Sulla L. Cornelius, 59, 65n67, 87n24, 116–17, 224n67

Sulpicius Severus, 144n10

surrender, terms of, 18–20, 50–57, 59–60, 64, 75–76, 78–79, 85n14, 92–93, 97–98, 115, 125–26, 129–30, 149–51, 154, 157, 160, 167, 178–80, 185–86, 189, 198, 200, 208, 213, 215, 220–25

Syracuse: sack of, 210, 212; siege of, 4n5, 107–12

Tacitus, 14, 19n39, 32, 38n57, 42–43, 51n11, 53n17, 55–62, 64n62, 68–69, 87n24, 143–44, 151n22, 209–10, 214–19, 222–23

tactics, choice or description of in siege assaults, 7–8, 22–23, 48–54, 65–77, 109, 120n5, 122–30, 139, 146, 174, 193n63, 195

technological change, lack of, 3n3, 9n18, 13–14, 41, 82n6, 171–73

technology, as narrative focal point, vii, 1–3, 48, 81–84, 92, 105n79, 107–8, 116–18, 122, 134–36; as digression, 3–5, 83, 96–99, 101n66, 121–22, 132, 137n50, 173n7, 184, 199n77. *See also* artillery; assault, heavy; gadget

testudo (as assault formation), 62, 68, 124, 163

Theodosius (fourth-century general), 185

Thilutha, non-siege of, 178

Thucydides, 3n4, 11n21, 33n39, 147, 154n28

Tiberius, 36, 216n37

Titus, 14, 30, 34–36, 38, 58, 60, 76, 142–70, 177n23, 179, 198, 221–22

Tolstoy, Leo, 8n14

Trajan, 36, 73–74, 199

Trajan's Column, 36, 67n76, 68n82, 73–74, 147n17, 170n, 224n68, 225n70

Trojan horse, 70, 88

Trojan Women, enslavement of, 218. *See also* Euripides

trumpets, 57, 70, 164, 190, 193, 196, 209
tunnel. *See* mine

undermining. *See* mine
unit cohesion, 25–30, 38–40, 45, 162, 182
urbs direpta (topos or catalogue), 93n44, 98–99, 209–14
Uxellodunum, blockade of, 130

Valencia, sack of, 218
Valerius Maximus, 15, 18n38, 29n23, 33n36, 44n80, 46n88, 67n78, 69n87, 217n39
Vegetius, 4n5, 14, 17n33, 24n5, 26n13, 40n65, 57–58, 62, 70, 129n30, 172n6
Veii, siege of, vii, 63n57, 86–89, 97nn58–59, 209
Velius Rufus, G., 31n32
Vellaunodunum, siege of, 65, 125–26
Vergil, 17n34, 32, 40n66, 60n46, 65–66, 110n94, 198n75, 207
Vespasian, 57n31, 64n62, 77n121, 142, 148
Vindolanda, 32n34, 40n65,
Viollet-le-Duc, Eugène-Emmanuel, 61n51
virtus (including as manliness and/or aggressive combat motivation), 6, 15, 24–28, 31, 35, 37–40, 41n72, 44n80, 57n29, 63, 69–71, 74, 84, 86n19, 87, 111, 122, 129, 134–36, 139, 141
Vitruvius, 10, 72n99

Volandum, assault on, 42, 68, 222
volunteers, siege assaults composed of, 24n9, 25n11, 28n22, 29–35, 37–46, 53, 61, 70, 94, 103–4, 110–12, 154, 158, 163–66, 171, 191, 202

wall: 1–5, 16–19, *passim*; assessing height of, 103, 105, 106n84, 110, 113; as backdrop, 5–6, 8, 36–37; as conceptual dividing line, 6–7, 16–19, 184, 209; Gallic, 32; rock opera, viii; as unfair, unworthy, and unmanly, 15, 84, 114. *See also* battering ram; breach; fortification; lines of circumvallation; lines of contravallation
wall crown. See *corona muralis*
Wellington, Arthur Wellesley, 1st Duke of, 8n14, 209n10
women, hair of, 17n3, 221; participation in and presence during siege assaults, 16–18, 134–35; victims of massacre and sack, 19–20, 50, 78, 87, 93, 131, 135, 203, 207, 209, 210–18, 221, 223–24, 226. *See also under* artillery

Xanthus, suicide at, 226
Xenophon, 19n40, 101n67, 215n33

Zama, assault on, 43–44
Ziolkowski, Adam, 208–9, 212–16, 222, 224n67
Zombie, history writing as, 11
Zosimus, 4n7, 37n55, 170n1, 201n79, 202